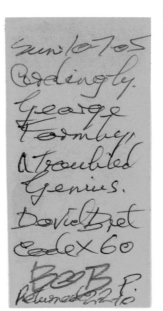

Sun 10.7.05
Accordingly.
George
Formby,
A Troubled
Genius.
David Bret
Codex 60
Bob P.
Returned 22.10

GEORGE FORMBY

GEORGE FORMBY
A Troubled Genius

David Bret

Robson Books

First published in Great Britain in 1999 by Robson Books,
10 Blenheim Court, Brewery Road, London N7 9NT

British Library Cataloguing in Publication Data
A catalogue record for this title is available from the British
Library

ISBN 1 86105 239 1

Typeset in Berling by SX Composing DTP, Rayleigh, Essex
Printed and bound in Great Britain by
WBC Book Manufacturers Ltd., Bridgend, Mid Glamorgan.

This book is dedicated to
Dennis and Pat Taylor
and Les Enfants de Novembre

N'oublie pas . . .
La vie sans amis c'est comme
un jardin sans fleurs

ACKNOWLEDGEMENTS

Writing this book would not have been possible had it not been for the inspiration, criticisms and love of that select group of individuals whom I still regard as my true family and *autre coeur*: Barbara, Irene Bevan, Marlene Dietrich, Dorothy Squires *que vous dormez en paix*; Montserrat Caballé, René and Lucette Chevalier, Jacqueline Danno, Hélène Delavault, Tony Griffin, Roger Normand, Betty Paillard, Annick Roux, Monica Solash, Terry Sanderson, John and Anne Taylor, Francois and Madeleine Vals. Also Caroline Clerc and Charley Marouani for the comfort you gave in times of great loss.

Very special thanks to Dennis Taylor and Dorothy Cottrell-Johnson. *Un grand chapeau-bas* to Simon Blumenfeld, Charlotte Bush, Irene Handl, Dorothy Hyson, Pat Kirkwood, Kate Mills, Dinah Sheridan, Pat Taylor, Dennis Poulter, Peter Pollard, Jacky Morley.

Especial thanks to my agent, David Bolt, to the magnificent team at Robson . . . and to my wife, Jeanne, still the keeper of my soul!

INTRODUCTION

The actress Thora Hird declared that he had been sent by God. Such was the devotion of his fans that over 100,000 of them turned up at his funeral. His record compilations, though dated and with many songs over-released, still outsell those of any other nostalgia artiste. His films, complete with their poor continuity and corny dialogue, represent the very best of British family humour.

George Formby successfully transcended every class barrier and was equally at home entertaining royalty in the most opulent surroundings as crawling through the mire, risking life and limb to cheer the lads at the Front. He brought joy to millions worldwide, yet never achieved lasting personal happiness. Throughout his career his loyalties were tested and torn between a grasping family he had been conditioned into respecting – but which he only ended up loathing – and a near-psychotic wife who made much of his private life a misery, yet without whose nagging and shrewd business sense he almost certainly would not have made it to the top.

On stage and screen, George Formby rapidly established himself as the seemingly inarticulate little man who nevertheless triumphs over adversity to ultimately prove that he is by no means as gormless as one has assumed – armed with the weapons of his particular trade: a ukulele, a clutch of catchy songs, a huge toothy grin, and a charisma which unequivocally placed him above all his contemporaries.

'I wasn't very good, but I had something the public seemed

to want,' he once said of himself. He was, of course, selling himself short. George Formby remains the ultimate all-round genius, a blazing lodestar of talent which will never be replaced.

CHAPTER ONE

A CHIP OFF THE OLD BLOCK

'I don't think anybody understood him. I don't know whether he understood himself.' Irene Handl, co-star.

His father, George Formby Sr, known in music-hall circles at the beginning of this century as 'The Wigan Nightingale', had the most inauspicious start in life. James Lawler Booth, born in Ashton-under-Lyme on 4 October 1875, was the illegitimate son of Sarah Jane Booth, a Lancashire prostitute who, in the space of ten years, was convicted 140 times for offences which included theft, vagrancy, brawling, and most frequently drunkenness.

In a thoroughly unfortunate childhood, James would find himself shunned by his mother, and shut out of the house whenever she was entertaining a man – which was often. Despite the fact that she was just four-feet tall and decidedly unattractive, there was never any shortage of clients. The youngster was beaten by his numerous 'foster fathers', such as the Frank Lawler who probably fathered him and whom Sarah Jane married when James was six months old. It is not known if his name was actually *changed* to Lawler at this time, or whether this was simply his middle name. Lawler certainly was no less cruel towards the boy than his mother, shutting him out of the house for hours and sometimes nights on end, allowing him in again only when he had earned enough coppers from singing in the streets to pay for their tobacco and Sarah Jane's gin. It is not surprising, therefore, that by the age of ten –

through sleeping rough and not eating properly – James had already developed severe chest trouble and acquired the 'graveyard' cough which would later form an essential component of his stage act.

By the time he was twelve – and his mother had been imprisoned for the umpteenth time – James had finally left home to work in a Todmorden cotton-mill. Showbusiness, however, was his only interest, albeit that he had never set foot in a music-hall, and he had supplemented his poor wages by singing in local pubs. It was here that he had been 'discovered' by an unscrupulous impresario and teamed up with another boy as the Glen Ray Brothers.

For several years, executing a badly-choreographed song and dance routine – like his more famous son, spontaneity would provide James with that integral element of magic, as opposed to organised patter – the Glen Ray Brothers had toured the provinces. According to the generally accepted story, it was whilst they were passing through a Northern railway station and James observed a number of coal-wagons destined for Formby – a small town situated between Ormskirk and the coastal area perhaps appropriately known as Mad Wharf – that he hit upon the idea of re-baptising himself George Formby.

Bearing in mind the fact that Formby Sr was unable to read and write until he was well into his teens, this seems extremely unlikely. According to the records of Birkenhead's Argyle Theatre, the entertainer was still being engaged as J H (never J L) Booth until 1897. When he was almost twenty the theatre *manager*, Daniel Clarke, suggested that he change his name to Formby after *he* had observed the lettering on the coal-wagons. The George, again according to Clarke, was chosen in honour of the great comic, George Robey.

As a solo entertainer, Formby Sr had slowly but surely amassed a following in his native Lancashire. Despite its limitations, his act had achieved immense popularity nation-wide, a success which had begun with a gimmick – an on-stage alter-ego, John Willie, whose catchphrase, 'I'm coughing better tonight!' accompanied by his rattling cough and droll repartee, would have them rolling in the aisles (even when audiences were well aware that he was terminally ill).

For two decades John Willie represented the then archetypal Lancashire lad: gormless but not *entirely* stupid, dry-humoured, inarticulate and well-intentioned, the sort of character working-class people adored and readily identified with, because this odd little man with the cut-down bowler, shoes on the wrong feet, and his pre-Chaplinesque antics always found a way of seeing the funny side of misery and destitution. In this respect, in years to come Formby's example would be followed by the likes of Little Tich, Jimmy James, Rob Wilton and Beryl Reid. His songs, on the other hand – numbers such as 'Since I Parted My Hair In The Middle' and 'I'm Such A Hit With The Girls' – were decidedly light-hearted and closely resembled the work of his Gallic counterparts, Dranem and Mayol, and the Anglo-Belgian chansonnier Harry Fragson. Formby Sr was also credited with 'inventing' Wigan Pier – when he confided to audiences that this was his favourite bathing spot, the less knowledgeable would rush off with their buckets and spades, only to discover that the 'pier' was actually a landing-stage of the Leeds–Liverpool Ship Canal connecting Wigan to Warrington!

It was in Wigan, in 1898, that Formby Sr met the woman who would become his wife. At the time he was involved with Ivy Caston, a music-hall hoofer of whom almost nothing is known. Caston was staying at a lodging-house in Marsh Lane run by a couple named Hoy . . . but when Formby called on her one evening and found she was not in, he promptly fell for the Hoys' feisty twenty-one-year-old daughter, Eliza.

Eliza's parents, devout Roman Catholics, were horrified to learn that their daughter had been asked out by a music-hall turn, and forbade her to have anything to do with Formby. When they found out that she had been seeing Formby behind their backs, her mother accused Eliza of being 'loose', and she received a thrashing from her father. Even so, the couple continued courting, and on 11 August 1899 they were married at Wigan Registry Office. Theirs would prove a happy, fruitful union. Possessed of a staggering consumptive virility, Formby is reputed to have sired several children on the wrong side of the blanket. He had thirteen children with Eliza, six of whom did not survive infancy, while their fourth child would one day achieve the international fame his father had only ever dreamed of.

Despite their initial dislike of their son-in-law, it did not take the Hoys long to accept him, particularly when his young wife persuaded Formby to convert to Catholicism, and over the next few months Hoy taught him another skill – equestrianism. In his younger days in his native Newmarket Hoy had worked as a jockey, and he was currently employed as an undertaker's 'horse-breaker', prior to the evolution of the motor-driven hearse.

Hoy rather hoped that the exercise, combined with plenty of good food and fresh air, would put a little colour into Formby's dreadfully pasty cheeks. What no one knew at the time, however, was that the twenty-four-year-old entertainer was already in an advanced stage of phthisis, or pulmonary tuberculosis, an incurable progressive wasting disease brought about by his childhood years of neglect. Indeed, Formby's condition was *so* critical that as early as 1900, when he was just twenty-five, Eliza began insisting that oxygen cylinders be installed in the wings wherever he was appearing.

After their wedding, the Formbys – they never called themselves Booth, and Eliza hardly ever addressed her husband as anything but George – lived with Eliza's parents. Their first three short-lived daughters were born here, but it was at their first home, 3 Westminster Street, on 26 May 1904, that George Hoy Booth – the future George Formby – came into the world. In the course of the next fourteen years he would be followed by Louisa, Frances, Ella, Mary, Frank, Ethel and Edward. Two more babies are thought to have been stillborn.

He was born blind, on account of a caul, or membrane, enclosing his head, and was unable to see for several months. In August 1939 the star took great pleasure in revealing to the *Daily Mirror* that he owed the miracle of regaining his sight to a simple sneeze:

> *Every time I sneeze now I think what a miracle it was. One day my mother took me across from Liverpool to New Brighton in the ferry boat. A gust of wind, or summat, made me sneeze. I sneezed so hard that the shock opened my eyes for the first time. Mother took me to the doctor's and he bathed my eyes. From that day to this I've never had any trouble with my eyesight. Even those big arc-lamps in the film studios don't affect me. A Manchester specialist is so interested in my case that I visit him every year for an examination. There's an old superstition which says a person born with a caul will never be drowned – the wife has it now, so it'll be handed down through the family as an heirloom. Ee, lad, I'll always have a soft spot in my heart for the blind!*

Young George did not have to suffer any of the hardships which had been imposed upon his father. At the time of his son's birth Formby Sr was earning £35 a week in pantomime, and as much as £15 a week on the legitimate music-hall. Within a few years he would be commanding £50 an appearance – a phenomenal sum at that time – and had progressed far and beyond his native Lancashire following a comment in a London newspaper by Marie Lloyd, the undisputed Queen of British Music-Hall, that in her estimation only *two* variety acts were worth seeing besides herself: Dan Leno and The Wigan Nightingale. George was therefore enrolled at the prestigious Notre Dame private school, not far from the family's new home in the more opulent Dickenson Street.

The arrangement would prove but temporary. A nervous, underweight child, George was inattentive in class. The nuns both terrified and intimidated him, particularly Sister Veronica, a sadistic individual who, he later claimed, never missed an opportunity to rap him over the knuckles with a ruler over the slightest misdemeanour. Sister Veronica was Notre Dame's music teacher, and it was probably on account of her that Formby Sr took his son away from the school when he was seven and doing *well* in music – the only subject that had ever interested him – though only through fear. The apprehension instilled in him by this woman would never leave him and, for the rest of his life, despite having the most astonishing sense of timing and ear for rhythm, George Formby would never learn how to read or write music.

From the summer of 1911, therefore, 'school' for George would be a succession of racing stables. Unable to forget his own appalling childhood, Formby Sr – who by this time owned several fillies – needed to give his son and heir a more privileged start in life. George was taken on as a stable-boy, firstly at Bishop's Cannings in Wiltshire, then by Jack Drake, at Middleham's Warwick House Stables. His father had every confidence that George would one day make the grade as a jockey.

The regime at Warwick House, however, was far harsher than it had been at the Catholic school. George had to be up at four every morning to clean out the horses, the other stable-boys bullied him on account of his puny size – at the age of eight he weighed just 55 pounds and he fell victim to every childhood ailment. Subsequently, every time he received a beating he would abscond and make his own way back to Wigan, only to be escorted back to Middleham the next day by his mother.

Whether George actually *wanted* to follow in his father's footsteps at this time is not known. He had successfully mastered the art of playing the Jew's harp and the mouth-organ, and he *is* known to have had a passable singing voice. Formby Sr, however, was virulently against George having anything to do with the stage. Indeed, he would not allow him to *see* his own act, not even when he appeared in the Royal Variety Show in July 1913.

George stuck it out at Middleham for another year until, weary of all the absconding, Formby Sr apprenticed him to Thomas Scourfield, at Epsom. His racing career would prove decidedly unenterprising. His first mount was in the Apprentice Plate at Lingfield Park – on Formby Sr's Eliza, named after his wife. The weather was atrocious, and George was suffering from mumps but insisted on competing with a field which comprised thirty-five runners. He came last. Over the next few years he would ride seven seconds, more than twenty thirds, but not one winner.

In April 1915, Formby Sr *was* persuaded to lift his embargo when a producer friend, Will Barker, asked him to 'loan' him George for four weeks to appear in his latest film, a five-reeler entitled *By The Shortest Of Heads*. The stars were Violet Hobson and Sidney Blackmer, a twenty-year-old hopeful who had just enlisted to serve in Europe with the American Expeditionary Forces. Another star was Moore Marriott, who later achieved notoriety as Will Hay's sidekick, Harbottle, in his famous comedies.

Sidney Blackmer, whose successful film and stage career would continue well into the Sixties, later dismissed this effort as 'goddam trash'. Few Formby fans have been able to form their own opinion, since only one complete print of the film is thought to have survived, and this remains locked in a London archive. Blackmer, however, appears to have judged it accordingly – the film *is* dire, with the exception of the final racing sequence. George also appeared briefly in another film at around this time – *No Fool Like An Old Fool* – of which absolutely nothing is known, and from which not even the stills survive.

By The Shortest Of Heads was shot at Epsom, and upon Formby Sr's insistence George was paid the princely sum of one pound for his appearance. He also demanded that his son be put through his paces for the film's gripping final race by the legendary Steve Donoghue, the Warrington-born jockey who had won that year's Derby and who would do so a record-breaking six times over the next decade. In addition Formby Sr arranged for the *Daily Mirror* to do a photoshoot, which appeared in the newspaper on 19 April under the heading: GEORGE FORMBY'S LITTLE JOCKEY SON WHO WEIGHS ONLY THREE STONE 13 LB.

In the film George played a stable-boy who, adopted by a trainer, outwits a bunch of criminals – setting a precedent for almost *all* of his future films – then wins £10,000 for his benefactor in a race. The film was not successful, though it did warrant a brief mention in *Bioscope* upon its re-release, during the summer of 1918:

> *It is an exciting photoplay of love and sport, capitally acted and redolent of the real turf atmosphere [though] it is the race itself which lifts the film above the ordinary, and the sight of the tiny jockey (George Formby Jr) gradually drawing away from his rival will raise the most phlegmatic audience to enthusiasm.*

Immediately after completing this film, which everyone expected to be a one-off, George's father secured him another position with a stables – this time in County Kildare, near the Curragh. Since there was virtually no racing in England during the war years, most owners, including Formby Sr, had transferred their horses to Ireland, and George was assigned to a trainer named Burns. In August 1915 he was enrolled at the school in Athgarvan, his first full-time education in four years, and that same week he rode a horse named Halfcast in Ireland's first-ever apprentice race and came second. On account of the hectic workload doled out by Johnny Burns he very rarely made it to class before lunchtime, and was frequently caned by the headmaster.

As had happened in England, George made innumerable attempts to run away from the stables, largely because of the unsociable hours and the bullying of the other stable-boys. The latter nicknamed him Cloggy, because he came from the same place as the much-lampooned footwear. Once, accompanied by another boy George named as Hamilton, he got as far as Dublin, only to be picked up by the police and locked in a cell for the night – such was the extent of his homesickness. On 10 October 1918, he sneaked away from the race-meeting at Baldoyle and, booking his passage on the *Leinster*, he sent a telegram to his father, asking him to meet him at Holyhead Docks.

When George had last seen them, his parents had been living at Hindley House, a large detached residence at Stockton Heath which Formby Sr had converted into a smallholding. In 1917, however, the family had moved to Hillcrest, a slightly larger house in Warrington's London Road, which George had yet to see. Fortunately, he never made the journey. Burns had reported him missing, and he was apprehended thirty minutes before the ship set sail. A little over two hours later, the *Leinster* with its 510 passengers and crew was torpedoed by a German U-Boat and sank. There were no survivors.

The incident had given Formby Sr a scare he could have well done without, and in November 1918 George was sent back to Middleham, this time to the stables owned by Dobson Peacock. His second period in the village, far happier than the first, was recalled by Dennis Poulter, the son of the local craftsman who, a few weeks after he arrived in Middleham, presented George with his very first musical instrument, a harmonica:

*George was befriended by three people: Jane and Violet
Parish, and my father Herbert Poulter. Jane, affectionately
known as Aunt Jin, was the eldest of a fairly large family, and
when orphaned at the age of fourteen she had decided to care
for the other children herself. By the time George came to
Middleham, she was also the stablelads' housekeeper. Her
sister, Violet, was in service at a town house in the village and
my father was the local shoemaker. Every year at
Middleham, on Whit Sunday, there would be a fancy-dress
parade, and in 1920 my father, accompanied by Violet,
wheeled him through the streets in a barrow. All three were
very fond of him – he was very small for sixteen, very nervous,
didn't see much of his family, and this adopted family
protected him from the other boys' bullying.*

George remained at Middleham until the end of 1920,
travelling occasionally to Newmarket to race for Formby Sr's
friend, Lord Derby, who owned a stable there. Exactly why he
decided to return to Ireland at a time when he was blissfully
happy and spending more time at Aunt Jin's cottage, adjacent
to the castle, than he did at the actual manor house, is not
known. He had only been in County Kildare a few weeks,
however, when on 8 February 1921 he received a telegram
from Eliza, bearing the sad news that his father had passed
away. Formby Sr had collapsed in the wings of the Newcastle
Empire, where he had been appearing in pantomime,
following a violent coughing fit which had ruptured the blood
vessels in his larynx, causing a haemorrhage. He was just forty-
five.

It had taken George Formby a good ten years to die, yet his
doctors had advised him that with proper medical attention –
by cutting down on his appearances in some of the smokier
flea-pit theatres, and by taking an occasional respite at a Swiss
sanatorium which, as one of the highest-paid acts in England,
he could easily afford – he might have lived a little longer. His

excuse had always been that he needed to provide for his wife and seven children, though George was, of course, providing for himself.

Towards the end of his life, many of Formby Sr's performances had been curtailed, or cancelled altogether by Eliza, a fiercely protective woman who only ever had her husband's best interests at heart. In the spring of 1917 her overtly caring nature had resulted in the couple being served with a writ by the Southport Palladium, when Formby Sr had failed to turn up for a show there, only to perform in London a few days later. Eliza had defended him by providing the London High Court with a doctor's certificate – and by giving the judge a piece of her mind – and the Formbys' lawyer had pleaded for clemency, describing his client as 'having one foot in the grave'. However Formby Sr had lost his case and had been ordered to pay the manager of the Palladium £175 in damages.

George's father was interred in the Catholic section of Warrington's Manchester Road cemetery – newsreel footage of the event has survived – and his grave was marked by an ornate marble tomb, embellished with an alleged replica of Manchester Hippodrome's proscenium arch within which there is a chiselled relief-portrait and the inscription, 'After Life's Fitful Fever He Sleeps Well'. And as if aware that he would one day be almost completely forgotten – having been majestically overshadowed by his son – Eliza had the word 'comedian' inscribed beneath his name.

After the funeral, leaving her other children to be looked after by relatives, Eliza took George on his first trip to London, hoping that the bright lights might help them through their grief. At the Victoria Palace, the scene of so many Formby triumphs, they happened upon a comedian named Tommy Dixon who, not content with purloining his material, had already begun styling himself 'The New George Formby'. George was appalled, and though he was totally unfamiliar with his father's patter, he made up his mind there and then that he *would* follow in his footsteps.

Eliza Booth, bereft of her anchor, approved wholeheartedly of George's decision and over the next few months devoted herself to launching him on the stage. In his later years George insisted that he had never wanted to cash in on his father's name, but this was not true. Although he refused to perform under the name Formby – choosing his first names, George Hoy – he did not argue when Eliza opted to use him as an excuse for 'resurrecting' her husband and put her son in his father's John Willie garb: the jacket which was several sizes too small, the concertina-bottomed trousers, the shoes which Formby Sr had always worn on the wrong feet, the cut-down bowler. Even the thick pancake make-up was copied . . . and so were the songs.

George Hoy's debut performance – he was sub-billed George Formby's son, just in case anyone did not know – took place between features at Harrison's Picture House (subsequently the Hippodrome) Earlstoun, between Warrington and St Helens, in April 1921 . . . just ten weeks after his father's death. He was accompanied by Harry Duckenfield, Formby Sr's pianist and arranger, and halfway through his first number dried up due to stagefright. He would have given up completely had not several of his father's more ardent admirers yelled encouragement, though George himself would always be the first to admit that as a 'green' sixteen-year-old, his John Willie interpretation had left a great deal to be desired.

This apparently third-rate performance did, however, have its compensation, for also in the audience was Daniel Clarke, the manager of the Argyle Theatre, Birkenhead. This was the man who had supplied his father with his stage-name. Invited to the show by Eliza Booth – 'out of respect for the lad's much-missed old man' – he offered George a one-week engagement at his notoriously difficult establishment . . . a ten-minute spot on a very full bill which was completely drowned by the hissing and booing from the galleries.

For the next two years, billed as George Hoy and engaged as the warm-up act – poorly paid, but supported financially by his mother – George toured the Northern halls and cinemas, always emulating his father. Then, quite unexpectedly in 1923, his whole life dramatically changed, on account of two impromptu 'acquisitions'. One was a musical instrument, the other a woman!

Exactly *where* George bought his first ukulele (technically a banjo-ukulele, *see* Appendix IV) is not known. The star himself claimed that he had paid fifty shillings for it from a hard-up comic, whilst his brother Frank maintained that it had come from a Manchester second-hand shop. What is certain is that George first introduced it into his act during a week-long engagement at the Barnsley Alhambra because, he said, he had never known what to do with his hands. Accompanying himself to 'Going Back To Tennessee', not a *deliberately* tuneless rendition of the classic, he received an unexpected standing ovation!

Afterwards, George would try to convince himself that such over-zealousness had been a mere fluke. The theatre's manager, Charles Lawson, had heard him plucking the instrument in his dressing room. While standing in the wings, waiting to announce the next act, he had observed that George was clearly on the verge of drying up. Therefore, to save his embarrassment, and to stave off a possible dilemma – if the warm-up was booed, the other acts on the bill frequently had a hard time calming the audience down – Lawson had sent on one of the stagehands with George's ukelele, and the young man had turned to the audience and quipped something along the lines of, 'Here, see if you can play this!' When he received *another* standing ovation the next evening, however, prompting Lawson to move him further up the bill, George knew that he was on to a surefire winner. Dispensing with his John Willie get-up, though not for the moment his father's songs, he announced that henceforth he would be known as George Formby.

CHAPTER TWO

COUNT YOUR BLESSINGS AND SMILE

'Wherever George had to go, Beryl had to go too. I just used to say all the time, "If you want George, you've got to have me." They always wanted George, so they had to put up with me!' Beryl Formby, wife.

Beryl Ingham, a twenty-three-year-old Accrington-born clog-dancer, had formed a variety act known as the Two Violets with her sister, May. Pretty, blonde – and feisty – she met George in 1923 when they were appearing on the same bill in Castleford, West Yorkshire.

It was hardly an auspicious occasion, for when George tried to show a little courtesy by asking the pretty blonde how she was, she snarled at him to mind his own business. She excused herself by declaring that her father had warned her never to talk to strangers. Commenting on George's act – for which he was now blacking his face, spouting an endless tirade of parrot jokes *and* singing his father's songs – she declared, 'If I'd have had a bag of rotten tomatoes, I'd have thrown them at him!'

A more sensible man might have given such a seemingly arrogant, outspoken creature a suitably wide berth. In retrospect, however, despite her domineering, conniving ways Beryl would prove the best thing that had ever happened to him as far as his career was concerned. On the personal level, however, this bossy, surrogate-mother figure was probably the personification of his very worst nightmares.

George, buck-toothed and loveable, and wholly unaware of

15

his unexplored, indeed immeasurable talent, was immediately attracted to Beryl, but terrified of making an initial approach. He was by no means a virgin, having enjoyed any number of one-night stands, mostly with dancers or chorus-girls. Beryl, however, was no woman of easy virtue. In the days when showbusiness was not generally regarded as an acceptable profession for young ladies the Ingham sisters were chaperoned virtually everywhere by one or both of their parents – an obstacle which George soon overcame when he learnt that Beryl's father was the landlord of a pub, the Black Bull in Darwen. With his natural wit and charm he very quickly befriended Ingham, and in next to no time was invited to the family home for Sunday tea. However during this and his subsequent visits to the house Beryl still looked down her nose at him every time he turned up on his newly-acquired motorcycle.

Their seemingly one-sided courtship dragged on for over a year, with George pestering Beryl to marry him – always receiving the same snappy negative response, usually in front of her family and friends in an attempt to humiliate him. Finally, in August 1924, he decided that he had had enough, that an ultimatum would provide the only solution. Any more rational man would have given up on her, of course, but Beryl had set his senses reeling, even though she would never see *him* even remotely as an object of desire. Therefore, borrowing his mother's car – a spanking brand new Rover which was the envy and talk of Wigan – he set off for Darwen, in the middle of the night, and in true 'Lancashire Romeo' fashion positioned himself under Beryl's window and began crooning, or so he later claimed:

> *How I love these Darwen girls,*
> *With their bright and sunny curls,*
> *From their red and ruby lips . . .*
> *I get the taste of fish and chips!*

The noise is said to have roused half the neighbourhood, though George stuck to his guns, shouting that he would *only* go away once Beryl had agreed to become his wife. Desperate to shut him up, now that the tables had been turned and *she* was the one feeling embarrassed, Beryl agreed.

George was nevertheless so convinced that Beryl had accepted a marriage proposal *only* to get rid of him, and that the next time she saw him, she would not mince her words in telling him so, that he said nothing to his mother. The proposal coincided with Beryl's acceptance, on his behalf, of a week-long engagement at the Alhambra, in London's Leicester Square. George was once more only the warm-up act – the part of the bill that all artists loathed, but in the days when entertainers were more or less *compelled* to work their way to the top via the ranks, an integral component of the music-hall regime.

The manager at the Alhambra had never heard of George Formby Jr, but had included him in the bill because his father's pianist, Harry Duckenfield, was accompanying one of the other artists and had recommended him, even offering to pay George's fee out of his own pocket, just to give him a break at one of the most prestigious music-halls in Europe. The Alhambra had been the first establishment to introduce a chorus-line, in the 1860s, and had been used as a model for the more famous Folies-Bergère, in Paris. George Formby Sr had regularly topped the bill, and though he too was unfamiliar with his son the orchestra leader, a snobbish individual named George Saker who rarely made an appearance on the podium before the interval – preferring to leave the 'amateurs and other riff-raff' to his deputy – actually *insisted* on conducting the young man billed as 'A Chip Off The Old Block' as a tribute to George's father.

George and Beryl's wedding took place a few weeks after the Alhambra season – on 13 September 1924, a Saturday, though he often joked that it had been on an 'unlucky' Friday. They married at Wigan Registry Office, with an aunt and uncle stepping in at the last moment as witnesses – and to vouch for George because he was still legally a minor. Indeed, Eliza did not find out that her son was married until the couple were due to return home from their honeymoon. To Eliza's way of thinking, Beryl was already a 'scarlet woman' who had lured her son to London; it did not matter that they had slept in separate rooms. Additionally, any marriage which had not been blessed by the Church was, she declared, invalid. Therefore, whilst he was living in 'open sin' with his 'floosie', neither of them would be welcome in her house!

Beryl had anticipated such a reaction, which was why she elected to stay in the car, outside Hillcrest, whilst George was facing the music – and she readily agreed to the church ceremony which took place two months later in spite of being a fierce agnostic. To a certain extent, Eliza was pacified by this, though she is said to have never really liked the woman who, in her eyes, not content with leading her 'Georgie' astray, had now taken over the development of his career.

Beryl's apparent psychosis almost certainly stems from the fact that in the days when wives were only too frequently regarded as subservient – particularly in Northern England, where traditionally the man worked to support his family, and the wife stayed at home to look after it – *she* had given up her own career to manage his. Just how far Beryl would have developed as an all-round entertainer as opposed to George's sometime stooge in pantomimes and stage-revues, is not difficult to ascertain. Clog-dancers were already going out of fashion when she met George, and though undeniably very pretty and an above average hoofer, she possessed neither the talent nor the temperament to progress beyond her own limited sphere. In contrast George was blessed with a tremendous *natural* presence and personality and would have made it to the top on these strengths alone. Mistinguett, Chevalier, his own father and even Marie Lloyd had already proved that one did not necessarily require the vocal ability of a Melba or Caruso, nor the dancing skills of a Duncan or Nijinsky, to fill theatres.

Beryl, however, would always appear to resent what she had given up for her husband, and their marriage began with her effectively holding the upper hand, a position she retained. *She* had paid for the honeymoon, and when George informed her that he was in the red to the tune of £70 – most of this was money he owed on his motorcycle – Beryl dipped into her savings and cleared his debts. It is no secret that he would spend thirty-six years paying her back.

Beryl also told George that they would never have children – not that she disliked them, but that they would end up getting in the way of his career if *she* spent time away from him bringing them up. George tried to argue but Beryl would not be swayed, and in a rare fit of pique he headed off to the nearest dog-pound, where for a few shillings he bought a brown and white mongrel which had been about to be put down. Beryl took to the dog at once – the first of many – and baptised him Mickey Dripping!

Neither was Beryl pleased when, early in October, George signed for a series of third-on engagements at a small Morecambe theatre, aware that the Two Violets had been booked with the Newcastle Empire for the whole of that week. Beryl was earning £10 a week in those days – twice as much as George – and, suspecting that he might start 'fooling around' so soon after their marriage, she tried to force the manager of the Empire to take George on too. He may have agreed, had she not tried to dupe him into paying George the same salary as herself, claiming that he never worked for less on account of his always being inundated with offers.

The manager, Thomas Convery, had been a close friend of George's father, and prided himself on the somewhat morbid fact that the great man had died only hours after his final performance at the Newcastle Empire. Convery checked

George out, and when he realised that Beryl had tried to con him, he came close to firing her. She, however, refused to be thwarted: having recognised her husband's enormous potential – something his peers have said *he* would not have done without her constant harping on and pushing – Beryl had taken George in hand. She taught him how to dress, stressing the fact that a Lancashireman would not be regarded as vulgar by Southern audiences if he abandoned the stereotyped flat-cap image and appeared on stage in a tuxedo. She taught him what to sing, how to use his hands when he was not playing his ukulele, what jokes to tell, and how to monitor audience reaction by playing mostly to the galleries, which contained the genuine fans, those working-class men and women who recognised within him so much of themselves.

Some years later, Beryl would offer a legitimate excuse for her frequently insufferable presence and behaviour, blaming this on her husband's tiresome indolence, and intimating that George actually gleaned pleasure from her incessant nagging:

> *George is hopeless when I'm not with him and is as miserable as sin. I always have to be in the wings when I'm not acting with him. I appear with him on the stage in his comedy act, but he does his famous ukelele act alone – when I have to be all the time in the wings, or anyway within hearing. And believe me, if I leave George alone for a minute he goes off and buys a new car or a new jumper . . .*

It was Beryl, too, who insisted that George stop 'plonking' his ukulele and learn how to play it properly. And ironically, his first major engagement – a six-month contract at £15 a week – was with the Newcastle Empire. Here, he was a big hit with the instrument, though at some venues, such as the Oldham Palace, he was specifically requested *not* to play it. In this part of the country his father's records were still selling well and some theatre managers, such as the Palace's George Collier, were actually receiving pay-offs from Formby Sr's record company to continue promoting his name. And what better way of doing this than to employ his sound-alike son to perform his songs?

The Palace revue, Thomas Convery's and Arthur Merts' *Formby Seeing Life* – subtitled *A Merrygoround of Laughter and Melody* – which opened on 2 November 1925, also saw George resurrecting his father's John Willie, complete with his graveyard cough, and was basically a hastily thrown together rehash of Formby Sr's sketches from the war years: 'The Wigan Railway Line', 'Mugs for Luck', 'Formby On The Boulevards', and a farce entitled 'The Interrupted Song', where George desperately tried to compete with a heckler.

For many, the highlight of the Palace revue was a sketch entitled 'Prisonville', which featured George's dog. Since acquiring Mickey Dripping, George had taken him everywhere and after each show the little mutt had trotted on to the stage to take a final bow with his owner. And now, in this highly emotive – some might say most un-Formby-like tableau – Mickey Dripping would jump on to the prisoner's lap and be sung to sleep with a tender ballad, 'Goodnight, Little Fellow, Goodnight'.

George's co-stars in *Formby Seeing Life* were husband and wife team Jenny Howard and Percy King, whilst Beryl and her sister May emerged from 'The Clog-Dancers' Retirement Home'. The critics, many of whom had turned up at the first night expecting to be disappointed, loved it. One anonymous scribe enthused in the *Oldham Chronicle*:

The name of George Formby has for years attracted all theatre-goers and it is well to know that, in all probability, George Formby Jr will prove as popular as his father – the revue presented at the Palace last night is as funny as the name led us to expect it would be. George Formby is the drollest comedian we have heard for a long time, and his

21

apparent simplicity, while always coming out on top, was obviously to the liking of the audience. At every appearance he was greeted with roars of laughter. With Formby in it, any revue is to be assured of success.

Despite the sterling reviews, George would continue emulating his father for several more years, partly because this was all the theatre manager expected of him, but largely because he was naturally indolent. As long as he could eat well, provide for himself and his wife and keep sending a little money home to his mother, and of course tinker around with his motorcycle, it did not matter much to him whether he became as famous as his father or not.

In February 1924, George and his mother had visited the His Master's Voice studios at Hayes, where Eliza had persuaded him to make a test-recording of Formby Sr's 1916 song, 'Rolling Around Piccadilly', though this had never been issued commercially. The pianist had been Madame Adani. Despite her exotic-sounding name she was a Cockney who, when not accompanying hopefuls for auditions, worked as a cook in the studio canteen! The previous year, Madame Adani had played on Gracie Fields' very first 78rpm recording, 'Romany Love' which, like George's first effort, never saw the light of day.

During the spring of 1926, Beryl Formby negotiated – with a great deal of tolerant wrangling – a one-off deal with the Edison-Bell Winner record company for George to cut six sides. Released that autumn, all were Formby Sr songs, with George sounding *so* much like his father that it is often difficult to tell them apart. With the exception of 'John Willie's Jazz Band', all were acoustic recordings done in a single take – and for good measure, George re-cut 'Rolling Around Piccadilly'. None of them sold well, however: the few fans who bought them were again interested only in the artist whose work was being covered, and some critics found them in very poor taste. On even accused George of 'digging up the dead', completely ignoring his own admission that he had not recorded them for financial gain, but to pay tribute to his father in this the fifth anniversary year of his death.

The advance on royalties paid by Edison-Bell Winner in 1926 was almost negligible – around £50 – but George was not allowed to do with it as *he* liked. Setting a precedent which would last another thirty years, Beryl placed £49 in the bank, and gave the remaining £1 to her husband for spending money. He used some of this to buy cigarettes and when Beryl saw him passing these around to friends, she told him in front of everyone that if they *wanted* to smoke, then they could smoke their own cigarettes and not his!

For the time being, Beryl was only being cautious. Though George *was* getting plenty of work – enough for the couple to purchase their first home, a semi-detached house at 836 Lancaster Road, Barton, near Preston, *and* a small flat in London's Great Portland Street – public opinion had become divided between the ones who liked to hear him 'honouring' his father, and those who reproached him for earning an easy living *off* Formby Sr's success. Therefore it was impossible to gauge audience reaction in some towns until the actual playbills had been posted. This meant that he could alternate between playing to two thousand spectators one evening, and a near empty theatre the next. The latter reaction often caused the management to cancel the rest of the week's performance, forcing the Formbys out of their hotel or guest-house into seedy digs. The couple's over-fondness for frugality, however, when times were far from lean, would almost take on an art-form, and within a few years George Formby would be regarded as one of the most tight-fisted entertainers on the tour-circuit, some said second only to Maurice Chevalier.

At the end of May 1926, coinciding with the Edison-Bell Winner recording session, George opened at London's Shepherd's Bush Empire in Thomas Convery's revue *Formby's Good Deed*. The week-long season was the end result of an almighty struggle, and a final heated row, between Beryl and a man named Gillespie – the assistant of Sir Oswald Stoll, the head of one of the most important theatrical emporiums in Britain at this time.

Three years previously, Gillespie had had a run-in with Archie Pitt, Gracie Field's entrepreneur husband, over his comment, 'There's nothing quite so common, Mr Pitt, as a Northern turn on the London stage!' During negotiations with Beryl, who had recently completed an elocution course, Gillespie repeated this in reference to George, and she understandably hit the roof, calling Stoll personally and reminding him of her husband's earlier London appearances at the Alhambra. Stoll, however, was less impressed by minor achievement than he had been after reading the reviews for the Convery revue in Oldham, and Gillespie's vow 'never to put on a Formby farce in a million years' was overruled.

Once again George placed the emphasis on imitating his father, performing all Formby Sr songs and recreating his 'John Willie At Home' sketch, though other tableaux such as 'The Jamboree', 'The Palace' and 'The Golf Links At Sunnydale' were original creations, and saw him dress as a particularly knock-kneed boy scout. His co-stars were Harry Brento, June Stirling – and Mickey Dripping – and at the eleventh hour Beryl was persuaded to put in an appearance. However, following a snide remark from Gillespie that one Formby on the bill was more than sufficient, she insisted upon being billed as Winnie Hardy.

Having witnessed several rehearsals for the show – and complained to Beryl that his stomach had ached through laughing so much – Sir Oswald Stoll wrote the press-release himself, part of which read:

George Formby in shorts, complete with pole and whistle, is a sight for the 'gods' – and for other parts of the house as well. 'Be prepared' is the excellent motto of this splendid [Scouts]

movement of which Our George is the latest member . . . a
magnificent combination of hilarious and original comedy,
superb vocalism, attractive dancing, tuneful melodies and
acrobatic novelties, one of the greatest and merriest
entertainments EVER seen on the music-hall stage. So rare is
it that the son of a stage favourite achieves the dizzy eminence
of his father that the tremendous success of George Formby
ranks as one of the most remarkable in music-hall history.

The London critics, of course, would always be greatly divided
in their opinion of George. Even when he became a megastar
many of them would still look upon him – along with almost
every one of his Northern colleagues – with a certain disdain,
and regard him as coarse, and on stage or screen he would
rarely make an appearance in the all-important West End.

As far as the recording studio was concerned, however,
Beryl's avaricious demands would prevent any serious contract
from coming George's way for another six years. In September
1929 he cut two sides for the Dominion label: 'In The Congo',
and the self-composed 'All Going Back'. There should have
been six more, but the managing director did not feel that he
was worth the money Beryl was asking for a carbon-copy of the
man he had admired, and for the sarcastic reviews he was
attracting, such as the one which appeared in the November
edition of *Sound Wave*:

> *This record gave us quite a shock. George Formby, the famous*
> *Lancashire comedian 'passed on' some considerable time ago,*
> *yet here he is once more, as large as life – speaking*
> *gramophonically – and his thousands of admirers should give*
> *him or rather his voice a warm welcome. How he 'came back'*
> *we confess we don't know.*

It was not until the spring of 1932 that the great Formby
recording boom was launched, when George signed a three-

year deal with Decca. This got off to a shaky start on 10 June when two acetates were completed at the company's small Chenil Galleries studio: 'Our House Is Haunted' and 'I Told My Baby With My Ukulele'. Despite the latter's title, George was too nervous to play his ukulele and had to be accompanied by a poor session-audition pianist. The recordings were subsequently rejected. The original pressing of 'Our House Is Haunted' – retitled 'The Ghost' because Gracie Fields was singing a song at the time called 'The House Is Haunted' – has recently resurfaced. It is more impressive than the later re-recording, because in this version George sounds *exactly* like his father, a comparison which is better appreciated today than it was sixty years ago. George positively drawls the tale of the 'ghost' who, were the narrator not quite so dim-witted, he would realise is no spook, but his wife's lover:

> *I used to have three sets of clothes once to wear,*
> *But now I can only find one,*
> *I said to my wife, 'Where's me clothes?'*
> *She said, 'Hush, I'll see if the ghost has 'em on,' . . .*
> *Each night I can hear him below,*
> *And the wife knows I'm frightened the most,*
> *She gets up and leaves me in bed pale with fright,*
> *Whilst downstairs she hunts him for hours left and right,*
> *I haven't seen her since eleven last night . . .*
> *Oh, I wish we were rid of the ghost!*

George fared slightly better a few weeks later when he recorded 'Chinese Blues' and 'Do De O Do' with the Jack Hylton Band – the latter an inferior number which is only memorable on account of Nat Gonella's superb trumpet solo – though there had to be several takes for both because George kept missing his cue. This made him so despondent that Beryl cancelled two further sessions which had been booked for that summer, and George did not enter the studio again until towards the end of the year.

'Chinese Blues' had been first offered to George by its composer, Jack Cottrell, in 1922, at which point he had turned the song down, claiming that it was too jazz-orientated. Later, he said he would not have recorded it at all had it not been for Jack Hylton, who heard him singing it at a party – and even then he only agreed to do the two takes providing Hylton accompanied him. Its title was subsequently changed to 'Chinese Laundry Blues', and though George had no intention at the time of ever recording a sequel, it would prove the first in a long-running saga about the ubiquitous proprietor of the Limehouse laundry, a stereotyping which is today regarded as most politically incorrect. Indeed, in 1995 when celebrations were being prepared for the 50th anniversary of the end of World War II, the BBC were specifically requested *not* to broadcast any of George's Mr Wu songs.

Born in Oldham in 1892, Jack Cottrell had tried his hand at any number of jobs before turning to the stage. He later formed the comedy duo Sid and Billy with the Kent-born singer Dorothy Sheepwash (aka Billy Morton) whom he married. Some time during 1931, when the pair had starred in Thomas Convery's revue *Just Plain Folk*, at the Oldham Palace, George had been signed up to make a guest appearance. Cottrell's widow, at the time of writing a very sprightly, still vivacious octogenarian, told me:

Jack was writing material for Sandy Powell at the time. He would often wake up in the middle of the night with a tune in his head and wouldn't be able to sleep again until it had been written down – later he would have our daughter's little toy piano next to the bed, ready for these flashes of inspiration. That's how most of his Formby songs came about. And of course, Beryl did her utmost to stop Jack earning any royalties by offering to buy the songs outright for a fiver apiece. Jack always took her money, but he also made sure that he got the royalties as well. With several small children to clothe and feed we needed the money! But the most *important thing Jack ever did for George Formby was never made public. Years before he persuaded him to record 'Chinese Blues' it was* Jack Cottrell *who got him to revert to the name Formby, no one else.*

Jack Cottrell supplied George with twenty-two songs over the next few years, fourteen of which were recorded. The composer's personal favourite was 'Levi's Monkey Mike', inspired by a visit to the Hampstead home of animal-mad Gracie Fields and her then husband, Archie Pitt, when he had been entertained by the couple's pet marmoset. The antics of Mike, the Tipperary anthropoid who is so bright that he plays the 'Wedding March', sneaks into an old maid's bedroom and ends up being elected Chancellor of the Exchequer, show the workings of a decidedly surrealist imagination:

> *He taxed the laces in our boots,*
> *And taxed our Christmas puddin' . . .*
> *Now, working men just give an ear,*
> *We're all right now, so never fear,*
> *Who's going to take the tax off beer?*
> *Levi's monkey, Mike!*

Cottrell's steadfast refusal to recognise George's 'composing' talents by allowing his name to be added to the credits infuriated Beryl and brought out her barely concealed mean streak, as Dorothy Cottrell recalled:

Beryl Formby was an extremely nasty woman towards just about everybody who came into contact with her husband. I don't know why she hated me. Maybe it was because Jack was quite a bit older than me, or because I was just as glamorous as she was. Even so, Jack and I were blissfully

happy together and I certainly wasn't amorously interested in
George Formby! When we were appearing in the Convery
revue our dressing-rooms were connected by a swing-door.
Beryl would hold it for me, then let it smack into my face. But
she was at her most cruel when we were all appearing a few
years later in a show in Blackpool. My little daughter, June,
was admitted to hospital with a tubercular abscess. Jack
would sneak in to see her whenever he could – the doctors had
told us that it was touch and go, and they were convinced that
she was only clinging to life because of her daddy's visits.
When Beryl found out, she stopped him from going – it was
either that or he would never work for Formby again.
Fortunately, Julie didn't die, though Jack was never the same
again.

Beryl's insensitivity resulted in there being no more Cottrell
songs for George, and started off this tremendously nice,
much-respected man's slow, tortuous decline. By 1936, when
Cottrell was still only forty-four, he would be bedridden and
virtually penniless, supported largely by a doting wife who had
taken employment as a dance-teacher and relocated her family
to Upton, near Pontefract in West Yorkshire. Yet even weighed
down by illness and near-destitution Cottrell put others before
himself, raising a large amount of money for the dependants of
miners killed in the Upton Pit Disaster through sheet-music
sales of one of his last works, 'Song Of The Pit'. And when
Cottrell finally succumbed to cancer in 1947, for all the wealth
and success he had brought George's way, Beryl would not
allow her husband to send flowers to the funeral, claiming that
these would only be a waste of money seeing as how Cottrell
would not be able to see them!

Unlike many 'visual' artists, George soon grew accustomed
to working in the studio, and even his most hilarious
performances here do not suffer when deprived of an audience.
Jack Hylton had been suitably impressed to *demand* to work

with him again, though not so much, it would seem, to allow George's name to appear on the record labels. Of the three numbers he recorded with Hylton on 13 October, for 'The Old Kitchen Kettle' George is referred to simply as 'vocal refrain'. To be fair, he could hardly complain, for he had insisted upon leaving his own name off the label of 'Chinese Blues'.

From this session came the side-splitting 'I Told My Baby With My Ukulele', an exercise in pure, unadulterated ragtime which is almost as appealing for its sizzling instrumentals as it is for George's uncompromising put-down of his latest flame:

> *Her hair was brunette type,*
> *It had pretty wrinkles like you see in tripe . . .*
> *Her face it is so bright,*
> *You can't see a blemish on a foggy night,*
> *And when she smiles of her own accord,*
> *Her face lights up 'cause she's lantern-jawed!*
> *Her teeth they are divine,*
> *All the colours of the rainbow there you'll find,*
> *Black, blue, green and red, you bet,*
> *She only wants a white 'un for a snooker-set!*

This little ditty ends with George complimenting his sweetheart on her lovely neck – by buying her soap and a sponge to wash it – before bashing her over the head with his beloved instrument!

The song was the first of over two hundred written by Harry Gifford and Fred E Cliffe, as a team, separately, or in collaboration with other composers. Half of these were issued on 78rpm recordings, whilst the others were either just performed on stage, or put on to acetates and consigned to vaults. Cliffe (Clifford Howcchin) was a stalwart Liverpudlian, forty-seven when he began working with Gifford (Henry Folkard), a middle-aged Devonian who had enjoyed a minor success with a revue, *Reflections*, which had toured London and the provinces in 1931. How these two vastly different men met is not known, though when George recorded 'I Told My Baby With My Ukulele' they were working in a tiny office in Streatham. Much of the time Cliffe would write the lyrics, which Gifford would set to music using basic melodies which rested easily on the ear, adhering to the music-hall adage that a song should stay in the memory after three airings. Astonishingly, despite the phenomenal success of their work, they would hardly ever see George save in the recording studio. Cliffe could not stand Beryl, and she was unable to tolerate Gifford, whom she often dismissed as 'one of them' on account of his single status.

The BBC played 'I Told My Baby With My Ukulele' and its flipside, 'If You Don't Want The Goods Don't Maul 'Em' to death – though they frowned on its 'companion-piece', Jack Cottrell's 'With My Little Ukulele In My Hand' when it was released the following summer.

The song was peppered with double-entendres, though fairly tame in comparison with other material George would perform in the not too distant future, setting a precedent which would largely be responsible for his becoming without any doubt the most fêted British male entertainer of his generation. Whereas Gracie Fields, his nearest female counterpart, provided an anodyne to the slight suggestiveness of some comedy numbers by offering audiences works of a romantic or religious persuasion, George hardly ever ventured far from his bouncy style and pulled few punches once he realised that he could get away with it. 'Bugger the critics and the snobs,' he once said, 'so long as the audiences like what I do and *they're* not offended, I don't care what anybody else thinks!'

Review copies of 'With My Little Ukulele In My Hand', coupled with 'As The Hours And The Days', were sent to the BBC and several music publications within days of its release, and a few hundred copies – subsequently to become much sought-after collectors' items – found their way into the shops.

Decca received so many complaints that the record was quickly withdrawn and instructions were given for the A-side to be replaced with the less risqué 'Sunbathing In The Park'.

The two stanzas of the song which caused the most offence, according to the moral watchdogs at the BBC, alluded to 'Mr Formby's preoccupation that his musical instrument represents for him a substitute phallus.' George has taken his lady-love, Jane, for a stroll along the sands. However:

> *I felt so shy and bashful, sitting there,*
> *'Cause the things she said I didn't understand,*
> *She said, 'Your love just turns me dizzy,*
> *Come on, big boy, get busy!'*
> *But I kept my ukulele in my hand!*

And, the subsequent birth of their baby:

> *My heart did jump with joy,*
> *I could see he was a boy,*
> *For he had a ukulele in his hand!*

During the autumn of 1932, Beryl decided that it was time to find George a manservant – someone who would be able to take care of his clothes, clean his cars, make sure that his ukuleles were set out correctly in the wings, and answer the telephone and his less important correspondence. Advertisements were placed in several local newspapers and there were dozens of applicants, though the man Beryl eventually settled upon would prove considerably more than a general factotum. Over the next twenty-nine years he would be regarded by George as a trusted servant and friend, a surrogate brother and a soulmate all rolled into one efficient, patient and loyal package. His name was Harry Scott, and many years later he would recount his stylised, albeit sometimes overbearingly sycophantic account of his life with Britain's top showbusiness couple in *The Vellum*, the official magazine of the George Formby Society:

> *My first week's wages with the Formbys was £5. It was still £5 a week nearly thirty years later when George died. George could be tight with his money when he wanted . . . in fact, I cannot honestly remember George buying a drink for anyone on more than two or three occasions all the time I was with him. I was rarely out of their sight. I went with them everywhere, and I enjoyed every single moment. Yet even though we did have our disagreements – I actually walked out on them more than once – I would do it all again, even for a fiver a week!*

There seems little doubt, however, upon studying Scott's *The Fabulous Formby* and reading between the lines – the story ran consecutively over fourteen issues of *The Vellum* in the late 60s – that whilst he nurtured an innate respect and admiration for George, for three more decades Harry Scott would carry a torch for Beryl, in spite of his own happy marriage – the only thing, some sources have said, which prevented their relationship from progressing perilously beyond the platonic:

> *Beryl was always full of generosity . . . She called me her brother. She was more a friend of mine than George was throughout most of the long time that I was with them. When I had a row with her – and that can happen with the best of pals in showbusiness – stage hands could ask her two minutes later, 'Is that your brother, Mrs Formby?' She would answer, 'Yes, that's my brother, Harry.' A marvellous woman, was Beryl Formby. She was the best!*

On 26 December 1932 George and Beryl opened in their very first pantomime, *The Babes In The Wood*, at Bolton's Grand Theatre. She had insisted on adding the 'the' to the title because, she declared, it would distinguish it from the inferior productions being staged up and down the country! Sitting in the audience during this first performance was Bert Loman, one of the North's most eminent impresarios, a man who, like Beryl, never minced words. When Beryl asked Loman for an honest appraisal of her husband's pantomime skills, which she had taught him, he told her, 'Not much.' Beryl's response to this – 'Can *you* do any better?' – was met with a tarty, 'Much better, Mrs Formby, so long as you have the brass!' A contract was drawn up there and then: Loman would 'mortgage' out his services for £300, to be spread evenly over thirty-six monthly payments, after which – providing George made the grade, which of course he did – he would be offered pantomime seasons in Loman's theatres.

It was public pressure – the fact that his records were getting a lot of airplay, or being noticed one way or another and selling well, and that now, wherever he was playing it did not take long for the HOUSE FULL signs to go up – which led Beryl into deciding that George was ready to begin making films. It did not matter that he was initially uninterested in the medium. From Beryl's viewpoint, anything Gracie Fields could do, *her* husband could do infinitely better . . . or so she thought.

Initially, Beryl approached Basil Dean, the head of ATP – Associated Talking Pictures, later to become Ealing Studios. Dean had recently produced Gracie's immensely successful *Looking On The Bright Side*, and had just contracted her for *Sing As We Go*. Over the telephone he had snarled at Beryl, 'George Formby? What are you planning on doing, dear, digging him up?' *She* had not seen the funny side of this, but before she had had time to give him a piece of her mind, Dean had begrudgingly arranged a meeting.

Gracie Field's stepdaughter, Irene Bevan, recounted the outcome of this:

Basil Dean was a miserable bastard. There's absolutely no

other way of describing him. He was thoroughly disliked in the business because he could be so nasty and spiteful. And George's wife was almost as bad, so you can imagine all the fireworks when those two met, all the demands she spouted for someone who was after all only a novice so far as films were concerned. Dean told her, 'I'm certainly interested in having Formby on my books, but I sure as hell don't want his fucking wife. Just make sure you trap your tongue in the door on your way out!' And that was that, at least for a couple of years . . .

Beryl was knocked back by virtually every studio in and around London, but this only fired her determination. Irving Asher, the British representative for Warner Brothers who soon afterwards would discover Errol Flynn, granted her an interview at Warner's Teddington Lock studios. Asher's speciality was 'quota quickies' – these were the cheaply made, usually direly scripted and acted B-movies which were churned out like factory products to compete with the big American productions being imported into this country. He told Beryl that although he had seen and appreciated her husband's act, there was no question of George ever making the transition from stage to film because he was 'too stupid to play the bad guy and too ugly to play the hero'. Beryl left Asher's office in tears – but only because she had wanted to throttle the man!

A few weeks after Asher's rebuff, George was in his dressing-room after his show in Warrington when he was approached by John Blakeley, the director of Mancunian Films, a small company which did not have a great deal of money, but which *was* interested in giving George a fair crack of the whip.

George's response – 'It's got nothing to do with me, lad. You'd better go see the wife!' – did not fill Blakeley with terror, as had happened with some of the others. The director was holding all the trumps, and told her that his terms were non-negotiable: a 15-day shooting schedule, a budget of just £3,000 which would include a £200 salary for George, and ten per cent of the profits for the star. The contract was signed at once, and to save money – and to keep an eye on George – Beryl announced that she would be playing his leading lady!

The result of George's first thrown-together enterprise with John Blakeley was *Boots, Boots*. Even before the film went into production there were problems with Beryl, as Dorothy Cottrell explained:

> *The songs and the* entire *script for* Boots, Boots *were written by Jack Cottrell, though Beryl tried to claim all the credit for George by saying he had written it – you know, so that he could rake in the profits, if there were to be any. Well, this time Jack was wise to her, though I was very angry with him for allowing George to sing 'Baby' to that horrible woman, particularly as he had written the song for me!*

Boots, Boots was shot in a disused warehouse above an Albany Street garage, just off London's Regent Street. Initially, this presented problems for the skeleton crew, headed by director Bert Tracey, who also appeared in the film which had to be shot over the clamour emanating from the workmen below . . . until Tracey installed a bell, which was rung each time a scene had to be shot. Then the men would disappear to the nearest pub, frequently with George in tow, which of course defeated the director's objective, resulting in much of the film being completed after the workmen had clocked off, when the pub was shut!

Boots, Boots has a very basic storyline, Roy Fogwell's camera-work is decidedly amateur – fixed position, with the actors walking in and out of the frame as if attending a badly-organised audition – and the acting is appalling. Only George and Beryl stand out, giving some indication of how scintillating their stage performances must have been, even in these, their formative years – in particular displaying how much Beryl had to offer, and how much she had given up to manage her husband. 'Shades of Libby Holman and a second-rate Mistinguett,' was how she was described by Irene Bevan – not by any means a back-handed compliment.

The dialogue, too, in parts smacks of the later Formby genius. John Willie is the cynical, inefficient 'boots' or factotum at a provincial hotel. Picked upon by the manager and the chef (Bert Tracey), he in turn intimidates the scullery-maid, Snooky (Beryl). Given his limited intellect this is the only way he thinks he can woo her, until he is taught the rudimentaries of seduction by Marie, the flighty chambermaid who is having an affair with her boss. Marie encouraged the intensely shy John Willie to put his arm around her and pretend that *she* is Snooky, though the outcome is not what she is expecting:

M: *Can't you feel a strange sensation, a peculiar feeling within you?*
JW: *Yes, I can – them pork pies I've had for me dinner!*
M: *Oh, John Willie. I'm bursting with love!*
JW: *Oh, don't burst. Undo something . . .*
M: *John Willie, look into my eyes. Don't you know that the eyes are the windows of the soul?*
JW: *Well, your windows want washing. But those eyes – like twin stars. Those nostrils – like twin cylinders. Those ears – like twin petals.*
M: *Petals? What kind of petals?*
JW: *Bicycle petals . . .*

Elsewhere in the scenario, John Willie confronts an effeminate client who, three decades prior to gay-liberation, demands a pink room. 'Oh, fairies!' he exclaims. Then, after they have pranced to 'Here We Go Gathering Nuts In May', John Willie flattens him. After another altercation, he throws the chef out of the window. For the lovebirds, however, all ends well when the manager becomes aware of their talent – the factotum's singing, and Snooky's tap-dancing, which John Willie gets her to speed up by standing her atop the kitchen stove.

The manager engages the pair for a cabaret spot when the billed artists fail to appear, and the transformation is remarkable as the characters become the actors portraying them: George in his dinner suit, singing two numbers with the Harry Hudson band; Beryl, debagged of her dreary uniform and bottle-bottom glasses, a vision of loveliness and grace. The film ends with them in one another's arms, crooning a delightful little love-song:

> *Although the skies be dreary and grey,*
> *Promise me that you'll never stray away,*
> *My baby, baby,*
> *You're my sweetheart . . .*

During the shooting of *Boots, Boots*, Beryl would set a precedent for being inexcusably catty towards George's co-stars, male and female. In theatres she had always done her utmost to discourage him from 'having a jar with the lads', and a murderous stare had kept chorus girls well at bay, but on the set her jealousy was taken to the extreme when she observed him chatting to a young actress named Betty Driver – three decades later she would portray one of Britain's best-loved television barmaids in *Coronation Street*.

In years to come Beryl would have good reason for suspecting her husband of 'meandering', for by this time she would have *driven* him into other women's arms. Betty Driver, however, was just twelve years old and any 'association' she may have had with George Formby was platonic. Not that the scheming Beryl believed this – Betty's scene in the film, performing a music-hall ditty during the cabaret sequence, ended up on the cutting-room floor.

CHAPTER THREE

HITTING THE HIGH SPOTS NOW!

'What a life George had with Beryl. There was no doubt as to who was boss. Almost the same situation as poor Arthur Lucan with the harridan Kitty McShane, though not quite as physical.' Arthur Askey, comedian.

Between the completion of *Boots, Boots* and its release, George made two visits to the Chenil Galleries, where besides 'Baby' he recorded several of his most roguish songs. 'The Wedding Of Mr Wu' was the second instalment of the Chinese saga and saw the church on Limehouse Way decorated with washing from the laundry, whilst the guests attempted to Anglicise themselves by using their chopsticks to eat peas, and a jazz-band replaced the ukulele interlude. And in 'Swimmin' With The Wimmin', George tells us what happened during a visit to the local swimming baths on a mixed-session day: the low point when the large woman he saves from drowning only turns out to be his wife – and the joy of being with his sweetheart, Adeline:

> *You ought to see her latest bathing costume,*
> *It's nothing but a little piece of trimmin'.*
> *And what I took to be her face*
> *Turned out to be a different place,*
> *When I went swimmin' with the women!*

This was one of the numbers George performed in *The Babes*

In The Wood, which played the New Theatre, Ashton-under-Lyme, in January 1934. He clomped on to the stage wearing an old pair of canvas boots two sizes too big for him. 'These belonged to my old man,' he told the audience, earning himself a standing ovation before the fun began. Formby Sr's boots would make an appearance in every pantomime premiere until George's very last one in 1960 – he would baptise them 'The Boot Repairer's Despair', and in 1940 pay as much to have them preserved and encased in leather as it would have cost to buy another ten pairs. He often said that they were his only superstition. 'A grand man wore them first, ma'am,' he would later tell the future Queen Elizabeth, 'and I'm proud to be wearing them now!'

A few weeks later, the Formbys attended the London opening of *Boots, Boots*. Southern cinemagoers, however, who had raved over Gracie Fields' screwball comedies, did not know what to make of this one, though it was *so* successful in the North of England that John Blakeley immediately contracted George to make another film, and this time the budget was increased to £8,000.

Off The Dole was adapted from a music-hall revue, one of which had starred George's younger brother, Frank. Unfortunately, it will go down in history as one of the worst British films ever made. It begins well. John Willie is thrown off the dole because he is too lazy to look for work, but is saved when an uncle asks him to take over his private detective agency. After the first ten minutes, however, the plot runs haywire. No one seems to have a clue as to what they are supposed to be doing, and one gets the impression that no matter how the mostly fixed-frame tableaux *could* have been edited and arranged, the film still would not have made much sense. Even more astonishing was the fact that this little horror was even *more* popular in the North of England than its predecessor – grossing some £40,000 at the box-office – whilst elsewhere it was deservedly ignored and assigned to obscurity.

Those sections of the film containing George's and Beryl's songs, however, were another matter – even the bungling John Blakeley had been unable to ruin these – and resulted in George being courted by Ben Henry, Basil Dean's Northern representative, who would in the not too distant future become the Formbys' agent. At this time, however, when Beryl learned *whom* he was working for, Henry was soon sent packing. Blakeley, meanwhile, upon hearing that Dean had made an attempt to poach 'his' star, decided to capitalise on George's success whilst he had the chance. Piecing together the songs from their two films, and supplementing them with a couple of atrociously edited sketches, he came up with *George Formby Cavalcade*, which starts off with the opening credit, 'Hear Again The Songs That Made George Formby The Idol Of The People!'

The ruse made Blakeley a tidy sum, but signalled the end of the road for his partnership with the Formbys. As soon as Basil Dean realised that George was wasting his talents with a 'two-bob outfit', he moved in on Beryl with a substantial offer which quickly enabled her to swallow her stubborn pride *and* put up with the man's arrogance and rudeness.

Gracie Fields' stepdaughter, Irene, was at the studios in the spring of 1935 when the Formbys arrived for their first meeting with Basil Dean:

Beryl barged in, dressed and acting like Lady Muck, with her poor little husband lagging behind like the lackey. She told him, 'Remember what I said. You speak only when you're spoken to, and you leave all the negotiating to me.' Gracie had just had a huge success with Look Up And Laugh *and was then shooting* Queen of Hearts, *a wonderful piece of slapstick being directed by her [second, but not until 1940] husband, Monty Banks, and Dean thought he would be the ideal director for his first film with George. He and Monty were such dear, funny men that any collaboration between those two*

41

would have to be a riot, so long as we all managed to keep
Beryl and Dean from going for one another's throats . . .

The film was *No Limit*, the first of eleven George would make under his five-year contract with ATP, starting out with a budget of £30,000. Dean, however, made it very clear from the signing of the document that Beryl would *not* be appearing in the production . . . indeed, that she would only be tolerated on the set in her capacity as 'Mr Formby's adviser' providing she kept her mouth shut and her opinions to herself. Unfortunately, Monty Banks' choice of Florence Desmond for George's leading lady did not go down at all well with the ubiquitous Beryl.

One year younger than George, Desmond's career had constituted one triumph after another. Having studied ballet since the age of ten, in 1926 she had augmented C D Cochran's dancing troupe and had appeared in several of his famous annual revues, holding audiences spellbound not just with her nifty footwork and fine singing voice, but with her startlingly accurate impersonations of Jimmy Durante, Ethel Barrymore and Tallulah Bankhead. Since then she had toured Britain on numerous occasions, appeared on the cabaret circuit and starred opposite Gracie Fields in *Sally In Our Alley*, produced by Basil Dean in 1931.

After witnessing Desmond's performance in the 1934 Cochran revue, *Streamline*, James Agate, one of the country's sharpest critics, had observed, 'She has not only a white-hot sense of the ridiculous, but can present it in a dozen different disguises.' But if the media adored her, many of those who worked with her had a different tale to tell. Desmond, a Londoner by birth, had made it quite clear what *she* thought of Northerners whilst working with Gracie Fields, as Irene Bevan explained:

Gracie condemned Florence Desmond for being such an out-
and-out snob. Their antagonism began one day when the

studio provided everyone with afternoon tea which they ate on their lap. Florence asked them to take the bread and butter back, saying she only ate brown bread. That stuck in Gracie's gullet. It was something quite silly, but it gives a good insight into her weird outlook on life, and the way she had been brought up. 'Stuck-up so-and-so. White bread's not good enough for her. Who does she think she is?' Eventually, Gracie and Florence did become friends, but Florence always loathed George Formby. 'That dreadful, slobbering little oaf,' she called him, whilst he always referred to her as, 'That snotty-nosed little minx,' and completely ignored her every time she threw a tantrum. The first of those occurred when Beryl warned her to keep her hands off her husband – not that she'd even tried such a thing. Florence screamed at her that she wouldn't be amorously interested in him, not if he was the last man on earth. And absolutely everyone at the studio detested Beryl. Poor George couldn't speak to anyone without her giving him the third degree. And if that someone happened to be a woman – even if she'd only smiled or said Hello – Beryl would accuse him in front of everyone of wanting to sleep with her.

Neither did Beryl see eye to eye with those running the studio canteen, in particular the French chef whom she accused of patronising them when he decided to surprise the Formbys by serving them his interpretation of Lancashire hot-pot. Beryl told him that she could not possibly eat such 'muck', to which the chef replied that if she could do better, then she would be welcome to have his job! The pair found themselves getting on like a house on fire, however, when Beryl barged into his kitchen and gave him an impromptu cookery lesson – the next time hot-pot showed up on the menu, the Frenchman received nothing but praise, though he flatly refused to have anything to do with the couple's other favourite 'delicacy' . . . beef-dripping toast!

No Limit was filmed mostly on location in the Isle of Man, in the summer of 1935 during the actual TT (Tourist Trophy) Races week. This enabled Monty Banks to hire several of the riders, who were paid £75 a week for their services whether they worked or not, *and* ensconced at the plush Majestic Hotel. The other 'riders', the studio stuntmen, received just £5 for each day they were called to the set and were expected to find their own accommodation. This resulted in the stuntmen going on strike for several days, until Banks capitulated – he saved the extra money he was compelled to pay the stuntmen by placing an advertisement on local cinema screens for crowd extras, most of whose only remuneration was the hope of seeing fleeting glimpses of themselves in a George Formby movie. Only the ones who appeared on the grandstand during the race scenes were paid the going rate.

George was firmly against the studio providing *him* with a stunt-double, though Beryl had insisted that he should – just about the only detail she and Monty Banks agreed upon all through shooting the film. George duped them both, however, during the scene where he rides his machine at break-neck speed, jumping clear a split-second before it somersaults over the edge of a cliff. Beryl had gone off to the studio canteen, and Banks had assumed the man on the bike to be a stunt-double . . . until a grinning George pulled off his helmet and goggles.

The director was suitably impressed with George's performance not to redo the scene with a stuntman, though he was obliged to report the matter to Basil Dean. George was not insured to take such inordinate risks, and had things gone wrong claims for damages at his level could have easily put ATP out of business. Beryl later said that she had only found out about the incident four months afterwards, when George confessed all at the film's premiere. This was not true: Dean had contacted her at once, in her official capacity as George's manager, and Beryl had shared his concern. Between them they decided that his future contracts should include a clause stipulating that he should never again be allowed to ride a motorcycle in any of his films . . . one which George would, as will be seen, promptly ignore.

As this was the middle of the tourist season, Beryl, completely disregarding Basil Dean's warning that she should take a back seat in the production, ensured that she milked the publicity for all it was worth. 'It's *his* film,' she told the press, whom she encouraged to photograph George acting the fool or chatting to the holiday crowds. 'And as you can see, the people are *only* interested in him, not in his so-called screen love-interest!'

This was very true, but the tension between George and Florence Desmond, which was bad enough *before* filming began, escalated sky-high when Beryl arranged for bills to be posted on the sides of the equipment vans which proclaimed, 'Associated Talking Pictures Now Filming *No Limit* With GEORGE FORMBY'.

Desmond saw red. She had already had a ferocious argument with Basil Dean because George was being paid more for the film than she was, telling the producer, 'The man's as thick as two very short planks. It wouldn't surprise me if he can't *read* his lines let alone remember them!' Dean had refused to give her a rise in salary, but he had been unable to ignore the terms of her contract, the fact that she *was* George's co-star, and entitled to equal publicity. She therefore told Dean that unless these posters came down immediately, *she* would walk off the set, and sue. Beryl merely scoffed at this, declaring that leading ladies were two-a-penny, which brought the most vociferous outcry from Monty Banks, a chirpy little Italian who hardly ever quarrelled with anyone, but who nevertheless tore a strip off Desmond for going over his head, and even threatened to fire her from the production. The situation was saved by George, who – waiting until his wife had gone off to the hairdressers – personally removed the offending posters, well aware that the public knew *exactly* who was the star of the film, and also aware that his actions would get him into hot water with Beryl.

One word describes *No Limit* – sublime! Indeed, it is virtually inconceivable that it is separated from the trashy Blakeley production by less than a year – or that, for such a bubbling, optimistic film, there was so much behind the scenes misery, for this certainly does not transpose itself on to the screen. George Shuttleworth, a mother's boy chimney-sweep's assistant from Flagdyke, adapts a 1928 Rainbow motorcycle in the hope that he will be able to enter it for the TT Races. Then, financed by his mother – who steals the money from her skinflint father's stash, which he has hidden in the sofa – George sets off for the Isle of Man. 'With my gears in reverse – the other way round, I'll finish first,' he sings on the train, to a collection of characters straight from a *Punch* cartoon.

Aboard the ship – the film's only *faux-pas* is that this starts off as the *Mona's Queen*, but changes mid-ocean to the *Manxman!* – George meets Florrie (Desmond), the secretary from Rainbow Motorcycles with whom he has been corresponding for a while, sending her photographs of 'George Shuttleworth, Speed Demon', in the hope that her company might sponsor him. Neither knows who the other is until George abseils down the side of the ship to retrieve Florrie's hat. He plunges into the sea, tears his suit, and she recognises him from the pictures she takes from his pocket whilst repairing his jacket. She then falls for the gentle, shy underdog, whilst spurning the advances of Rainbow's boorish ace-rider, Bert Tyldesley (Jack Hobbs).

As George's champion, Florrie helps him out when his money is stolen: blacking his face with soot, she parades him on the beach, where he entertains the crowds until sprung by his fussy landlady, who concludes that he may not be able to pay his bill. No problem, here – George is not really hard-up, just collecting for charity! He then enters the TT Trials, breaking the speed record when his brakes fail and the throttle jams wide open, but ending up with the shakes and vowing never to ride another bike – a vow he is persuaded to keep when a rival company sends a pair of thugs to pay him not to participate in the main event, and to smash up his bike by riding it over the edge of a cliff. The machine takes George with it: he grabs an overhanging branch and backflips on to the clifftop, offering one of the film's few moments of slapstick. He then uses his bribe money to offer his sweetheart a good time.

Meanwhile, George's mother and grandfather (Edward Rigby) arrive on the Isle of Man. The old man, who has always dismissed George as useless, changes his tune now that the lad has made good. He pays off George's rivals, whilst Florrie presents him with a prototype machine on behalf of Rainbow, who have nominated him their official rider. This incurs Tyldesley's wrath – henceforth, he is the enemy engaged by another rival manufacturer.

The big race is tremendously exciting, with George doing almost all of his own stunts. Before the start, the two men fight – stepping out of character, George bashes Tyldesley. From here on the hero comes up against every obstacle, crashing through fences and gates, several times falling off his machine, always neck-and-neck with the foe, whilst around them the other competitors drop like flies – until the last lap, when Florrie spurs him on by holding up a sign, 'I Love You'. 'Must have been a summons,' observes the commentator, 'he shot away like a bullet!' Then, 500 yards from the finish, George runs out of petrol and has to push, collapsing as he passes the post – authentically so, on account of the heat and the fifteen takes demanded by Monty Banks – just seconds before his rival screams past.

The songs in this film are arguably the best performed in any of George's Ealing comedies. From the zippy 'Riding In The TT Races' to Florence Desmond's big production number, 'Riding Around On A Rainbow' – which has everyone joining in aboard the ship and which is made all the more effective by the curious camera angles. And from George's and Desmond's romantic little *chanson*, 'Your Way Is My Way', to the comic-strip humour of 'In A Little Wigan Garden', these musical delights all represented a sparkling antidote to the dark days of the Depression:

> *Crocuses croak with the frog and the smoke,*
> *From the gas-works near.*
> *The one thing that only grows*
> *Is the wart on my sweetheart's nose . . .*
> *'Neath the Wigan water-lilies,*
> *Where the drainpipe overflows,*
> *There's my girl and me,*
> *She'll sit on my knee and watch how the rhubarb grows!*

It was during the shooting of this film that George substituted his John Willie bowler with his infamous grey felt trilby – which subsequently became a fixture in almost every one of his celluloid appearances. Beryl bought it for ten shillings, and after each day's work it would be locked away in a steel box in the studio's props department. No one but Beryl and George were ever allowed to touch it, it had its own chair in the studio canteen, and always occupied the seat between the Formbys when they were in the cutting or projection room – giving way to rumours that they hardly ever spoke to each other whilst they were on the set, which of course *was* partly true.

No Limit was released in March 1936, and despite being awarded a thumbs-down by the London critics it was a huge success nationwide, finally bringing George the recognition he deserved, though not yet by any means putting him on a level with Gracie Fields. Basil Dean, however, knew that he was on to a winner, and therefore decided to stick to the tried-and-tested formula with George's next film – using the same director, scriptwriter *and* leading lady as before, and as many songs as George's team could come up with at such short notice.

George and Beryl were not told that Florence Desmond was going to be in his film until Desmond had been sweet-talked into doing so by Basil Dean. This was not an easy task, for the actress was still of the opinion that George was a 'dirty little man', an 'amateur' who had no interest whatsoever in acting or trying to remember even the simplest parts of the script, preferring to improvise as he went along. Desmond told Dean that if she *did* sign the contract, he would have to swear that Beryl would never be allowed on to the set. Dean did so with his fingers crossed behind his back, though he did worm his way into Desmond's good books by offering her the same (undisclosed) salary as George, for which she signed a pledge that this would never be made public.

Having secured Desmond, Dean went to see the Formbys. Beryl called him all the names under the sun, but instructed George to sign the contract all the same, and George reiterated that he did not mind *who* his co-star was so long as he was getting his 'brass', and so long as his 'management team' – in other words, Beryl – had access to the studio and set at all times. Dean attempted to take him on one side and explain that this might prove difficult, for Monty Banks and some of the other actors had petitioned Dean, begging him to banish this troublesome woman. Beryl, however, got the first word in: unless Dean and everyone else agreed to her terms, she would go looking for another producer.

Technically, as George was contracted to ATP until at least the summer of 1941, Beryl could not do this. He had, however, already been courted by several other top producers – including Elstree Studios' John Maxwell – and it would not have been impossible for one of these to buy him out of his contract with Dean. He therefore decided not to take any chances, though such was the tension during shooting – with George and Desmond not exchanging a single word unless it was part of the script and the cameras were rolling – that Dean gave his own studios a wide berth for almost a month.

Keep Your Seats Please was based on the Petrov play, *Twelve Chairs* – though in this particular instance their number had been reduced to seven – and also featured that fine character actor, Alastair Sim, portraying a creepy, over-the-top lawyer. An elderly millionairess, Georgina Withers, bequeaths her fortune to charity to prevent her greedy relatives from getting their hands on it – anyone who wants a memento of her, she declares in her will, will have to buy one! – but she has concealed £90,000 in jewellery and bonds in the seat of an antique dining chair, one of a set which is about to be auctioned. In view of this, she has left a letter at the lodging house where her favourite nephew George, the family black sheep resides, urging him to purchase them so that his other relatives will not be suspicious.

The action cuts to George, an out of work concert-party artist, plucking his uke in a pawn-shop. He tries to pawn his instrument to raise the money to pay for his room, but is unable to do so and when he gets back to the lodging house he discovers that the landlady has rented it to Florrie (Florence Desmond). She is being pursued by welfare officers who are trying to take away Binkie (Fiona Stuart), her dead sister's child whom she has promised to look after. When it emerges that she cannot afford to pay for her room either both are evicted and set off for the auction rooms. What George does not know is that one of the chairs has already been sold to a drunken sailor. He therefore buys the six under the hammer, holding up the proceedings by informing the auctioneer that he has no money – no problem, he says, for he will borrow this from Drayton, his aunt's lawyer (Sim). Drayton, however, knows what is inside one of the chairs, and wants them for himself. He burns George's letter of proof, though their subsequent conversation is overheard by conman Max (Gus McNaughton), who agrees to help George and Florrie in exchange for a percentage of the booty, which increases with each step of the search.

By now all the chairs have been sold, and the trio set off on a quest to recover George's inheritance. The first has been bought by Madame Louise, the celebrated voice coach – a visit which ends up with George and Max being suspected of being her lovers, and manhandled out of her house by an irate husband – though not before George has serenaded her with 'When I'm Cleaning Windows', the most accomplished song in the film. Elsewhere, Florence Desmond emulates Tallulah Bankhead and Gracie Fields when she duets with Fiona Stuart in 'Standing On The Tip Of My Toes', and she and George sing to the child, harmonising beautifully in 'Goodnight Binkie', though the film's title-track is far less memorable.

With Drayton and the welfare workers still in hot pursuit, the trio also draw a blank with the next purchasers – an incompetent doctor with a buxom nurse who attempts to undress George for his examination, with hilarious slapstick consequences, and with a bungling magician who has acquired three of the chairs. George and Florrie are invited on to the stage to participate in his latest illusion, and George slashes the chairs – from which emerge a psychotic duck which attacks him, a mischievous monkey and a flock of doves . . . but still no valuables.

Convinced that his legacy must be concealed in the sixth – and he thinks final – chair, the friends head for the home of a pair of eccentric sisters, only to discover that the contents of its seat have been devoured by the pet goat. They therefore kidnap the goat and rush it to the nearest hospital – on a bus. The goat is disguised as a dog and wears a mask which George has seemingly produced out of nowhere, has his uke, with which he now accompanies himself whilst entertaining the passengers with a few couplets from 'Keep Your Seats Please'. 'It's a hippopotapig!' he tells the bemused conductor. The goat, however, has merely scoffed a number of metal objects.

George then learns that a seventh chair was snapped up by the drunken tar, who is about to set sail on his ship, *The Bumblebee*. The final pursuit ends up with George and Florrie missing the ship, though Max gets there before it leaves, beaming triumphantly because he believes he has duped the other two. The sailor, however, has pawned the chair, enabling George and Florrie to buy it back – once he has pawned his ukulele, and all their clothes! And of course, he finds what they have been searching for, and asks his sweetheart to marry him.

This time, the London critics *did* sit up and take notice of a Formby film. 'Wigan's George Formby is now funny enough to take on the West End,' quipped one, though virtually *no* cinemas in this part of town were remotely interested in screening his films, with 75 per cent of their profits still coming from the North.

'When I'm Cleaning Windows' remains one of a select handful of 'property' songs which, his most ardent admirers believe, may not justifiably be performed by anyone but George Formby. In her biography of sorts – *My George* was written for the George Formby Fan Club at the end of 1938 – Beryl states that George himself had composed the song during a 2½ minute break on the set of *Keep Your Seats Please*, and that she had helped him. This, of course, was pure invention. Fred E Cliffe had written the lyrics in early 1936, and Harry Clifford had set them to music. George had simply 'kited' the credits, as usual, to get a third-share of the royalties which he was legally not entitled to – something the pair had 'consented' to when informed by Beryl that to refuse would result in her husband not performing any more of their songs.

George recorded the first version of 'When I'm Cleaning Windows' – a saucy series of Peeping Tom anecdotes, brilliantly set to ragtime – along with three other numbers on 27 September 1936, at Blackpool's Feldman Theatre. This unusual location nevertheless gives each performance a 'bouncy' feel which might not have easily been achieved in the caustic confines of the studio. It proved his biggest success to date, selling 150,000 copies within one month of its release and earning George his first silver disc. Like the earlier 'With A

Little Ukulele In My Hand', however, it attracted media condemnation on account of its prurient lyrics – offering some critics proof, they alleged, to add to the rumours being spread by the likes of Florence Desmond that George really was 'a dirty little Northern would-be Casanova'.

> Now there's a famous talkie queen,
> She looks a flapper on the screen,
> She's more like eighty than eighteen . . .
> She pulls her hair all down behind,
> Then pulls down her – never mind,
> Then after that pulls down the blind,
> When I'm cleaning windows!

The lyrics, of course, were *intended* as considerably more than innuendo, though George would later argue that since *he* never let on exactly *what* the talkie queen was pulling down in front of the window, the idea of filth came from the listener's mind. Since 1932, however, when he had begun performing his own material as opposed to his father's cast-offs, each number had been gauged by audience reaction, and for most fans – as with Frank Randall and Max Miller – there appeared to be no limit to how far George could actually go without offending *them*.

> The blushing bride she looks divine,
> The bridegroom he is doing fine,
> I'd rather have his job than mine . . .
> Pyjamas lying side by side,
> Ladies' nighties I have spied,
> I've often seen what goes inside,
> When I'm cleaning windows!

It was this last stanza which resulted in the recording of 'When I'm Cleaning Windows' being consigned to a drawer at the BBC – in those days controlled by the puritanical John Reith –

marked NTBB . . . Not To Be Broadcast. 'If the public wants to listen to Formby singing his disgusting little ditty,' Reith declared, 'they'll have to be content to hear it in the cinemas, not over the nation's airwaves!' Strangely enough none of the cinemas screening *Keep Your Seats Please* received a single complaint, for the film footage containing the 'naughty' bits had ended up on the cutting-room floor. And the record *was* broadcast, infrequently and late at night, for the mere fact that some announcers persisted in referring to 'the banned Formby song' which only stimulated listeners' interest, resulting in the record selling more copies than it might have done otherwise. 'The windows are not yet *clean* enough,' quipped one snooty request-programme host – the day after which shops reported running out of copies of *all* Formby recordings and sheet-music. And the windows would get even dirtier! Six months after cutting the original, George would record 'The Window Cleaner No. 2', and this one would include several stanzas which would upset the usually unshakeable Beryl:

> *To overcrowded flats I've been,*
> *Sixteen in one bed I've seen,*
> *With the lodger tucked up in between . . .*
> *Now lots of girls I've had to jilt,*
> *For they admire the way I'm built,*
> *It's a good job I don't wear a kilt,*
> *When I'm cleaning windows!*

George himself found it hard to comprehend what all the 'to-do' was about. As the son of the infamous 'John Willie' and the product of a Wigan backstreet he had been raised on what he took to be harmless innuendo. In his part of the country the predominant interest among the locals was and always had been whatever the other locals were getting up to. This fact, and the front parlour gossip which little boys were not supposed to hear, all this provided George with a rich array of source material for his work. It was also a good enough excuse for his name to be included amongst the song-writing credits, though his *actual* contribution as a composer as opposed to a 'supplier of ideas' has been much overestimated. The ideas for some songs are even said to have come from Beryl – her expression when bored, 'I'm sitting pretty with my fingers crossed', being but one example. The broadcaster Peter Clayton, writing in the *Sunday Telegraph* in 1974 on the occasion of the publication of a volume of Formby songs, made another interesting comparison:

> *Possession of a book of George Formby songs is roughly the equivalent of having your own rotating wire stand full of seaside comic postcards. 'When I'm Cleaning Windows' is pure Donald McGill set to music, an aria about honeymoon couples, bathrooms, underwear and old maids. Verses about Blackpool rock, flannelette nightshirts, violin bows and the prowess of the handyman constitute a crescendo of innuendo in song after song. As you read through them you see why adults would exchange significant glances over your then innocent head when George Formby records were plonked on the wind-up gramophones of your childhood.*

Donald McGill (1875–1962) remains the most popular post-card artist ever, drawing an estimated 25,000 cards in a 50-year career. He was renowned for his malapropisms and double-entendres. George's personal favourite postcard is said to have been the one which depicts an agonised casualty patient, and a bungling nurse being told by her superior, 'No, nurse. I said *prick* his *boil!*' McGill's speciality, outsized women strolling alongside feeble, henpecked husbands would also remind many of the Formbys, later in life.

Beryl, meanwhile, was incensed at the BBC's suggestion that her husband's work was apparently unfit for human con-sumption and she quite rightly defended him. Marching into

John Reith's office, she gave the Controller such a piece of her mind that he personally read out an apology that evening before the 9 o'clock news. The ban on the song, however, was not lifted.

The media were so busy attacking 'When I'm Cleaning Windows' that they completely ignored an equally 'rude' little gem from the same recording session. 'Sitting On The Sands All Night' was written by Jack Cottrell and told of what happens on the beach after dark, where the police 'perve' on courting couples, where girls shine electric torches up Scotsmen's kilts, and where blisters appear where they should not. And where ultimately:

> *You start feeling rather stiff,*
> *Then find that you're stuck tight,*
> *With a boat-hook sticking in your Westward Ho!*
> *Through sitting on the sands all night!*

George began work on his next film, *Feather Your Nest*, at the Ealing Studios during the summer of 1936. He and Beryl were now living in London – and apparently hating every moment of it – but driving back to Barton on Friday evenings when the set had closed down for the weekend. Here, on 18 July, they were interviewed for the women's page of the *Blackpool Gazette & Herald* and photographed with their Alsatian, Peter, who, George said, was training to become a postman! 'Whenever Mr and Mrs Formby are away,' observed the young woman reporter who signed her feature only as Sylvia, 'Mrs Formby's father re-addresses the letters, and Peter takes them to the village post office some distance away and posts them. He has never been known to drop one. And when meals are ready, he trots up the garden to find Mrs Formby's father and gently lifts that gentleman's hat off.'

During the interview, which barely touched on his career, George managed to get the date of his marriage wrong, declaring that he and Beryl had tied the knot in August 1925. Sylvia was then shown around the house, and marvelled at the costly features: the glass panels of the sun porch which contained reproductions of Formby Sr's tomb design, the Tudor panelling in the dining room into which was set his father's portrait, the inch-thick velvet curtains emblazoned with the arms of Lancaster, the metallic wallpaper in the bedrooms, and the Chinese box-room which was there just for show – whose ceiling slanted, George cracked, like Mr Wu's eyes.

George's new film was less troublesome than the last two. Now that he was a household name, Beryl was more or less able to dictate her own terms, and she had given Basil Dean *orders* that this time there should be 'no Eye-Ties and stuck up little trollops' – she was, of course, referring to Monty Banks and Florence Desmond.

Dean agreed wholeheartedly. He too had grown weary of all the on-set squabbles, so he brought in the less excitable – and less amenable – William Beaudine to direct, and the little-known Polly Ward was engaged as George's leading lady. This resulted in a film which was nowhere near as funny as its predecessor, with a lack-lustre script by Austin Melford and Val Valentine, and a clutch of songs which – with the exception of the one which would become immortal – were comparatively bland.

Willie Piper works as a technician for a record company, along with his fiancée, Mary (Ward). The couple have secretly bought a house which they plan to move into after their wedding, which will take place once the hyper-nervous Willie has been given a pay-rise. Unfortunately, this may never happen on account of his tendency to drop and break something every time the factory whistle blows, and because of his disrespect for his boss, Mr Murgatroyd, whom he dismisses as 'a bow-legged, bandy-legged, knock-kneed old stingy tight wad'. Mary, however, has such faith in her bungling young man that she has filled their house with furniture, all purchased on credit.

Now enter one Rex Randall, a famous crooner – and utter pain – who, after umpteen takes, finally completes a wax of 'Leaning On A Lamp Post' in Willie's studio. Willie drops the wax, then he and Mary set about tracking down Randall to cut another whilst the studio is closed. Their trail leads them to the Turkish baths. 'You can't go in there – it's full of Turks with nothing on,' he tells Mary. Inside, he is mistaken for an overweight boxer and given the works by two burly masseurs. Eventually he emerges from his ordeal looking a wreck, having missed the crooner, who has left the baths for Brighton. Mary tells him not to worry. She has had a brainwave: she and Willie will break into the studio, and *he* will cut the recording! The film's great *faux pas*, of course, is that the scriptwriters never thought of giving the subsequent disc a B-side.

Willie Piper's version of 'Leaning On A Lamp Post' proves a huge hit, by which time Murgatroyd has given him the sack. Randall threatens to sue the company, yet even they do not know who the mysterious singer is. Finally, Willie comes clean . . . after a frantic race against time, with his sweetheart on the pillion of a purloined motorcycle, to prevent their house and furniture being repossessed. *He* then signs the contract the arrogant Randall only ever dreamed of, and he and Mary are married. In the final scene Willie is about to carry his bride over the threshold when the factory whistle blows and he drops her – into a muddy puddle!

At the beginning of October 1936, George found himself in hot water with Basil Dean when he made a £5 wager with a producer pal, Jack Taylor, that he would climb Blackpool Tower by way of its intricate inner network of staircases and ladders. Taylor announced this in the *Blackpool Gazette*, and on the morning of the climb George and Beryl arrived to find 6,000 people clustered in front of the 500-foot structure. By this time, however, he had received a telegram from Ben

Henry, his manager as well as the general manager of ATP. Henry stated that if he went ahead with this madness, his contract with Dean would be terminated forthwith. Clutching his ukulele case – it had been his intention to sing a few choruses from 'When I'm Cleaning Windows' from the summit of the tower – George shrugged his shoulders and told reporters, 'Ah, well. I suppose even I can't lose £50,000 for a five-quid bet. But don't worry. Both our wagers have been given to the hospital. The sad thing, of course, is that I could have done it!'

Having failed to 'ascend' in the world, so to speak, George was allowed to travel in the opposite direction when, on 18 October, he and Beryl were invited to appear at the venue where he had first plucked his ukulele – the Barnsley Alhambra. The occasion was a benefit concert in aid of the families of the 58 miners who had recently been killed in the Wharncliffe Woodmoor Pit Disaster. Beryl had initially been against the idea of George's fee being handed over to charity, so she 'hyped' up the event by arranging for George to address the Alhambra's audiences, by way of a link-up from the Blackpool Opera House, on three consecutive evenings prior to the concert. This way, she reasoned, their arrival in Barnsley, a town she loathed, would take on all the proportions of a royal visit and allow her to demand – and receive – almost as much in expenses as George's fee would have been, had this been a regular show!

The ploy worked. The Formbys were greeted at the railway station by 5,000 fans, and escorted to the hotel by the Dodworth Colliery Band. For a 'small fee', in the event of her expensive clothes getting ruined, Beryl consented to an underground visit to the recently repaired coalmine a few hours before the show.

Feather Your Nest was premiered in the spring of 1937, and proved another smash hit. It also provided George with the number most associated with him . . . a rare love-song, one of the few entirely void of innuendo, and one which did not come from the 'Gifford-Cliffe Smut Factory', as the BBC had dismissed his current songwriting team.

Noel Gay's sublime 'Leaning On A Lamp Post' was first recorded in September 1937. From its first public airing two months before, until almost the day of his death, George would never be permitted to leave the stage without performing what the *Sunday Times*' Harold Hobson applauded as, 'The true theatre, the real thing, the golden coin and the gates of pearl.'

> *There's no other girl I'd wait for,*
> *But this one I'd break any date for,*
> *I won't have to ask what she's late for,*
> *She wouldn't leave me flat,*
> *She's not a girl like that . . .*
> *I'm leaning on a lamp-post*
> *At the corner of the street,*
> *In case a certain little lady walks by!*

Beryl, however, had been firmly *against* her husband recording 'Leaning On A Lamp Post'. The more famous George became, the more grasping she became – in this instance arguing with Noel Gay that, as George had created the song, *his* name should be added to the songwriting credits as had happened with Harry Gifford, Fred Cliffe and several others. Beryl was unable to blackmail Gay into submission by threatening to 'take her business elsewhere'. For a start, he was not a regular Formby composer. Also, as he already owned copyright on the song *before* the public had even heard it – when *Feather Your Nest* was released in the summer of 1937, though the trade-show screening had taken place five months previously – George had to ask Gay's *permission* to record it. By this time, there were plenty of other artists waiting in the wings, so to speak, to record cover-versions.

Beryl attempted to twist Noel Gay's arm by declaring that no *other* artist would be able to get away with performing a number which was by this time unquestionably George Formby's theme-song . . . that if Gay *allowed* anyone else to record it, or refused to include George's name in the credits, she would personally sue him. Gay hit back by declaring that if this happened, he would let the media in on Formby's most closely guarded secret – that *such* were his musical talents that he was not even capable of tuning his own ukuleles. Gay was referring to the fact that whenever George was on stage there would always be several pre-tuned instruments ready for him in the wings, each set in a different key to save time and not affect the continuity of his performances. One must, however, assume that he always pre-tuned them personally, for on some of his live recordings George can actually be *heard* tweaking his ukes between songs. All the same, Beryl conceded defeat and Noel Gay's name was added to her list of enemies, which is a great shame . . . Gay later confessed that he would have liked to have composed more for George than he did. His only other contributions to the Formby repertoire would be 'The Left Hand Side Of Egypt' and 'Who Are You A-Shoving Of?' in 1941, neither of which were written especially for him.

Neither did Beryl approve of George's choice of B-side for 'Leaning On A Lamp Post'. 'Hi-Tiddley-Hi-Ti-Island' was a 1922 number he had been singing for some time, again not especially written for him. Beryl objected to the stanza which, she declared, would give people the impression that the Formby marriage, now entering its fourteenth year, was not the rock-solid institution they liked to present to the world. George told her that she was being 'just daft'. In years to come comics such as Tommy Cooper and Les Dawson would get away with 'slagging off' the wives they otherwise adored, though George *was* having personal problems with Beryl, not that this was the reason for insisting that the 'offending' verse stay put. He was simply in his Donald McGill mode once more.

On this particular surrealist, cannibal isle, everyone lives in style, nude bathing abounds, cows chew pins to enable the milk to come out in shilling tins. But this is not all . . .

> *The girls out there are full of sport*
> *And wear their frocks a trifle short,*
> *Some are simply wrapped in thought . . .*
> *The life's so fast and swift and gay,*
> *You live two weeks, then fade away.*
> *I'm taking the wife for a fortnight's stay*
> *On Hi-Tiddley-Hi-Ti Isle.*

CHAPTER FOUR

THE FIDDLER KEPT ON FIDDLING

'There was nothing gormless about George, although he appeared so in his films. He was just a hard-headed Lancashire lad!' Eddie Latta, songwriter-mortician.

Beryl certainly had cause for concern when George began shooting his next film for Basil Dean. *Keep Fit* was a send-up of the craze sweeping Britain at the time, spurred on by the League of Health and Beauty. His co-star, Kay Walsh, was *the* perfect specimen of womanhood and unlike most of the others did not mind George's wink-and-nudge flirting technique whilst they were on the set. The young actress also took pleasure from the effect she was having on George – detected by Beryl's stern, ever-watchful gaze – and made it patently clear from Day One that she was a star in her own right and not about to be bullied by this 'snooty little hoofer'. The director, Anthony Kimmins, was so terrified of George's wife that he neither questioned nor reproached her whenever she barged on to the set – most often when the red NO ENTRY sign was lit – to bawl him out in front of the actors and crew for what she declared was incompetence. Walsh had, in fact, wanted her friend Monty Banks to direct the film, but the otherwise placid little Italian had told Basil Dean, 'The only time you'll ever get me directing anything where that fucking Formby woman is concerned will be when she's playing the murder victim, and the scene's for real!' Monty was able to offer Walsh a little moral support, however, for he had persuaded Anthony Kimmins to give him one of the bit-parts.

Needless to say, the tension was almost unbearable. Beryl tried her utmost to get Kay Walsh fired from the production, threatening Basil Dean that she would 'persuade' George to break his contract unless Walsh was replaced with a less attractive actress, or 'de-beautified' by being put into ugly clothes and by having a less feminine hairstyle! During the subsequent showdown in the producer's office, to which George was not invited, the producer told Beryl that, not only was Walsh going to complete *this* film, she had also been contracted to appear opposite George in another, *I See Ice*, which would begin shooting immediately after *Keep Fit* had been edited. Beryl tried to argue, but Dean silenced her for the time being by informing her that George's salary for the new film would be £25,000.

Keep Fit was not quite as witty or well-scripted as George's previous Ealing films. Most of the 'fringe' characters were bland, as were the songs, aside from the whimsical 'I Don't Like'. This was no doubt because the ever-meticulous Basil Dean had objected to George's non-existent songwriting skills being fêted in the opening credits. Fearful of being dropped by George, Fred E Cliffe and Harry Gifford had offered the excuse that, given the tight shooting schedule, they had been unable to come up with any big production numbers, the likes of which had made George's first two Ealing films sparkle. Even so, this one was just as hugely successful, though today it rarely shows up in television and cinema retrospectives.

The storyline was pure escapist fantasy, and centred around the circulation war between two rival newspapers, the *Gazette* and the *Country Echo*. When the former poaches readers with its cookery competition, the *Echo* decides to organise a keep-fit contest which is part-sponsored by the local department store. Enter one George Green, a timid gentlemen's barber whose love for a pretty manicurist, Joan Allen (Kay Walsh), has thus far been unreciprocated because she is attracted to the store's resident beefcake, Hector Kent (Guy Middleton). Now enter Ernie (George Benson), George's 'nervous Nellie' pal from the menswear department, whose task it is to deliver the sports kit samples to the gymnasium, but who is pressed for time because he has to attend an amateur dramatics rehearsal. George offers to go in his place, and the man whose sole claim to athletic prowess is that he once came second in a two-contestant egg-and-spoon race finds himself mistaken for one of the competitors. 'If that's the result of physical exercise, thank heavens I had a mis-spent youth,' observes one of the adjudicators after George has tackled the horizontal bar, only to fall off and end up dangling upside-down from a trapeze.

George is nevertheless championed by a crooked photographer (Gus McNaughton) who gets him to pose for a picture which George naively assumes will be published in the newspaper . . . it is for the 'before' half of a before-and-after fitness poster, with Kent taking up the other half as the preening, musclebound hero. We then learn that Kent has a criminal record, and that, with his cronies, he is intent on creaming off funds from the sponsors.

When Kent has to postpone taking Joan for a trip on the river – he is about to pull off a heist – George takes her instead. Kent likes rowing, George can only punt. Even so, when Ernie secures him an Avon Rowing Club blazer and boater from his department, the pair set up a scam: in order for George to impress Joan and sweep her off her feet, Ernie will turn up disguised as an elderly toff and recognise George as the man who once saved him from drowning! Joan, however, realises that she has been set up when both men fall into the water and have to be rescued by Kent, who just happens to be passing. George then attempts a hasty exit, and he leaps over a hedge and is carried off on the back of a broncoing bull!

As happens in all Formby films, of course, the underdog comes out on top. Joan falls out with Kent when she discovers that he has rifled the store's till and pinned the blame on George – who resigns – whilst the doting Ernie is given the sack for procuring him the Avon Club uniform. This results in a confrontation with the enemy, who accidentally knocks himself out by stepping on to a broom. Arrested, George is hauled before a judge who berates him for being a bully, and unaware of his own strength.

Ernie, meanwhile, genuinely believing that *George* has knocked out the other man, suggests that the two should settle their differences at the keep-fit contest's boxing finale. Kent agrees, but because everyone assumes that it will be a walkover, no bets are laid. Kent then hits upon the idea of sending a couple of sparring-partners across to the 'Battling Barber' training-camp – a farm – to feign being knocked out, thus giving the punters a misguided notion that George really is as dangerous as the judge made out. He is, but only on account of his lucky mascot – a lock of Joan's hair, which Ernie has concealed in his glove. 'Get up, I want to do it again,' he exclaims to his barnyard audience, after felling Kent's hench-men and the referee. 'I'm a killer and didn't know about it!'

Finally, the big fight takes place, with George – having had his mascot stolen by the referee – almost getting annihilated in the first round. He picks up, however, when Joan snips off another lock of hair, only to be floored again when Kent cheats by sprinkling pepper on his gloves. This calls for drastic action from George's sweetheart – in the form of a kiss, whilst he is seeing stars in his corner. Completely revitalised, he knocks out Kent during the final round, and as the lovers are jubilantly 'stretchered' out of the arena, the crowd bursts into a chorus of 'Keep fit'!

According to Irene Bevan and a number of others, it was Fate which enabled George to have a brief fling with Kay Walsh. On 18 June, shortly before the film stopped shooting, Beryl was admitted to a private nursing home in London to undergo an operation for appendicitis – or so the press were led to believe – following a fall from a horse whilst she and George had been judging a gymkhana event. The clinic in fact specialised in gynaecological treatment, and the real reason for Beryl's sudden departure from the set was to book into the clinic – under an assumed name – for a hysterectomy. As Irene Bevan explained:

As George was a Catholic, he naturally wasn't supposed to be practising birth-control, but religion didn't prevent Beryl from making sure they would never have children. It was a well-known fact at the time that the Formbys had hardly ever slept together – and she often used to say that as she wasn't even remotely interested in having sex with him, no one else would look at him twice. But with all those pretty girls hanging around the studio she was convinced that he would stray sooner than later, so she 'had everything taken away', as they say, so that hopefully George wouldn't go looking elsewhere for what she'd never given him. The ruse worked for a little while – until she started telling everyone about his shortcomings in the boudoir. And who wouldn't have had problems, having to put up with that sort of thing?

Beryl would always rue her decision not to have children, as the ever-doting Harry Scott intimated in *The Fabulous Formby*:

Years later, George and Beryl realised as thousands of other self-centred, over-ambitious couples have realised, that wealth and fame are no substitute for the love and trust of a child of your own. All of her creative and physical energy was spent in driving the Formby fortune up to a staggering figure. George and his career were her babies. Yet it was Beryl who, most of all, regretted that they had a room that was never turned into a nursery.

There was also considerable behind-the-scenes speculation

that Beryl also 'misbehaved' whilst George was making *I See Ice*. 'There's absolutely no doubt about that,' Irene Bevan told me. 'Beryl was absolutely besotted with Gavin Gordon, a young actor who starred in the film, so she allowed George to sow a few wild oats for once whilst she went off and did the same. After all, it wasn't often that a woman like her had the opportunity to sleep with a man who'd bedded Garbo and Dietrich!'

Gavin Gordon was around the same age as George, but out of make-up he looked much younger and his almost ethereal beauty complemented Beryl's own. In 1933, weighed down by what Marlene Dietrich had dismissed as 'a silly moustache and a ten-cent wig', he had played resident stud to her Catherine the Great in Josef von Sternberg's *The Scarlet Empress*. Prior to this, he had portrayed a virgin priest opposite Greta Garbo in *Romance*. Well over six-feet tall and extremely muscular, Gordon spent the whole of the thirties notching up a string of lovers on both sides of the Atlantic, so his brief relationship with Beryl Formby is hardly likely to have been any more serious than all the others. Even so, it must have been gratifying for her to learn that other men did find her attractive, and that some would-be suitors were not deterred by George's super-star status. Gordon may have been the first, but he certainly would not be the last.

I See Ice was again written and directed by Anthony Kimmins, and co-starred Betty Stockfield and Garry Marsh. The latter (Leslie Marsh Geraghty), two years George's senior, had actually had a part in 1920 Formby Sr revue, and until the mid-thirties had featured in dozens of B-movies, mostly thrillers. Marsh later confessed that he had only agreed to appear in a Formby film because Basil Dean – never the most tactful of men – had told him that with his rapidly receding hairline he would make the perfect straight comedian-villain. Dean was proved right, but though he enjoyed countless such roles until his retirement in 1967 (he died twelve years later), there would only be three more films with George.

The story was more convoluted than ever and contained several sub-plots which were removed from some prints when the film was re-released as part of a Formby double-bill during the fifties. He played George Bright – a misnomer if there ever was one! – a photographer's apprentice who invents a tiny camera which he conceals in his bow-tie. Assigned to a job in Birmingham, George is befriended by Judy, a pretty young skater (Kay Walsh), after he has saved her from a pile of luggage at the railway station. She and her partner Paul Martine (Cyril Ritchard) are on their way to London to participate in an ice-show, after which Martine is to play in the London Cyclones–Canada Buffaloes ice-hockey final at the Imperial Rink. All travel on the same train, though what George does not know is that the vehicle is scheduled to divide at Birmingham.

'I'm told I look pretty good with my skates on,' Judy tells him, whilst George offers to share his sandwiches and pig's trotter – to which he innocently replies, 'Ee, you'd look good with nothing on!' Then she is dragged off by the toffee-nosed Martine, just as the train splits and George discovers he is in the wrong half and on his way to London. In a panic he pulls the communication cord and is nabbed by the guard, who offers him an option: an on the spot £5 penalty, which he cannot afford, or two weeks in prison. This leads to the film's first mad-cap chase: George wrecks the dining car, gets menaced by an ugly dog, and finally hides in Judy's carriage. Sprung by Martine, he is saved by the young woman, who persuades her partner to take him on as their property man. The police, however, are waiting for him at Euston, so he leaves the train disguised as a woman – the script called for a Sybil Thorndyke lookalike. 'I'm a Tiller Girl,' he coos, sparking off another chase wherein he again evades his pursuers.

Judy, meanwhile, has developed a soft spot for George, and she coaxes him into putting his camera to good use. Burmanov, the legendary explorer, has just returned from the North Pole and is tetchy about being photographed. George manages to snap him at the rink where Judy and Martine are about to perform, but he is caught out. Harried into one of the dressing-rooms, he emerges clad as one of the Cossacks who are about to assist in Martine's spectacular ice-jump over the backs of eight men. George, naturally, ends up as the eighth man. Ordered to kneel, his false beard becomes frozen to the ice. Judy's and Martine's act is ruined and the couple are fired. Martine exacts his revenge by shopping George to the police.

Nonplussed, Judy helps George to develop his film. The picture, however, reveals more than the burly explorer. In the background George has inadvertently caught Galloway, the editor of a leading newspaper (Garry Marsh), canoodling with the wife of an influential sports supremo. Initially, George does not cotton on to this . . . or the fact that Galloway thinks he is blackmailing him by trying to force him to buy the picture. More mayhem ensues when George announces that he does not want *money* for the snap and the negative – just an assurance that Galloway will print another photograph which he has taken, of Judy, on the front page of his newspaper in the hope of someone offering her a lucky break.

George, meanwhile, is hired to take sneak-shots of the ice hockey final, an event from which photographers are barred, by a rival paper. He is still being pursued by the police, and by Galloway's henchmen, who believe he has the negative. The editor has paid for them to dine at the plush Lotus Club, where salmon is on the menu. 'Ask him to open a fresh tin,' George tells the waiter, before the slapstick resumes. This time, however, the police apprehend him and he is thrown into jail and gets out just in time for the big match, in which Martine is the Cyclones' star player.

Judy has been engaged as the pre-tournament entertainment, and George is sneaked into the referee's box so that he can get good shots. He is, of course, called to referee, causing pandemonium on the ice and getting rumbled by the players, who scramble all over him to get at his camera . . . which he has tied around his leg. George therefore gets his pictures, and with them the position of ace reporter from the rival editor, and most importantly he ends up with the girl!

For *I See Ice*, Anthony Kimmins commissioned *two* endings – one to please Beryl, in which George and Kay Walsh are left sitting on the ice and merely appear to be *about* to kiss – and another, the one most commonly seen, where their lips actually meet not once, but twice. There were also three fine songs: 'Mother What'll I Do Now?', 'Noughts And Crosses', and Harry Parr-Davies' 'In My Little Snapshot Album' . . . which Gracie Fields' arranger and personal composer had written for her, only to be told, 'Better give that one to Formby, love. It's a bit too rude for me!'

> Now I've got a picture of the vicar's wife,
> Chasing the curate with a carving-knife,
> Now what he did was all in fun,
> But that's not the kind of thing that's done,
> I could see he'd pinched her hot-cross bun . . .

George was visited on the set of *I See Ice* by *Film Weekly*'s Leonard Wallace, who had arranged to interview him some weeks previously. Beryl very quickly put the dampers on this, however, when she asked Wallace for a list of the questions he was going to ask – a common prerequisite, so that she could 'guide' George through his responses. Wallace had scribbled the heading, 'Introducing George Formby – Next Year's Comedy King', across the top of his pad, and as in her estimation George was definitely the flavour of the moment who needed absolutely *no* introduction, the interview was scrapped, and Wallace was warned to watch his step. His feature, published in the 6 November 1937 issue of the magazine, was nevertheless amongst the most praiseworthy ever written about George. It certainly offered his career, 'South of Birmingham', a tremendous boost:

> *Unknown to half of England a couple of years ago, I doubt if*
> *any other star, with the possible exception of Gracie Fields,*
> *has made such a quick climb into the favour of British*
> *filmgoers. I'll give him another year, and I'll bet he'll be*
> *running level with Gracie for the honour of being Britain's*
> *most popular film star. George has buck teeth and a feckless*
> *grin. He is a broad comedian, a knockabout clown, a ukulele*
> *strummer, a comic-song singer, and still half a variety artist*
> *in a strange element. He also has that spark of personality*
> *that breeds universal appeal and commands universal*
> *affection. The teeth and the dumb grin are his properties, like*
> *the clown's red nose and white diamond patch.* But the spirit
> of Formby is in his eyes. *There is a smile in them that can*
> *turn to the most touching pathos, like the eyes of a spaniel.*
> *There is also in them an unquenchable optimism that sums*
> *up the very essence of his character, that of the good-natured*
> *simpleton who is put upon and badgered, but who always*
> *comes back smiling. He is the perfect pattern of all the timid*
> *men, the dunderheads, the bullied, pushed around*
> *underdogs. In his ultimate triumphs all these little men*
> *triumph also; and as most of us have a streak at least of that*
> *sort of thing, we get a vicarious pleasure in a vicarious victory.*
> *With his honest broad appeal, and his closeness to the hearts*
> *and psychology of the ordinary person, he is one of the most*
> *important discoveries British studios have made for years.*

Meanwhile, at the end of June, mere days after finishing the film – and for the first time in thirteen years without Beryl – George opened at Blackpool Opera House in *King Cheer*, Jack Taylor's latest revue. Sylvia, the editor of the *Blackpool Gazette*'s women's page, was allowed to sit in on rehearsals and told George that in her humble opinion the revue's best songs were 'With My Little Stick of Blackpool Rock', 'The Lancashire Toreador', 'Hindoo Man' and 'Sitting On The Sands All Night'. This pleased him. 'I'm writing most of my own melodies today,' he said. 'I strum out the tune on my uke, and a couple of lads I have jot it down as music. *I* don't know a thing about music – and there you are!'

The revue kept George occupied for the rest of the summer, during which time the house at Barton was sold, and he bought a five-bedroomed property at Little Singleton, five miles from the centre of Blackpool. 'Garthallen' was set in four acres of landscaped gardens and woodland, and boasted a full-sized tennis court which, George joked, would be handy for keeping chickens in! The couple moved in on 9 September, Beryl's thirty-seventh birthday . . . by which time the house, like all the others, had been rebaptised 'Beryldene'.

On 15 November 1937, George appeared in his first Royal Variety Show, alongside fellow Lancastrians Gracie Fields and Norman Evans. On the morning prior to this, George succumbed to a colossal attack of nerves. Beryl later said that she had helped him through one crisis by instigating another. 'A moment's serious thought told me that there was no time for half measures,' she recalled. 'George was a bad case, so we had a row – and row we did, as we had never done since we'd been married. I told him off left and right. He'd been so nervous he hadn't wanted to get out of bed, but when I began rowing at him he was *glad* to get out!'

According to Beryl, the couple had kept at it, hammer and tongs, until late in the afternoon, when they had gone off on a shopping spree and George had bought a chromium sports cycle. After riding around the store to the amazement of the other shoppers, he had taken it for a 'test-drive' up and down Oxford Street before finally setting off, nerves-free, for the Palladium:

By then George was so exhausted with the day's row and the excitement about the new bike that he hadn't a trace of stage nerves! I do believe that he was one of the calmest people backstage during those antagonising seconds before the first curtain. I was in my usual position in the wings when George went on with his ukulele. I'd pinned on him the tie-pin which King George had given his father . . . and I gave him a kiss as he went on, just to show him once more that the row had all been a fake!

The Royal Variety Show set another precedent as far as Beryl's impeccably organised routine was concerned. George had been told that his spot would amount to twelve minutes exactly – not a second more. Beryl therefore went out and bought a stopwatch to augment an already-present notebook and clipboard which were used to keep a record of the songs George performed in every show, along with a number-coded record of his self-confessed abysmal jokes. Like Tommy Cooper after him, only George could have an audience in hysterics with such deliberately dire patter. The idea behind this was that Beryl was able to gauge the public's reaction to George's work, enabling songs which had not gone down particularly well to be revamped or even removed from his repertoire – there were always dozens more, ready to take their place, many of which he never got around to airing. And now she began timing them, bringing the comment from the stridently acerbic critic, Hannen Swaffer, 'Not content with keeping her husband on a leash like a pet monkey, Mrs Formby has now taken to *clocking* his every movement.'

In the spring of 1938, with the threat of war-clouds lurking on the horizon, Basil Dean's morale-boosting crusade began with him putting his biggest star, Gracie Fields, into *Keep Smiling*, an exceedingly optimistic vehicle directed by Monty Banks, whom Dean also assigned to the next Formby film, *George Takes The Air*. Shooting was scheduled to begin as soon as the Fields film had been completed. Beryl, however, objected to Banks *and* the title, but especially to Dean's decision to engage Kay Walsh as George's co-star for a *third* time. Subsequently, Anthony Kimmins was again brought in to direct, Walsh was dropped and replaced by Polly Ward – who was read the 'keep-your-hands-off-my-husband' riot-act by Beryl – and the title was changed to *It's In The Air*.

The storyline was extremely improbable, but the slapstick remains amongst the most perfectly-timed and side-splitting that George ever performed. He played George Brown, a would-be recruit who is rejected by the RAF for being too gormless. Not only is he unable to distinguish his left from his right, when he turns up for enrolment with his dog, Scruffy, but without his gas-mask, he remarks that he had only been provided with one . . . which he has given to the dog. He then wanders into the communications room where, filling in for the operator whilst he takes a break, he serenades a couple of pilots over the air with a few choruses of 'They Can't Fool Me', before pulling the wrong lever and blowing up the set – causing Scruffy to put on his own gas-mask , a masterpiece of bungled editing!

Disappointed, George returns home, where he cannot resist trying on his sister's boyfriend's uniform when he goes on leave, and in the pocket he finds a letter addressed to an RAF official, which he delivers to the HQ in his motorbike and sidecar. Here the CO (Garry Marsh) mistakes him for a dispatch rider and orders him to drive him to the Glenbridge airbase – ploughing through farmyards, gates, road-works and fords. Here he is mocked by the other recruits on account of his Northern accent, bullied by the sergeant major, and befriended by his pretty daughter Peggy (Polly Ward). Initially, she dismisses him as a 'headquarters nitwit', but she and the others warm to him after he sings a song berating the sergeant major, a man who is so hard, he declares, that he would strangle his own mother:

His medals break our hearts,
He won them playing darts . . .
His feet fill up the road,
Knock-kneed and pigeon-toed,
We'd sooner shoot him than salute him,
Our Sergeant Major!

If this is not enough, George is tricked by a snooty officer who has designs on Peggy into billeting in the sergeant major's quarters, and, after a hilarious Faydeau-esque routine, wakes up next to him in bed. For this and his other peccadilloes he is brought before the CO and made to perform the song again. And, of course, he has changed the words.

He's as generous as can be,
So sentimental, kind and gentle . . .
He's got a heart of gold,
So fearless and bold!
He's like a Samson – strong and handsome!
Our Sergeant Major!

After this episode, the sergeant major rumbles George's true identity and enlists him for flight-training, where a pilot about to fly a prototype plane mistakes him for an engineer and asks him to 'run up' the engine. Still confusing left and right, he takes off in a series of aerial loops and death-defying stunts – at one stage switching off the engine! – which would have rivalled Von Richthofen. Scoring a perfect hit whilst accidentally dropping a bomb, he so impresses his superiors that he is elevated to a fully-fledged pilot. The film then ends with George performing the show-stopper title-song . . . on stage in a revue, in a model plane which subsequently drops to bits!

Although they did not work together as frequently as George would have liked – on account of being more or less tied to Gracie Fields – George enjoyed Harry Parr-Davies' company.

'A cheerful antidote to that fucking viper,' was how Monty Banks described the on-set presence of the man who would supply Gracie with some of her most celebrated songs – 'Wish Me Luck As You Wave Me Goodbye' and 'Pedro The Fisherman' were but two – though there would never be any really big songs for George.

A moody, totally unpredictable Welshman, Parr-Davies was just twenty when he wrote his first song for George, 'Your Way Is My Way', in 1935. Around this time he also became Gracie's pianist and arranger. Harry was the perfect foil for George's decidedly off-beat sense of fun, and the only person who could call Beryl a 'miserable bleeder' to her face and get away with it. Effeminate, thin, pasty-faced and unable to see a thing without his trademark bottle-bottom spectacles he and George spent a lot of time together whilst shooting *It's In The Air* – mostly at the pub near the studio, and with Beryl's blessing. Her naivety stretched to the point where she thought her husband would be safer in the company of a 'grumpy nancy-boy' than being pestered by the likes of Polly Ward. She had lately revised her opinion that Polly was only slightly less promiscuous than Kay Walsh or Florence Desmond – an opinion nurtured by her own paranoia. Snooty they may have been, but thus far *all* of George's co-stars had been respectable young women.

'It was Harry's constipation that always made him grumpy,' Irene Bevan said. 'That troubled him more than anything. He used to come down to breakfast on a morning and say, "The Chooser's been!" We all knew then that he'd been to the lavatory and that he would be in a good mood!'

Another drinking partner, and homosexual to boot, who could not stand Beryl was Garry Marsh, who genuinely believed that her domineering was becoming detrimental to George's health. Marsh, however, preferred a more salubrious kind of entertainment to smoky pubs, as he explained in a 1967 interview:

One day I said to George, 'Let's got out to the Café Royal for a few drinks and a bit of grub.' He said, 'Ee, I'd love to!' And suddenly I noticed that his face dropped. He said, 'Beryl, she'd never wear it. Besides, I can't afford it!' I said, 'What do you mean, you can't afford it? You're getting thirty-thousand a picture!' At that moment Beryl came across the set. I said, 'Beryl, I'd like to take George out tonight, give him a few drinks. What about it? It'll do him good. He's been working very hard, it'll take his mind off things.' She said, 'Off what things? Off me? Do you know what would happen if he went out with you? He'd come home in the early hours of the morning, stinking drunk, with lipstick all over his chops. No, he's coming home with me. Aren't you, George?' And that was that!

Whilst shooting *It's In The Air*, George took delivery of his first custom-built car – over the next twenty years there would be another 130! – a fabulous Rolls Royce. He still hung on to his six-cylinder SS1 Coupé, which he had purchased second-hand in 1933. Both cars were registered in Beryl's name, it was later claimed, to prevent George from 'fooling around'. If he ever *did* decide to walk out on the wife who was so in name only, Beryl would at least be left with a small fortune in metal.

Why George continued to allow himself to be picked upon is not easy to understand. Perhaps he was afraid of creating a scandal by leaving her; or perhaps he actually *enjoyed* being henpecked. His career would certainly have collapsed without her domineering spirit, for while Beryl only *nagged* her husband, she could prove a veritable vixen as far as songwriters, producers and theatre managers were concerned. She demanded and got the very highest fees, argued 'nit-picking' contractual details which anyone else might have ignored and swelled the Formby coffers beyond even her expectations. Yet though George was by this time the highest-paid male entertainer in Britain, it was common knowledge amongst the showbusiness crowd that his wife allowed him just five shillings a day pocket money – less, if he could get through the day without spending it all. Good friends such as Tommy Trinder, whom Beryl just managed to tolerate, believed that George often used his wife's ruling as an excuse to get out of buying a round of drinks – or to rid himself of hangers-on and scroungers, such as certain members of his family who might have regarded him as a soft touch. 'Beryl never missed a thing,' the comic said in a television interview, shortly before his death in 1989, 'She always felt, "Well, here's the goldmine and I'm not going to let anybody else take their pick and shovel there!" I'd say, "Why don't you give him a couple of pounds and let him live it up?" Beryl would get very haughty at that!'

Beryl would also accompany George to his tailor's, bartering with the assistants for a bargain, and frequently not even paying for his finished suits, claiming that to boast the logo, FORMBY SHOPS HERE, would bring them all the business they could handle without them having to charge her for her purchases!

For her own clothes, Beryl visited only the more exclusive and of course expensive fashion emporiums, causing a sensation whenever she turned up at a premiere or function clad in the finest silks and furs, invariably dripping with diamonds, and wearing trademark bird-of-paradise hats. George invariably trailed behind in his tuxedo, or nervously clung to her arm like he was escorting his mistress to some coy, adulterous rendezvous.

On 15 October 1938, as much for his own personal pleasure and satisfaction as for the publicity stunt it really was, George returned to the racetrack for a single meeting, riding Lucky Bert in the October Handicap Hurdle, at Northolt Park. The horse was the 6–4 favourite, and everyone at ATP had a bet on it – though the jockey was given explicit instructions by Beryl not to waste his money. He risked one pound, the horse refused a fence and was disqualified. To teach him a lesson

Beryl yelled at him in the middle of the members' enclosure for spending money they could 'ill afford' – at this time the couple had around £50,000 in the bank – and deducted the cash he had lost from his following week's allowance!

And George *was* making a lot of money. Between February 1938 and the end of 1939, Regal Zonophone, with whom he had signed a contract in the summer of 1935, released his records on average at the rate of one a month. Few would be regarded as Formby classics, but they sold extremely well and helped his bank balance to stay healthy. He also earned a great deal from radio appearances – firstly from his *A Lancashire Lad* series which began in January 1938 and ran for several months, followed by three *Formby Do* broadcasts during the summer, and ending with some thirty twice-weekly programmes on Radio Luxembourg, sponsored by Feenamint laxative. The signature tune for these, a parody of the theme-song from one of his films, had him warbling,

Keep fit and take a hint,
It will give your eyes a glint,
If you take Feenamint!

In the autumn of 1938, George began shooting *Trouble Brewing*. Anthony Kimmins again directed, though this time not under the auspicious gaze of Basil Dean who, having had enough of dealing with Beryl, had passed the reins to Jack Kitchin. George's leading lady was Googie Withers, then twenty-two and virtually unknown, and playing the chief crook was Ronald Shiner, a beady-eyed, raucous-voiced Cockney comedian whose huge trademark nose had recently been insured for £20,000. 'If he breaks his conk during the action sequences, he'll end up getting as much for the film as me,' George told the press. He and Shiner got on very well, despite Beryl's interference, and they often went off to the pub together – they said to get away from the 'brewery' in the film – during shooting. Shiner would become a Formby regular, appearing in six more of his films.

George Gullip, who is described as 'Sherlock Holmes and Sexton Blake rolled into one', is a printroom operator at a newspaper office. He invents an indelible ink finger-marking system which he puts to good use whilst tracking down a counterfeiting gang – known to the trade as 'slushers' – assisted by his sidekick, Bill (Gus McNaughton) and Mary (Withers), the young secretary who has stolen his heart.

At the racetrack, George and Bill have won a tidy sum, backing an outsider which George – standing in for his newspaper's absent horoscope writer – has predicted will win. Bill – McNaughton in his usual con-man role – has, however, taken possession of the winnings, and offers drinks all around in the bar. The barmaid cannot change a £10 note, so up steps one of the counterfeiters who changes this and the others in Bill's hand for fivers – fake notes which are confiscated by a detective. The two friends then observe the crooks getting into a Blue Star Brewery wagon, and on hitching a ride they end up not at the brewery, but at the local swimming baths. Bill, the coward, purloins a bathing suit for George and sends him in after them – only on this particular evening the baths are holding a free-for-all wrestling match. In a hilarious sequence, George ends up taking on the Terrible Tiger . . . and only he, of course, can win the bout aided by a hatpin, a bar of soap, and a lighted cigar which he shoves down his opponent's trunks, setting his posterior alight! The crooks get away!

Meanwhile, the newspaper's owner has offered a large reward for the apprehension of the criminals after finding fake notes in *his* winnings at the racetrack. Initially, George and Bill suspect the feisty opera star, Madame Berdi (Martita Hunt), to be the head of the operation because they have seen her speaking to one of the crooks at the afternoon meeting. They gain access to her house by masquerading as waiters at a party. George manages to get Madame Berdi to leave a fingerprint on a piece of paper, but she tucks it into the top of her stocking. He eventually retrieves it by crawling under the table and sticking his hand up her dress, a scene which had Beryl really hitting the roof, until the statuesque Miss Hunt threatened to *throw* her off the set unless she left of her own accord. The print on the singer's finger, however, fails to match that found by Mary on one of her boss's banknotes. Suspicion then falls on a certain Major Hopkins – though Mary and George do not at first know that the 'slush' money he and Bill have seen in his apartment is there because Hopkins is the Chief of Police and examining the notes.

It is Mary who discovers the identity of the real culprit – the editor, Brady (Garry Marsh), who subsequently kidnaps her and incarcerates her in the brewery whilst arrangements are made to ship her out of the country so that she will not blab. She does, however, manage to leave a message for the sleuths, who set off in hot pursuit. The film then ends with the usual, frequently speeded-up mayhem, during which all the crooks end up being pushed into fermentation tanks and getting drunk. It also contains the most controversial scene in any Formby film when George and his sweetheart topple backwards into one of the tanks, surfacing to enjoy a passionate mouth-to-mouth kiss!

This latter sequence – horror of horrors! – caused a furore within the Formby household. Upon reading through the script, Beryl had ordered George to deliver a fleeting peck on his leading lady's cheek, and no more. The director, however, had other ideas. Anthony Kimmins told Googie Withers, 'Make it a whopper!' which she did . . . and though Beryl fumed for days afterwards, demanding twenty-three takes until she was certain that George's ardour for Withers had cooled, and choosing the least sensual one, it was the 'whopper' which stayed in the finished print.

One of the songs pencilled in for this film, 'I Wonder Who's Under Her Balcony Now?' – George called it 'a tale of

lost love' – had been cut out during production because
Anthony Kimmins had been worried that it might be mis-
construed:

> Will he kiss her under the nose,
> Or underneath the archway where her sweet william grows?
> If he's fresh and gets too free,
> I hope a bulldog bites him in the place it bit me . . .
> I hope he catches the lot
> When she empties out her old geranium pot!

One may readily assume what some of the snootier critics
would have made of this one, had George performed it in the
film. 'Fanlight Fanny' *was* left in, resulting in a savage attack by
Picturegoer's Hubert Cole, though one fails to understand why,
with the passing of sixty years.

> She dances underneath a magic spell,
> She's full of charm and beer and stout as well . . .
> You can't tell if she's brunette or a blonde,
> She's like something you drag out of a pond . . .
> She's a peach, but understand,
> She's called a peach because she's always canned!
> That's Fanlight Fanny, the frowsy nightclub queen!

An influential but extremely prudish individual, Cole had
earlier accused Gracie Fields of 'inciting perversion' because she
had used the popular Northern expression, 'acting the goat' – a
euphemism for clowning around and not, as Cole had wrongly
concluded, one which alluded to oral sex! 'You've got a dirty
little mind,' Gracie had told him angrily. Cole particularly
objected to the word 'fanny' – in this instance, of course, a
woman's name and not a slang word for vagina or buttocks,
depending on which side of the Atlantic one happened to be on.
In the magazine's 30 September 1939 issue, he admonished:

George caters for family audiences who don't want near-the-knuckle jokes. Yet when the latest Formby film came along a few weeks ago, I found that it contained two or three jokes in the worst possible taste. They were so 'blue' that they staggered me. It may be true that George finds this type of joke popular on the music-hall stage. Music-hall audiences have a right to demand whatever humour they most prefer. But cinema audiences don't want that kind of stuff. The screen is too intimate a medium to be used for coarseness. 'Blue' gags are not going to entertain George's millions of film-going admirers. They are going to embarrass and annoy them. He should give them up at once before they do him serious harm.

The extraneous takes for the final scene in *Trouble Brewing* had pushed George to the limit. At the end of January – halfway through a season of *Dick Whittington* at the Manchester Palace – worried that the chill he had been suffering from for several weeks was getting no better, Beryl took George to Harley Street, where he was diagnosed with an acute respiratory infection. He was told to stop smoking, and not to speak for a week: two things he later said he could not have done to *save* his life. He was, however, obliged to pull out of the pantomime – the couple were replaced by another popular duo, Billy Caryll and Hilda Mundy – and George agreed to take his first holiday in five years. In the middle of February, therefore, he and Beryl joined a five-week cruise to the West Indies.

The couple were accompanied by Beryl's parents who, George told Sylvia shortly before leaving Blackpool, would be able to keep his wife company whilst he was catching up on his songwriting. 'I've just completed five songs, including one called "It's Turned Out Nice Again",' he added, 'I got the inspiration for that one from the fact that I've been ill, and now I'm better.' The song – its title referring to his famous catchphrase – had been sent to him a few days previously by Fred Cliffe and Harry Gifford!

Gifford and Cliffe had also sent George two more instalments of the Mr Wu saga: 'I'm The Husband Of The Wife Of Mr Wu', and the biting 'Mr Wu's A Window Cleaner Now'.

Next on the ATP production-line was *Come On George*, a horse-racing comedy perfectly suited for George who, having had first-hand experience of the sport, insisted upon doing most of his own stunts. For once, Beryl agreed with him, telling the press, 'What George doesn't know about racing isn't *worth* knowing!' And this time there were two female co-stars: Meriel Forbes, and Pat Kirkwood, who played his love-interest.

The film opens at the racecourse, with the jockeys emerging one by one from behind a fence – followed by George, mounted on an ice-cream cart. The slapstick begins at once. Two pickpockets steal a wallet which ends up in his cart. The owner, a top trainer, spots it and sets the police on to George, resulting in a wrecking chase through the clubhouse and on to a train – all the while George is clutching his ukulele case. Here, he hides in the wagon transporting a psychotic horse named Maneater, which he manages to soothe. The stable are impressed, and take him on to ride Maneater in the forthcoming Bargrave Stakes, not telling him the truth about the horse's nasty temper – adopting the theory that the beast, rebaptised the Lamb, is only unmanageable when those around it show fear. 'My uncle Joe made *his* living following horses,' George says, appreciatively, before adding, 'with a bucket and shovel!'

George finds digs at the local police station where Anne, the sergeant's pretty young daughter (Kirkwood), shows him to his room – the disused cell. When the police arrive looking for a pickpocket, he opens the door disguised as the maid. Then off he goes to serenade the horse:

> *I joined the gym for exercise,*
> *A lady instructor put me wise,*
> *She made my spare parts twice the size,*
> *I'm making headway now!*

Elsewhere in the song George makes the obligatory reference to window cleaners, and has a sly crack at the BBC. Then, after singing the sergeant's obnoxious, catapult-wielding grandson, Squib, to sleep with 'Goodnight, Little Fellow, Goodnight' – the number he had sung to Mickey Dripping in *Formby Seeing Life* – and crooning 'Pardon Me' to Anne, he takes his sweetheart to the funfair where the real hilarity begins.

In the flea-circus tent, Squib empties a tube of fleas inside the back of George's trousers, whilst the trainer pronounces, describing the insect battle taking place in an adjoining tank, 'The troops are about to fall into no-man's-land. Yes, they are now giving a stinging attack to the rear!' Later, when Anne comments on a troupe of scantily-clad Parisian dancing girls, he tells her, 'You'd look better than *them* with *nothing* on!' Then the police-chase resumes – into a trailer from which he emerges in the guise of the world-famous acrobat, the Golden Phantom, creating yet more mayhem before making his way back to the stable – where he is told the truth about the horse he is about to ride.

Terrified, George tries to back out of the race – a problem which is effectively solved by a visit to a brain-specialist who reveals that, whilst under hypnosis and barring any knocks to the head, our hero will remain fearless. *En route* to the racecourse, he is pursued by thugs sent by a rival stable, but outwits them by stealing their car. When he puts his foot down, however, mere minutes before the race is due to begin, the accelerator jams and he again ends up wrecking the clubhouse. *Then* he is told that the race is a steeplechase, something he has no experience of riding!

Setting off at last, George is thrown at the water-jump and the horse continues without him. He whistles it back, it crouches for him to remount, and he tears past the post, emerging as the victor of a nerve-racking photo-finish. And whilst the crowd are cheering, Maneater throws him the ten yards on to the trailer upon which Anne is standing – which they both fall through. George finally gets to kiss his love *almost* on the lips, whilst the horse pokes his head through the flaps behind them. A masterpiece!

The 'doctored' climax to this film is *so* badly spliced – George actually changes direction, mid-air, in some prints! – that it has become legendary. It is, however, by no means the only clanger. In one of the earlier scenes, when George dashes on to the train after being pursued through the clubhouse, it is being drawn by a LNER 4309 locomotive, though by the next scene this has changed to a LMS *Dreadnought*. In addition during this same sequence the editor has combined two vastly differing backdrops – the fabricated one of the Fells whilst George is running across the tops of the carriages, and the Kentish location which was used for the setting of the Avonbury Goods Yard! Later on, when he is singing 'I'm Making Headway Now' to the horse, he plays one ukulele for the song – then walks off with another model, leaving his case behind, though by the next time he sings he has been united with the original. And finally, during the scene prior to the big race, George is speeding along a country lane when he almost runs into the back of a removal van – only when he overtakes this, he is suddenly careering along a triple-carriageway!

To the cinemagoer, *Come On George* may have appeared an over-frothy, light-hearted romp where no one takes anything seriously, and where even the crooks do not get their comeuppance. For the cast, however, shooting had been anything *but* pleasant. Neither George nor Beryl could stand the child actor, Ronald Stagg, who played Squib – nor Meriel Forbes, of whom George quipped, 'When she talks, she sounds like she's got a gob full of marbles!' George also loathed Pat Kirkwood, a feeling which was obviously mutual.

Just sixteen when she appeared in *Come On George*, and with a few film credits tucked under her belt, Kirkwood was first and foremost a singer-dancer who aspired towards a career in the West End. She was also very pretty and elegant, which to Beryl's way of thinking meant only one thing – George would immediately make a play for her. In her opinion that would be even more likely if the director was able to get away with the scene he planned – pre-dating Marilyn Monroe – which would have a wind-machine blowing Kirkwood's skirt above her head, exposing her bloomers. Incensed, Beryl ordered a 'deglamorisation' programme, informing Anthony Kimmins that unless the young actress was shorn of her lovely tresses and put into dowdy clothes, George would not make the film.

Many years later, Kirkwood would confess how she had hated the whole experience of working in a Formby film, denouncing George as 'cretinous' and 'lacking in intelligence'. 'Try to converse with him and you'd find there was no one at home,' she told one interviewer, adding somewhat smugly, 'They wanted a plain, English rose, and I was never that!' Kirkwood was also disappointed that she was not allowed to duet with George on 'Pardon Me', something which would have worked inordinately well. In fact, everyone connected with the film had *wanted* them to do the song together, and again Beryl had put her foot down. 'Even serenading a girl on the screen was tantamount to his having sex with her, in Beryl's eyes,' Irene Bevan said, 'so George sang the number on his own.'

Another British actress who experienced problems with George – or so she claimed in a 1981 interview – was Phyllis Calvert, his co-star in *Let George Do It*. Twenty-four at the time, Calvert had recently appeared with Arthur Askey in *Charlie's Big-Hearted Aunt*. Confessing that George had always been the great hero of her childhood – though he was only eleven years her senior – she explained what it had been like working with him:

It's the highlights that remain in your memory, and meeting George Formby, there weren't many highlights . . . and like a lot of people you make films with, once you've met them they're just perfectly ordinary people. So he was a bit of a disappointment. I think the thing I admired most about him was his technique. He was a very dull man. I don't ever remember holding a conversation with him. But when you watched him doing his stuff on the floor, then he became a completely different person.

Calvert then went on to explain how, before any Formby film got under way, the girls were forewarned of his reputation, though all through shooting he steered clear of him. She suspected this was because Beryl was watching his every move. Until the last day, that is:

It was quite extraordinary how he couldn't resist trying to make it with all his leading ladies. Beryl had to do some Christmas shopping, and I was in my dressing-room in the lunch-hour. A knock came at the door, and George stood there rather like a little boy and said, 'Ee, I'm crazy about you!' And that was all!

Beryl's absences from her husband's side were rare, but he took advantage of these occasions. Some sources have stated that no sooner was Beryl out of sight than he would have a woman – more often than not a dancer or extra, but occasionally a co-star, such as Coral Browne, who was in *Let George Do It* – if not in his dressing room, then back at some discreet hotel, depending upon the length of his 'parole'. Dorothy Hyson, who auditioned for the new film but failed to get the part, said:

George doted on his wife, there's absolutely no doubt about that. But he was even less interested in having sex with her now that she'd had the operation, not that he'd ever been passionate about her in that sense. Beryl was more like a nagging mother than a partner, yet he was so reliant on her for guidance, for handling the business side of things, that as

much as she was starting to wear him down he would never
have been able to have coped without her.

Let George Do It was a bubbly, hugely successful entertaining
propaganda vehicle, rich with melodious tunes and possessed
of a good script, and marred only by a silly ending. Much of the
action takes place in Norway, during the early months of the
war, where the eminent bandleader, Mark Mendez (Garry
Marsh) is based and doubling as a Nazi agent, sending
musically-coded messages over the air to German U-boats so
that they can sink Allied shipping.

When one of Mendez's musicians – a ukulele player – is
discovered to be spying for the British, he is disposed of . . . shot
whilst the orchestra is playing 'Oh, Don't The Wind Blow
Cold', and whilst the audience's attention is diverted by the
dancing of Mendez's partner, Iris (Coral Browne). A
replacement is requisitioned from London, but unknown to
Mendez this musician too works for British Intelligence. In
Dover, however, there is a blackout, and Mendez is sent the
wrong man – George Hepplewhite, a member of the Dinky-Do
concert-party which has just returned from France and who,
instead of boarding the ship for Blackpool with his colleagues,
ends up bound for Bergen.

Here, George meets his 'contact' – Mary (Calvert), who
leaves a note in his ukulele case instructing him to meet her for
a briefing. This is signed 'M', and when he shows this to
Mendez's sidekick he is told that the bandleader always does
this when discussing contracts. Mendez, meanwhile, sends
along Iris to seduce George into giving himself away. She fails,
of course, because he does not know that he is supposed to be
a spy, though when he eventually meets Mary and she confides
in him, he is only too willing to help. Sneaking into Mendez's
room, he finds the code document and photographs it. Then he
escapes out of the window, plunging through an adjacent
bakery roof and dropping the camera. It, and George, end up

in the flour-bin, then the dough-mixer, but he retrieves it and, in supplying Mary with the evidence she requires, wins her love.

Together, the pair set up Mendez by sending a copy of the code to the Admiralty so that British destroyers can sail to the spot indicated by Mendez's message, and wait for the U-boat. 'Wallop, Mrs Ducket – your mother's won a bucket!' George gleefully exclaims, and their mission succeeds when the British sink three enemy craft.

Mendez now suspects George of espionage and, whilst Mary – her task completed – prepares to leave for England on the *McCaulay*, he is administered a truth-drug, and confesses all before passing out. There then follows the most extraordinary dream-sequence, at that time the most powerful piece of propaganda on British screens:

Mendez and his sidekick, wearing enemy uniforms from the First World War – an allegory that the Germans were beaten then, and will be again – try to capture George, informing him that he and Mary are about to be executed. Imitating James Cagney, George produces a machine-gun and shoots at them. Their trousers fall down, revealing Swastika undershorts, and George escapes to rescue Mary, whom they have imprisoned in the bakery. 'George, I'm half-baked,' she screams, about to be shoved into the oven. Together, they face the foe, throwing hand-grenades made of dough. George asks her to marry him: she responds that true marriages are made in heaven, and very soon they are following the sign marked PEARLY GATES. George is not permitted to enter paradise, however, until he has captured the Führer. He therefore embarks upon his quest riding a pallet-lift attached to a barrage balloon, and descends upon Hitler whilst he is addressing a rally. 'You're my last territorial demand in Europe,' he opines, bashing him senseless, whilst all the Nazis rush to congratulate each other . . .

91

Mendez, meanwhile, now that his plan has been foiled, opts to deliver his next message to the U-boat in person, declaring that one of the next ships to be destroyed will be the *McCaulay*. Prior to this, during their broadcast the orchestra plays 'Oh, Don't The Wind Blow Cold', Mendez's cue to have George killed. He is tipped off, however, by another player (Ronald Shiner in his smallest ever role), and gets away, only to find that Mary's ship has set sail. Not to be beaten, he stows away on the motor-launch conveying Mendez to the U-boat.

The film ends with the usual free-for-all mayhem. George intercepts Mendez's message, contacts Mary on the *McCaulay*, and sends the U-boat's controls haywire so that its first torpedo goes off-course. The craft is then captured by the British, but before he is taken away, Mendez makes a last bid to sink the ship by firing another torpedo. George, however, has hidden in the shute so he and not the shell is shot into the air . . . to make a perfect landing at the feet of his sweetheart on the deck of the *McCaulay*, with the quip, 'Turned out nice again, hasn't it?'

The Americans were so impressed by this film, and in particular with the dream-sequence, that when it was released in the United States its title was changed to *To Hell With Hitler*. The biggest surprise of all, however, was the film's success in Russia. Dubbed and retitled *Dinky Doo*, it opened at a small theatre in Murmansk – the country's most important fishing-port, in the north-west – primarily to entertain sailors stationed there who were then being fed a diet of Laurel and Hardy, Chaplin, and the Keystone Cops. Within weeks, however, it had transferred to Moscow, where for ten months it broke all cinema box-office records . . . resulting in a feature, published in *Russia Today*, which declared, it has to be said only half-seriously, that George Formby was fast becoming the most popular figure in the country after Stalin and Churchill! The publication's editor, Richard Bishop, concluded:

Mr Formby has kept the entire film industry of Moscow busy making copies of his films. And however our two ideologies might differ, we must have reciprocity and tolerance. The closer our two peoples can be brought together, the easier it would be to persuade the Russians to take from our way of life that which was best, while we, in turn, could take the best from their way of life.

This may well have been true, but the publicity gimmick attached to the *Russia Today* spiel – that George, the 'celluloid ambassador', had been awarded the country's highest honour, the Order of Lenin, was pure propagandist tosh.

The film critic Leslie Halliwell, the greatest authority of the day, regarded *Let George Do It* as the finest of all the Formby films, and awarded especial praise to the song which tells of the old family heirloom within which its narrator is baptised and wed:

> *In the train, my bride gave a shout,*
> *'Ee, what is that you are pulling out?'*
> *I said, 'It's old-fashioned*
> *And it's tattered and torn,*
> *But I've brought it honeymooning with me, Gert!'*
> *When she said, 'What is it, dear?'*
> *I whispered in her ear,*
> *'It's my grandad's flannelette nightshirt!'*

Another big hit from the film was the next instalment in the Limehouse saga. For the laundry has now gone bust, and our honourable Chinese friend has a new profession:

> *When he goes out working, interest he arouses,*
> *Polishing the windows with worn-out ladies' blouses . . .*
> *With a Hi-di-hi! and a long-one-too!*
> *He's had his eyesight tested,*

A most important matter,
Through a bathroom window a lady he peeps at her,
His eyesight's getting better,
But his nose is getting flatter,
'Cause Mr Wu's a window-cleaner now!

CHAPTER FIVE

SWINGING ALONG . . . SINGING A SONG

'George has forgotten what it's like to have a bit of leisure, and apparently he's not likely to begin learning whilst our country is at war. [Beryl Formby, wife]

Ever since the start of the war in September 1939, George had been begging Basil Dean – now the head of ENSA – to temporarily release him from his film contract and grant him a permit to entertain the troops in Europe. Dean had repeatedly refused, declaring that George would be better off touring English army camps and Navy bases. In the first week of February 1940, during a pre-trade screening of the rough print of *Let George Do It*, Beryl took Dean to one side and told him in no uncertain terms what she thought about his idea. Ten minutes later, the Formbys' names had been added to the ENSA list.

A few days later the couple were informed that they would be sailing for France on 2 March. This came as a surprise to George, who had not expected to be leaving so soon. After her 'ding-doing' with Dean, Beryl had assigned George to several shows, which she now said could be cancelled owing to the mitigating circumstances . . . including a marbles competition in Castleford, in aid of Finnish refugees, which George vowed he would never postpone, not even if the instruction came from the King himself! Incredibly – which goes to prove *how* important George was in these days – the sailing was held up for four days until this engagement had been fulfilled. 'It's not that I'm particularly fond of marbles,' he told the *Blackpool Gazette*, 'but it's for a good cause, and I've a sort of romantic attachment to Castleford because it's there that I first met a charming lady – my Beryl!' And after the contest, which his team lost, George swiped all the marbles, signed them GF with the tip of a dart, and raffled them for the charity!

Beryl, meanwhile, had set up a 'Jump Fund' – so named after a Hertfordshire housewife who had sent her six woollen balaclavas which she had knitted herself, for Beryl to pass on to the soldiers in Europe. Beryl placed advertisements in all the local newspapers, urging female readers to follow Mrs Jump's example and supply her not just with headgear, but with scarves, socks and gloves. The response was quite unexpected: within three days Beryl received over a thousand articles of clothing, and others were sent to the local offices of the Thornton Home Guard, in which George and Harry Scott had enlisted as dispatch riders. This was more than a mere honorary gesture, too. Both men took their duties seriously, and whenever George's tight schedule permitted they mucked in with everyone else. 'It's a nice bit of twig, is this!' George cracked, whilst posing for photographs with his rifle – he was a crack shot, too – though most of his fans would have begged to differ, arguing that the only 'weapon' they ever wanted to see in his hand was his ukulele.

In Brest, on the coast of Brittany, George and Beryl were amongst the small pioneering concert-party which entertained the 40,000-strong British Expeditionary Force. For the first show of 26 March 1940, the couple improvised a hilarious 'Dick Whittington' sketch, and George performed his most popular numbers, including 'Imagine Me In The Maginot Line', which he had recorded the previous December. Parts of the show were shown on cinema newsreels throughout Europe, and much of it was taped – however, though several acetates were pressed, the actual recordings would not be released during George's lifetime.

George's next concert, at Quimper, was heard on the radio by the *Blackpool Gazette*'s Sylvia, who became a friend and over the next few years acted as the Formbys' unofficial champion in the press. Their association got off to a bad start when Beryl took exception to the headline, 'George Is No. 2', and Sylvia's opening comments:

> *I should rank George Formby as second to Gracie Fields in the affections of the B E F. Not since Gracie visited the B E F theatre have I heard such a hullabaloo on the air. George sang his new song, 'Imagine Me In The Maginot Line', which, so he announced, his wife had written for him. Afterwards the audience was so excitable and undisciplined in its demands that George had to ask for order. Half of this young comedian's success can be ascribed to his unaffected intimacy with his audience. Last night he invited them to shout messages home. They nearly blew up the microphone. And when he invited them to tell the people in England if they were happy, their 'Yes' could have been heard in Hamburg. No wonder they love George!*

George and a very apprehensive Beryl invited Sylvia to tea at their Singleton home on 5 May, a few days after their return from France – predictably enough, Beryl was terrified that this journalist had been worshipping her husband from afar for one reason only! In fact, she was pleasantly surprised: Sylvia was well into her fifties, plump and bespectacled, and had a husband and a family. Beryl did, however, gently rebuke her for daring to suggest that Gracie Fields was a greater star than her husband. However, the two women hit it off like a house on fire when Sylvia informed her that she too had put out an appeal for the Jump Fund during the Formbys' absence, one which had brought in dozens of sacks of knitwear.

Sitting in his living room, under the auspicious gaze of Formby Sr, whose portrait hung over the fireplace, George spoke of his experiences in 'Garlicland'. The looks on the men's faces, he said, would stay with him for ever, as would the stench of the converted fish-van which had been the company's only means of transport over the last five weeks. And only one thing had been worse than the dreadful seasickness he had endured each time he had stepped on to a boat – French food. 'They were beginning to call me Tommy Tucker before we left,' he grimaced. 'I used to go along to the cookhouse and offer to give them three songs for a real English meal of bacon and eggs.'

Beryl also spoke of their 'privileged' return journey from Honfleur, where their last show had taken place less than an hour before they were due to set sail. After the performance, George had told an English admiral how he was dreading the overnight crossing because a storm was brewing and he had already left 'half his insides' at the bottom of the Channel. The admiral had told him not to worry: an empty ship was scheduled to leave for England the next morning, and the 23-strong ENSA party would be welcome to travel on that. 'George was very happy,' Beryl concluded. 'He said he could be ill in every room.'

The very next day – both of them suffering from a heavy cold – George and Beryl embarked on a four-week tour of munitions works in the North of England to raise money for the Fleetwood Fund, which gave aid to the families of killed or missing trawlermen. This constituted more than a hundred 30-minute concerts, many taking place during the workers' lunchbreaks which, the managers repeatedly informed ENSA, boosted output considerably more than any increase in wages would have done.

'Workers move about with a lighter step. Smiles broaden on their earnest faces,' reported the ubiquitous Sylvia, 'they eat a bigger lunch – that's a sure sign that they're feeling happy!' And at a gas-mask factory in Manchester, Basil Dean himself introduced his least-favourite 'employee' on to the stage, and swallowed hard when forced to read the brief speech prepared by the manager:

> *The North-West is a storehouse of rich things, of which the most prized, perhaps, is humour. And the leader of funsters is your own George Formby. He has carried his uke everywhere in the service of his country. In barn and cowshed, hangar and canteen, field and tent, there goes George, the modern minstrel. Everywhere he carries the language of commonsense, and when the band of victory plays, the star artist will be George!*

In June 1940, having raised well over £10,000 for the trawlermen's dependants, George began work on his next ATP film, *Spare A Copper*, directed by John Paddy Carstairs and co-starring Dorothy Hyson, the Chicago-born actress who had recently triumphed in the Old Vic's production of *A Midsummer Night's Dream* alongside Vivien Leigh and Anthony Quayle.

Hyson was a rarity – a leading lady whom Beryl actually approved of, largely because whilst 'researching' her she had learned about Hyson's clandestine involvement with Anthony Quayle, the great love of her life whom she would eventually marry. Hyson, however, found out during the first week of shooting that Beryl had 'fixed things' with Michael Balcon so that she would fail her audition for *Let George Do It*, and her attitude towards Beryl was now openly frosty. Throughout the film, Hyson would refer to Beryl – and sometimes to her face, as 'the diamond-studded bitch'.

The screenplay and three of the film's four songs – not amongst George's most enduring, primarily because their composer is said to have purposely avoided the requisite double-entendres – were by Roger MacDougal, the Glaswegian chiefly remembered for scripting two comedy classics of the next decade, *The Mouse That Roared* and *The Man In The White*

Suit. Even so, the numbers would prove popular enough with George's fans for MacDougal to be commissioned to write for him again in the near future.

Spare A Copper was amongst George's better films, for though the editing and script are poor and Dorothy Hyson is unconvincing as his leading lady, *he* is in sparkling form. The action takes place in Birkenhead on the eve of World War II. The battleship HMS *Hercules* is about to be launched – and also about to be sabotaged by enemy agents, an operation which is spearheaded by the amusement park proprietor Edward Brewster (George Merritt), a plot which is ultimately foiled by bungling War Reserve George Carter. George makes an uneasy entrance on a bicycle he has 'borrowed' from Jane Gray (Hyson) – causing traffic mayhem. Henceforth the slapstick is continuous: numerous escapades when George inadvertently gets on the wrong side of the police *and* the crooks, culminating in a high-speed chase in a miniature racing-car which sees him zooming around a Wall of Death, after which he launches HMS *Hercules* himself just seconds before the bomb goes off.

The story, of course, *was* only secondary to the slapstick – with George once more doing most of his own sometimes quite dangerous motorcycle stunts. Ignoring the clause in his contract which prohibited him from even *riding* a machine, he heralded himself as 'an angel with 200 horse-power wings' before charging around an obstacle course and ending up in an exploding first-aid hut. Jane works in a music-store, which just happens to have a large selection of ukuleles. He therefore sings 'I'm The Ukulele Man' with an invading children's choir, after which he wrecks the place whilst rushing off to take his motorcycle test. 'On The Beat' starts off quietly enough, but ends up as a rip-roaring free-for-all stomp complete with male trio, marching feet, and a raucous female obligato . . . delivered by Beryl Reid in one of her earliest screen appearances! Later, accompanied by a novachord, he croons 'I'm Shy', and in the

midst of a wild chase through a theatre he pauses long enough
to participate in an amateur talent contest . . . where once more
a uke is close at hand. The song was yet another that had been
frowned upon by the BBC:

> *I went into a nightclub where a lady did a dance,*
> *She'd nothing on but pigeons,*
> *And she left the rest to chance.*
> *She didn't seem to feel the cold,*
> *The birds knew where to stay,*
> *I clapped my hands and shouted,*
> *But they didn't fly away!*
> *I wish she was down on our farm –*
> *She'd have nothing on whatever,*
> *'Cause our pigeons aren't so clever!*

The continuity errors in this one are few, but amusing
nevertheless. In the scene where George sings 'On The Beat',
filmed in sections on different days and spliced together only
after the director had decided to use Beryl Reid, the chain of
his pocket-watch alternates in length and between the second
and fourth buttons of his coat. Later, when he and the
saboteurs are being pursued by the police and George ends up
in a falling barrel, the frame pauses for a split-second, revealing
the attached safety wire. And towards the end of the film,
during the car-chase when the crooks' vehicle backs into a side
road, the fumes are actually sucked *back* into the exhaust
because the cameraman, Ronald Neame, had filmed the car
travelling forward and reversed the shot!

Shortly after completing *Spare A Copper*, George was
approached by Charles Forsythe, a Canadian comic-
entrepreneur who was visiting Britain to put together a team of
top-notch stars for a tour of North America, to raise funds for
the Spitfire Fund. Forsythe's project had been given full
backing by the Ministry of Information, and he was confident

that if he could talk George into participating, other artists of a similar calibre would soon follow suit.

Forsythe, however, had not reckoned on the Formbys' patriotism. Even if Canada was a part of the British Commonwealth, to their way of thinking in troubled times – when the emphasis was on 'looking after one's own' – it was just another foreign country which should have been able to take care of its own fund-raising. 'If we want Spitfires, we'll pay for them ourselves without asking for help from foreigners,' Beryl opined, whilst George cracked, 'The only time *I'll* be leaving Britain is when they *blow* me out!'

This latter statement worried Basil Dean, who initially was led to believe that the Formbys would also refuse to do any more shows in France. George soon put him straight on this score. 'So far as I'm concerned,' he said, 'France and Britain are the same, especially those bits of France where our lads are. In the time it takes us just to get to Canada, Beryl and me can do a dozen shows across the Channel. Tell the Canadians to get Bing Crosby if they're so desperate to be entertained!'

The work for the Fleetwood trawlermen continued. Beryl placed announcements in the local papers that, for the time being, knitted articles sent in to the Jump Fund would be donated to this cause, adding, 'And if any of you hard-working ladies out there do have a few moments to spare, please knit me a few pairs of bootees for all those poor, fatherless babies.' Within the week, more than 1,000 pairs were sent to Singleton.

Beryl also began charging George's fans for his autograph – a few coppers, or whatever they could afford, which was dropped into a tin and counted up at the end of each day so that the money could be added to the fund.

In August, George and Beryl turned up at a RAF base near Newcastle to find an in-house concert-party in full swing and a young officer named Ted Coates impersonating George. Coates had written to him a few weeks previously, asking his permission to do this, wondering if George might see his way into loaning him an old ukulele which would be looked after and returned to him after the war. George had a far better idea: marching up to Coates, on the stage, he pushed a ukulele into his hand and told him, 'That thing you're trying to play's out of tune. Here, have mine!'

George *should* have left for London in the middle of September to begin shooting his next film, but just as a game of marbles had delayed his journey to France, so too he was held back by a series of events which for him were of great significance. Firstly he stood in for an indisposed Bud Flanagan at Blackpool's Palace Theatre. After the show he was reunited with Fred Harrison, the manager of the Earlstown Hippo-drome where he had made his first professional appearance nineteen years before. Harrison was celebrating his quarter-century at the theatre's helm, and suggested they get together and put on a concert. George said that he would be delighted to, but that it would have to be that weekend. For old times' sake he left his ukulele in the wings until the last two songs, and was accompanied at the piano by a Mrs Clements, who had played for him back in 1921. He raised over £100 for the Spitfire Fund.

The third event took place when illness forced Arthur Askey to drop out of *The Show of 1940* at the Blackpool Opera House, and George insisted upon taking over for the last twelve performances – providing the producer agreed to hand over his salary and all the profits to the war-effort. This brought an angry reaction from Ealing's Michael Balcon, since George's new film was still waiting to begin shooting and the leading lady, Phyllis Calvert, was getting restless. George, however, was not wearing this. At such critical times, he declared, helping others less fortunate than oneself was far more important than making films, and he put the phone down on the man who was ostensibly his boss.

Balcon is said to have become wild with rage upon reading a

copy of George's immediate itinerary, which Beryl had printed in several local and national newspapers. This was the first in what would be a series of campaigns aimed at proving how much George was doing for his country, as opposed to some of his 'conscientious objector' contemporaries who, over the next few years, would be constantly under the threat of being exposed by him:

> *I'm at Llandudno tomorrow night. I should have gone today. Instead I'll have to remain at home and prepare material for the Opera House. I'll go to Llandudno tomorrow and drive back in the middle of the night in time for rehearsals on Monday. On Tuesday I'll open a mile of pennies at Cleveleys. Wednesday's a dickens of a day. I'm appearing as Henry Hall's guest star at the Palace. In between I have a matinee at the Opera House, a couple of shows there at night, and a couple of Palace appearances in between. On Thursday I may go to Manchester for a consultation about the new film. On Friday I have two munitions concerts. On Saturday two more, and a lunchtime broadcast. And seeing as I'm in the Home Guard as well, I won't be forsaking them – I'll be out on patrol all Sunday. After that, who knows? We all have to do our bit, Mr Balcon!*

At the beginning of November, George and Beryl were finally free to make what would prove his final film for ATP: *Turned Out Nice Again*, again directed by Marcel Varnel. Many of his friends, however, were concerned about George filming so close to London, the main target for the air-raids. George's journalist friend, Sylvia, even warned him that this might prove an 'unlucky thirteenth' production – to which he responded that thirteen was his *lucky* number, for had he not wed 'the girl of his dreams' on this date? Then he told everyone not to worry. *He* had given Michael Balcon an ultimatum: he and Beryl would spend just three weeks in London – which would include a full day at the recording studio – and the rest of the shooting schedule would take place in the North of England. This was not because he was afraid of remaining in the capital, but because he was still working flat-out for his Northern war charities *and* about to open in a pantomime at the Blackpool Opera House. Balcon then informed him of ATP's latest dilemma – following the delays caused by George, the production would not be able to begin shooting because it no longer had a leading lady. 'Miss Calvert has made such a success since her appearance with George Formby that it is feared she will be too busy,' read the statement in the *Evening Standard*. This did not bother George, who just went off and did a few charity shows until Marcel Varnel summoned him back to the set.

George was next warned that the script had a jinx on it. It had started out as a successful West End play, *As You Are*, but its author, Hugh Mills, had yet to collect on his investment because he had been visiting Paris when the Germans had moved in and occupied the city. A homosexual, Mills had subsequently been interned and his London agent – fearing that he might be dead already – would not give ATP permission to transfer the play to the screen. The producer, Michael Balcon, got around this by signing a contract with Mills' mother, wherein it was agreed that the author's earnings from the film would be placed in a London bank account, and in the event of his demise be shared out amongst his relatives.

Like all its predecessors, *Turned Out Nice Again* would have its share of backstage problems. When told that his leading lady Peggy Bryan, was a former elocution teacher straight out of drama school, George steeled himself for 'some pain-in-the-arse snob' . . . as he had once dismissed Polly Ward. Bryan, however, was not posh at all. She hailed from Ireland, but had spent much of her life in Birmingham and her accent was a combination of the two. Beryl, however, disliked her from the start. *This* actress was going to portray George's *wife*, the first time this had ever happened, and she anticipated that he would be expected to say and do all manner of things in front of the cameras!

Before Beryl could get round to reading Bryan the riot act, however, part of the studio was hit by an incendiary bomb and almost totally gutted. Only George's ukuleles and Bryan's costumes were saved from the fire by quick-thinking, unnecessarily brave technicians. The fact that the actors and crew had vacated the area only hours before brought Beryl to her senses and reminded her that there were better things to argue about than co-stars who were only 'flighty' in her overworked imagination.

While he was in London, George joined a shelter group organised by ENSA, for a series of underground shows in and around the capital. One of these, at the Aldwych tube station, was broadcast by the BBC on 27 November 1940 as part of their immensely popular *Let The People Sing* series. George, one of several entertainers who participated in the event, cringed as he was introduced to the stage by Admiral Sir Edward Evans – who pronounced in his Etonesque accent, 'You will hear George Formby, so typical of this country, and Geraldo and his orchestra. And you will hear London, below ground, making a night of it. George Formby. He needs no introduction. Good old George . . . not so old!'

When George realised that Evans had delivered his spiel from a script, and that he disliked Northern entertainers, he denounced him as a 'snotty-nosed old bugger'. The people, of course, were only interested in George, and roared their appreciation even when he quipped that many of them would be spending the night underground, when he had a comfortable flat to go back to – not that he would have minded roughing it for once. Pointing to a middle-aged woman, he chirped, 'Shift up, missus, I'm coming in!' On a more serious note, he concluded, 'I can't tell you exactly what I feel about the English people today. We've got a King and Queen and I think they're marvellous people for us lot to look up to. I think the way they're carrying on, they've got as much good in their little finger as Hitler and Gower-ring and all the damn lot put together. Don't forget, it's wonderful to be British!'

The four songs which George performed at Aldwych were recorded by the BBC, though they never made it past the acetate stage. They included Fred Godfrey's 'Bless 'Em All', written in 1917 and newly-revised by him especially for George, with additional verses . . . and Gifford and Cliffe's 'Down The Old Coal Hole'.

At the end of the month, shooting on *Turned Out Nice Again* transferred to Preston, where Horrockses-Crewdson & Co had placed their huge textile mill at ATP's disposal, giving the workers the week off and some of them an opportunity to become extras in the film. At their Singleton home, George and Beryl had once again invited their journalist friend, Sylvia, to tea, but instead of doing the interview there and then, George had suggested that they meet the next morning on the set – at six on the dot! Sylvia had tried to argue that this was far too early, until Beryl had announced, 'But you'll have to, dear. George has already told the director that you're going to be one of the extras!' George had also decided that 'Sylvia' was not an appropriate name for a 'film-star', albeit that the journalist would only ever appear in a single scene in just one film – two minutes into the scenario, she is the matronly factory girl with her hair in a bun – henceforth she would write under the pseudonym which George gave her: Phyllis!

Turned Out Nice Again – named after the catchphrase which he uses umpteen times in his other films, but only once in this one – was, for most Formby fans, an inappropriate ATP swan-song because it contained no slapstick. It did, however, deliver a neat slap in the face for those detractors who had accused George of being unable to act. Indeed, *because* it brought George's true thespian skills to the fore, with its blend of pathos, humour and down to earth histrionics, in this respect it may justifiably be regarded as the best of all his films. Peggy Bryan – despite a sometimes 'dodgy' Northern accent which reverts to her natural Irish-Brummie one when her temper flares – can likewise be deemed the most adept of his leading ladies.

George Pearson, the foreman at Dawson's underwear factory, suddenly finds himself promoted when Nelson, the overseer (Ronald Ward) is fired for fraud and goes to work for a rival firm. George is delighted, for this now means that he and his sweetheart, Lydia (Bryan) can wed. The Pearsons' homelife, however, is anything but harmonious. George's Uncle Arnold (Edward Chapman) is paranoid because his prize pigeon will not lay an egg. Ruling the roost is George's mother, who interferes in every aspect of the couple's lives, including accompanying them on their honeymoon . . . feigning heart-attacks and persistently reminding her son how she spent four and a half hours 'under the chloroform' bringing him into the world. The part had originally been pencilled in for Thora Hird, an actress from Morecambe who was several years younger than George, though one cannot imagine a more immaculate portrayal than that by Elliot Mason, a stone-faced harridan – in real life nothing of the kind – almost a British Marie Dressler who, a few years later, would support Robert Donat and Deborah Kerr in *Perfect Strangers*.

The action jumps to the Pearsons' first wedding anniversary, when Lydia buys George a dinner jacket and is berated by her mother-in-law for living above her means. 'Nothing's nice to look at till it's paid for,' she chides. George, however, cannot make the party: he has to stand in for a colleague at an underwear exhibition in London. Here, he bumps into Nelson, showing off only the chicest lingerie whilst Dawsons parade its old-fashioned stays and bloomers. At the show, Nelson is sold the rights to a prototype yarn which, when he realises that the vendor may be a crook, he passes on to George. The next day he explains this to Lydia, in such a way that she at first believes he has been with another woman. 'It all started at the party last night . . . It was Mr Nelson who suggested it. I admit I rather liked the idea, but I didn't know what you'd think about it . . . So I went back and did it quickly. It cost three hundred pounds . . . I gave an IOU for it.'

When the penny drops, Lydia is only enthusiastic. 'Nothing ventured, nothing gained,' she says. Then the Pearsons' marriage hits a rocky patch on account of the domineering old woman. The rows are vociferous and most un-Formby-like, and even continue into the office when in a quick volte-face Lydia attacks George for failing to stand up for himself, and he resigns after the boss insults her. All turns out well in the end, however, when Lydia pretends to walk out on him. She has actually gone to London to model his samples, and when her picture appears in the newspaper, the bartering begins for George's yarn – just as the couple's furniture is about to be repossessed. George opts to go into partnership with Dawsons, even though the wily Nelson outbids them – so that he and Lydia can work at their London factory, where they will be rid of his mother. And adding to the blissful ending, Uncle Arnold's pigeon finally lays an egg!

Turned Out Nice Again contained four excellent songs, amongst them Eddie Latta's pastiche – and another Formby 'property' number – to the inventor of the potion, sold at every chemist for 'one-and-a-kick' (1s 6d), which cures all ills:

> *Now if you get lumbago, rheumatics or gout,*
> *Or a pain in your Robert E Lee,*
> *Don't kick up a shindy,*
> *You'll never get windy*
> *With Auntie Maggie's Remedy!*

Like Fred E Cliffe, Eddie Latta (Bruce Williams) was a gregarious Liverpudlian, born in 1900 into a family of undertakers – a trade which he reluctantly continued his whole life.

Latta wrote just nine Formby songs, though no doubt there would have been more had he taken a leaf out of Gifford's and Cliffe's book and *demanded* his share of the royalties. He did not. Upon Beryl's insistence, George paid Latta a flat fee for each song, added his name to the songwriter credits so that he got *all* the proceeds. When Latta realised that he had been duped he focused his talents elsewhere, which is a great pity. Songs such as 'Auntie Maggie's Remedy' and 'Guarding The Home Of The Home Guard represent George at his most astute, and there should have been many more.

Meanwhile, the Formbys' first Blackpool concert, *Dick Whittington* – with George playing Idle Jack to Beryl's Polly Perkins – opened to fabulous reviews, despite the fact that there had only been sufficient time for one rehearsal. George donated his first week's salary – £1,000 – to the Manchester Air-Raid Distress Fund, and despite Beryl's protestations actually registered for military service. The press turned up at the Labour Exchange, and jokingly asked him how, as one of the highest-paid stars in British showbusiness he would be able to get by on such a colossal drop in salary, should he achieve his ambition and be accepted as an army dispatch rider. George cracked back, 'I get less pocket money each week from the wife that they'd pay me, so I'd be laughing!' The examining board, however, gave him a Grade Four classification and rejected him when he was discovered to have arthritic toes and a minor chest ailment.

For George, the pantomime run could not end soon enough. He was convinced that he had 'bled the North dry' so far as his and Beryl's fund-raising was concerned, and was anxious to return to London and raise more money there, risking the dangers of the Blitz by joining the ranks of Flanagan and Allen, Elsie and Doris Waters, Max Miller, and Al Bowlly – the much-loved crooner, who, early in 1941, would become the Blitz's most celebrated casualty. 'If London's good enough for her Majesty,' he declared, referring to the Queen's stolid determination not to leave Buckingham Palace even though persistently advised to do so, 'then it'll do for Beryl and me!'

George was a tremendous favourite with the royals, and at around this time there occurred his and Beryl's much-publicised visit to Windsor Castle, where they entertained the royal family and several hundred troops. A few weeks before the show, George was informed that he would be expected to sing all his big hits, including 'When I'm Cleaning Windows', and fearful of offending 'sensitive ears' he had at once contacted Fred E Cliffe and commissioned a set of 'alternative' lyrics. When he and Beryl arrived at Windsor, however, they were told by a royal aide that the King and Queen were interested only in hearing the *uncensored* act with which George had delighted the troops – even though the young princesses Elizabeth and Margaret would be present. The show proved a triumph – afterwards the King presented George with a set of gold cufflinks, and Beryl with a silver powder-compact, and three weeks later the Formbys appeared in a command performance for the Marlborough Troop, presided over by Queen Mary, the King's mother – a strait-laced woman who nevertheless requested George not to spare her blushes. *She* loved 'When I'm Cleaning Windows' so much that George was asked to sing it again, and the next morning news of this was relayed to the headquarters of the BBC, hoping the ban on the song would be lifted. It was not.

Before leaving London, George – or rather, Beryl – had informed Basil Dean and Michael Balcon that he would not be renewing his contract with ATP. *Turned Out Nice Again* had provided George with an opportunity to portray the kind of half-serious character he felt better suited to his acting abilities – one which was *not* suited to Ealing comedies – and no amount of persuasion or even a substantial increase in salary would get him to change his mind.

Being on the open market, so to speak, naturally brought in a flood of offers, and when George finally signed a new contract, in March 1941, it was for Columbia Pictures. In a deal worth in excess of £500,000, George would head his own company, Hillcrest Productions – so named after his mother's Warrington house, though he hardly ever saw Eliza – and over the next two years he would do a minimum of six films, with his own choice of director, scriptwriter and theme, though his leading ladies would be chosen by the studio.

The Columbia contract had been greatly influenced by the recent poll in the *Motion Picture Herald* which had placed George's films at the top of the British cinema box-office returns, just slightly ahead of Gracie Fields and Charles Laughton – and Number 5 in the International list, ahead of Errol Flynn, Bette Davis and even Bing Crosby. George himself had stipulated just the one condition: although his films would be American-backed, they would have to be made in Britain.

George's defection to another company – one which was not British – caused considerable ill-feeling in some circles. Anti-American detractors accused him of 'selling out' on his country for the sake of lining his own pocket, and it was also suggested that he had only agreed to do charity concerts because his and Beryl's 'expenses' included a percentage of the takings. This upset him so much that he began estimating how much each show would raise, and always made a point of making up any 'deficit' – ridiculously unnecessary, of course.

The Formbys began receiving poison-pen letters and threatening telephone calls, and on one occasion a brick was thrown through their car windscreen, narrowly missing Beryl's face. When interviewed by the police and press, George attempted to make light of the situation by suggesting the culprit had been a fan, too shy to ask for a conventional autograph. He agreed to sign the brick, should its owner come forward, which of course he never did. The incident shook him badly, however, and for several days he tried to get out of his Columbia contract. This was not possible, though George's attackers were placated for the moment by a statement issued by his film company, declaring that thus far in the conflict he had raised over £25,000 for the war-effort. Columbia were effectively selling George short, for he had actually brought in almost twice this amount.

In May 1941, Beryl set about organising a lightning, fifteen-day 'shilling' tour of those cities and towns worst affected by the Blitz. 'I know these people will get compensation after the war,' George told the press, 'but we don't know when that'll be, and they want help now.' The idea behind the concept was that if just ten per cent of those who so far had been unaffected or not had properties damaged during air-raids could subscribe a single shilling each, top-notch artists such as George could quite easily raise as much as £10,000 a week. Advertising was essential, of course, and the BBC had given over each Sunday evening for personal appeals from the stars, so that large sections of the public who would not normally have had a chance of seeing them in their neck of the woods would now know how to acquire tickets. Basil Dean and ENSA had agreed to handle any artists participating in the project, and Oscar Deutsch, the managing director of Odeon Cinemas, had promised to supply the theatres free of charge.

Beryl at once hit a snag when she learned that the BBC, who clearly *did* believe that the Formbys had been dipping into the war-effort funds, declined to offer him air-time to make his appeal – claiming that all their Sunday evening appeal-slots were fully booked until the end of the year.

For once, Beryl was justified in giving the BBC's director general a piece of her mind, though her victory was decidedly Pyrrhic: George was allocated a mere two-minute slot in *Monday At Eight*, broadcast from North Wales, and he was not allowed to give out the address where contributions had to be sent. The BBC later admitted that because of this 'oversight' just over one thousand contributions had been forwarded to their London headquarters, a mere fraction of Beryl's target.

Fortunately, Beryl was not the kind of entrepreneur to give up easily. The tour kicked off at Southampton on 10 June, and over the next two weeks took in Portsmouth, Plymouth, Bristol, Liverpool, Sheffield, Hull and Glasgow, in that order. Prior to each engagement, Beryl arranged to have slides projected on all the circuit cinema screens, informing fans exactly where George would be appearing, and where to send those all-important shillings. The tour would bring in a staggering £23,000 in its first week, and even more in the second.

On 22 June, after Glasgow, George and Beryl played theatres in Stirling, Pitlochry and Fort William, before travelling to Inverness. Then – ignoring ENSA's warning that such a trip was too perilous to undertake – the couple flew to the Orkneys. Whilst here, they learned that a detachment of just twelve men were stationed in the Shetlands, but that their request to have George visit them had been turned down because their camp was out of bounds. The Formbys waited until after dark, then bribed the captain of a small boat to ferry them across. Other fans, over the last few weeks, had had to be content with thirty minutes of George's valuable time: these soldiers, however, had him for four hours, sipping mugs of cocoa laced with rum between songs, most of the time huddled around a camp-fire.

On 27 July 1941, George loaned his services to the London Tank Fund, taking part in the heavy infantry parade which 'invaded' the West End. Driving a tank, he manned an unloaded tommy-gun to the delight of the 12,000 people who turned up to witness the event. Afterwards he appeared at the Tank Matinee at the Odeon Leicester Square – a snobbish occasion part-hosted by Ben Lyon and his wife, Bebe Daniels, who boasted to all and sundry of how much *they* had raised for the fund – whilst George quietly handed over a cheque for £3,000, telling one of the organisers, 'Buy rivets, cock. That way I'll get more for my money!'

A few days later, the Formbys returned to Singleton for a well-earned rest. 'We're going to put our feet up, or maybe catch up on a bit of gardening,' he told a reporter from the London *Evening Standard*, adding, 'Well, hopefully. Ee, there's no rest for the wicked!' He was right. The pair ate one meal at their home before dashing off to a show in aid of the Fleetwood trawlermen, and the next morning George *did* get to tend his garden – digging up the potatoes he had planted outside his house. 'If you can't eat it, it's a weed,' he told passers-by who stopped off at the sign SPUDS FOR SALE, gasping at the exorbitant price he was charging for his produce . . . until they learned that the money would be augmenting Beryl's Jump Fund.

At the end of August, following innumerable troop, factory and shelter concerts, George began shooting his first film for Columbia. *South American George* saw him in a dual role – playing a gormless but loveable busker, and a Brazilian operatic tenor whose singing voice in the film is thought to have been dubbed by Giovanni Martinelli. The latter, 'disgusted' by the way in which Verdi's *Rigoletto* was sent up, subsequently asked for his name to be removed from the credits. The music, suffice to say, is not always what one would come to expect in a Formby film!

The story begins at a provincial theatre, where the great Gilli Vannetti is giving the last performance of the opera season. When one of the non-singing extras fails to turn up, the producer sends out his scout who engages George Butters, whom he finds serenading an unappreciative barmaid at the nearby pub. George makes his stage debut dressed as a soldier: he drops his musket, and creates havoc with the soprano, in mid-aria. 'Beg your pardon, missus,' he says, then panics when he sees two relatives in the audience – his father loathes the stage because his sister-in-law, Mable, formerly a Gaiety girl, is now a has-been residing at the Fernlands Artists' Retirement Home.

In the wings, George meets Vannetti's personal assistant, Carol Dean (Linden Travers), and overhears an argument between Ricardo, the theatre manager (Jacques Brown) and his lawyer. He learns that this last performance has been played to an entire house of concessionary ticket holders, for away from his own country no one wants to hear the arrogant Vannetti if they have to pay! Unfortunately, Ricardo has booked him for the next season, so to save his theatre from bankruptcy he must now find a way of getting the tenor to break his contract. In a fit of pique, the tenor leaves for his next recital overseas, leaving Carol in the lurch – she has secured him a charity engagement, presenting a cheque to the residents at Fernlands.

George, meanwhile, leaves the theatre and on the way home – having told his parents, upon leaving the house that morning, that he is looking for a job, and having received only half-pay for his stage appearance – he accepts payment from a market-trader for demonstrating hair-curlers. This new hairstyle results in his becoming the spitting image of Vannetti, and when he visits Fernlands the next day to see Aunty Mable, he bumps into Carol, who transforms him – aided by a mascara brush and false moustache – into a carbon copy of the star and saves herself from the embarrassment of having to tell everyone that Vannetti is not really a charitable man. When a shot of the presentation gets into the local newspaper, however, Carol persuades George to keep up the charade, and the remainder of the film has the pair outwitting the wily Ricardo – for George knows that if Vannetti does break his contract, he will never see Carol, with whom he has fallen in love, again.

Because Vannetti's contract decrees that he must obey every instruction given to him by the manager, Ricardo forces his double to dance in the ballet corps. Then he makes him clean the stage, even getting him to count every flake after he has switched on the snow-machine, before ordering him to climb the scaffolding outside the theatre to erect the neon lettering. Carol is impressed by his naive determination. 'I think you're

116

the biggest little man I've ever met,' she tells him, to which he replies in song that, no matter the challenge, so long as it is to please her, he will do it with a smile.

Having failed to break George's spirit, Ricardo next attempts to catch him out with the contract's 'undesirable publicity' clause. Hiring hammy actors, he sends a scantily-clad woman up to George's apartment, trailed by a jealous 'husband' who will find them in a compromising position. Before this can happen, we hear George being berated by Jiminy Cricket – the voice of his conscience which he chooses to ignore. 'I love her,' George says of Carol, to which his other half responds, 'You *love* her! What could *you* give her? If turkeys were sixpence a pound you haven't enough to buy her a feather from a tomtit's ear-hole!' Then Carol arrives on the scene, and the floosie is trussed up and shoved inside a blanket box until Ricardo and his cronies have left.

As a last resort, Ricardo hires the spivvish thug, Swifty (Ronald Shiner) to kidnap Vannetti and spirit him out of the country, but whilst Swifty is masterminding his plan the manager gets a call from the infamous entrepreneur, George White: his *Vanities of 1941* is about to open, but his star has gone missing. White offers Ricardo a huge fee to take Vannetti's contract off his hands, leaving George and Carol with a seemingly unsurmountable predicament – if the real Vannetti cannot be located and brought back to England in time for the opening night, George will have to sing opera! And of course, now that Ricardo is about to rake in the money, he is all over the little man he has thus far treated like dirt.

The big performance takes place, with Aunty Mable and her pals opening the show – George's condition for helping out, now that Ricardo has been told his true identity – and with George having been forced to mime to one of Vannetti's recordings. The real Vannetti has also turned up, and been knocked out by Ricardo's hitman. After George's successful opening aria, however, mayhem ensues when Swifty and his sidekick, assuming their quarry has got away, chase him up and down the props and the scenery is wrecked before *they* are knocked senseless by Carol. And finally, before blurting out that he loves her after she has presented him with a showbusiness contract – with her as his manager – George whips off his troubadour garb, under which he is wearing a matador's suit-of-lights. As 'Don Tonsillitis' he entertains the crowd, having replaced his ukulele with a more appropriate instrument, with one of the finest of all the Formby film-songs, 'My Spanish Guitar':

> *I've had some hard fights and I've had a few frights,*
> *There was one when the bull got me down.*
> *He jumped on my corns and stuck both of his horns*
> *In my shanty in old shanty-town!*
> *His eyes they were staring and glassy,*
> *I could feel his hot breath in my ear,*
> *So I stabbed him three times in the chassis . . .*
> *That bull got a shock so,*
> *He turned into Oxo,*
> *You'll find him on sale at the bar!*

South American George was completed in just six weeks, and its press-showing set for the end of November. Because many of George's fans had bemoaned the lack of slapstick in his last film, the distributors hit upon a clever gimmick by taking out a pukka insurance policy with Lloyds. At some cinemas, notices were pasted to the playbills, declaring, 'The aforementioned underwriter vows that for the receipt of a £1 premium, an agreement will be made wherein a sum of £500 will be paid in respect of each person who may die laughing whilst and as a result of viewing this film.' As far as is known, Lloyds did not have to fork out: it was not that the film was unfunny, quite simply that few of George's admirers could afford the hefty premium!

The Formbys, meanwhile, had ended up in the middle of yet another bust-up with Basil Dean. Since turning down Charles Forsythe's offer to tour Canada, George had been pestered by Dean to join ENSA's official package to the country, which had been scheduled to leave for Toronto in the New Year. Time and time again, George had told Dean that he was not interested, begging him to send him back into France, or even out to the Middle East. Dean, however, knew that it would prove difficult to put on any tour of North America without a headlining name to attract other artists, and he piled on the pressure to such an extent that George almost gave in. Then on 13 October – a 'lucky' day – George read a letter from an elderly fan, Frank Hannan, in Sylvia's column in the *Blackpool Gazette*:

Dear George. I feel very sorry for you, old boy, but you cannot please everybody. We all know that Canada would like you, that America would like you, that every country would like you, that even Hitler would like you. He would reckon it one of his biggest successes to get you. Anyway, take a tip from an old Lancashire lad and stop with us. You DO buck us up in these dark days and we shall not forget when this mess is over. I am talking to you as your father would. Stay put and carry on the good work!

When George read in Hannan's postscript that he had once worked the music-halls – more than this, he had actually appeared on stage with Formby Sr – George called Basil Dean. The head of ENSA, however, still would not take no for an answer, so Beryl paid for a piece to be placed in the national press in which her husband proclaimed:

George Formby is NOT going to Canada, Mr Dean. I appreciate your invitation, but I can't accept it. I've decided that I ought to remain with the lads in THIS country, singing to them whenever they want me. Sorry, but there it is!

George even made light of the situation when his agent, Ben Henry, remarked that Basil Dean was extremely angry with him for so publicly forcing him to 'eat humble pie'. 'If he doesn't like humble pie he can always join us for hot-pot,' George told Sylvia. The occasion was a hot-pot supper at Fleetwood's Marine Hall, for 120 dependants of dead or missing trawlermen, after which he presented the mayor with a cheque for £1200.

With Dean out of their hair for the time being, George and Beryl spent several days entertaining troops on Salisbury Plain, and on 28 December they put in an appearance at the Royal Albert Hall – in an ENSA concert in aid of the King's Fund For Sailors. Basil Dean was conspicuous by his absence.

The following afternoon, the Formbys paid their second visit to Windsor, where they put on a sketch, 'The Casting Office', and George sang seven songs accompanied by Geraldo's orchestra. The King requested 'With My Little Stick Of Blackpool Rock', and Princess Elizabeth 'Frank On His Tank', and after the show George and Beryl took tea with the royal family. The King and Queen presented them with a signed photograph, so it was only natural that Beryl should dip into her handbag and return the compliment!

On 5 January 1942, the Formbys embarked on a tour of Northern Ireland, one which should have begun four weeks previously, and for which George had foregone his annual pantomime. This offered detractors a little more ammunition to attack – concluding that if he had sacrificed £1,000 a week, he would be sure to be getting his money elsewhere. This was untrue. Starting off with a 'command' performance before the Ulster Prime Minister, he appeared in a minimum of three shows a day for six weeks, donating every penny of his earnings to Belfast air-raid victims. His travelling and hotel expenses also came out of his own pocket. 'Just keep me supplied with Guinness, and I'll do the rest,' he cracked at an impromptu press-conference, before launching into a snatch from 'The Cook House Serenade':

> *My uniform is an apron,*
> *I'm learning to cook and bake.*
> *Now when I get out of the army,*
> *What a wonderful wife I'll make!*

It was during a troops concert in Belfast that George first publicly expressed his opinion – with no prompting from Beryl – about the 'top brass' and their wives. Many of them did not even bother applauding between sketches and songs, although they invariably took up the first few rows of the concert halls – whilst the fighting men, his true fans, were relegated to the back of the auditorium. And when one rather stuffy Irish-woman was overheard to say that she hated these 'tiresome little shows', but that at least they got her out of the house on an evening, George put his foot down. Marching on to the stage, he placed his ukulele at his feet and announced, 'I've come all this way to entertain the troops, the whole troops, and nothing *but* the troops!'

This brought gales of laughter from the boys at the back, though the military hierarchy were not amused, and George was cautioned never to say such a thing again. He promised the commanding officer that he would think about this – then adopted the saying as his war-time catchphrase, invariably causing pandemonium whenever he walked on to a stage. On one occasion he even called out for a telescope so that he could see his real fans, and on another he arrived early for a show – before the officers and their wives – and invited everyone to take their seats up front, declaring that he would personally 'carry the can in the event of a bollocking'. For this he was actually summoned to explain his actions to the War Office,

121

though he did not attend the subsequent meeting, preferring to issue a simple statement that he was just an ordinary citizen doing his bit for England – and for nothing.

The Irish, however, did not always appreciate George's off-beat sense of humour. It was all very well for him to sing about the 'Hindoo Man', and slant his eyes before emulating Mr Wu, but another matter, some thought, to crack jokes – in the days before racial equality, when it was not considered *wrong* to do so – about 'Micks' and about Irish potatoes being better than English ones 'Because they make thicker chips!'

George's rank-and-file fans, in general, never found him in the least offensive because everything about his delivery was done only in fun, without the slightest touch of malice. One very strait-laced commanding officer's wife, however, complained so virulently about George's 'vitriolic attack on this our beloved Emerald Isle' that within a few days the smear campaign mounted against him by her Limerick Ladies' Circle brought about an embargo on his films in that part of the country. Beryl was so annoyed that she contacted all the local newspapers and offered a £100 reward to be donated to a hospital of the editor's choosing, should he name this woman. Both ATP and Columbia pictures offered similar incentives, and though George's detractor was not exposed, the embargo was lifted.

Early in 1942, George began shooting his second Columbia feature, *Much Too Shy*, co-starring Eileen Bennett, Hilda Bayley and Kathleen Harrison. More fascinating than any of these, however, was Jimmy Clitheroe, the tiny, squeaky-voiced star who later appeared in British radio's longest running comedy series ever, *The Clitheroe Kid*. Sixteen when he made the film, though he looked about seven, Clitheroe was, like George's friend Wee Georgie Wood, a perfectly-formed midget, and he made the production glow from start to finish. There was also a fine cameo role from future *Carry On* star Charles Hawtrey, and others from Formby regulars Wally

Patch and Gus McNaughton.

Much Too Shy was a gentle, part-sophisticated comedy, very much in the Ernst Lubitsch vein, set in the rural hamlet of Standstilton Green, where everyone knows everyone else's business. The story centres around three local women – Amelia Peabody (Harrison) who runs the village shop, the snooty Lady Driscol (Bayley), and farmgirl Jackie Somers (Bennett), who is George's love-interest.

George Andy is the village handyman, and an amateur artist. The walls of his trailer, which he shares with little brother Jimmy, are hung with head-and-shoulder portraits, and pride of place is awarded to Jackie's. Jimmy does not approve of George's infatuation with her because he never charges her for the odd jobs he does. 'Show me a woman and I'll show you trouble,' Jimmy persistently opines.

Sadly, Jackie is engaged to be married to the stuffy lawyer who serves George with a writ for non-payment of rent. His rent-money comes from what he earns designing posters for the local cinema, and the manager has dispensed with his services because he wants pretty female bodies, which George cannot draw. 'I'd give a thousand pounds this minute to be a millionaire,' he complains to Jimmy over his lack of cash. Then he sees an advertisement in his chip-paper for art-classes which boast an easy income even after the first lesson, and decides to give it a go.

At first the students, who are all into abstract art, poke fun at George, though he soon wins them over with a song . . . and when he draws three female heads on a canvas – copying a newspaper photograph of Peabody, Driscol and Jackie – the students add *naked* bodies. Outside the college, George leaves the painting with a pavement artist whilst making a telephone call, and the artist sells it to a pair of entrepreneurs, giving George half of the proceeds. The picture, however, ends up as part of a soap advertisement in newspapers and on hoardings, resulting in George being served with a writ for libel by the outraged Lady Driscol. The painting, she declares, suggests that she has a 38-inch bust, whereas she claims she is a mere 36! 'They've added two inches to my bust,' she cries, whilst George responds, 'Well, isn't that making mountains out of molehills?'

The village women wreak their revenge on the hapless handyman. Marching on his trailer, they attempt to burn him out. The trailer breaks free and rolls down the hill into the village, flattening everything in sight and finally crashing into the shop. Then the court hearing takes place, with George defending himself, aided by Jimmy and Jackie. He proves that the offending portrait has in fact *benefited* the three ladies. Miss Peabody's fame has finally enabled her to find a man, Jackie has seen sense and dumped her tiresome fiancé, and Lady Driscol has actually been complimented by being given a 38-inch bust . . . Jimmy has provided the court with a portrait of her, taken before she was married when she was working as the showgirl, Connie Silver, and this is supplemented with evidence from a variety agent which states that in those days her bust measured thirty-*nine* inches! The case is therefore dismissed, and George – still shy – rides away from the court-house in a hackney carriage with his sweetheart!

George described *Much Too Shy* as a 'human interest story', though it was not well-received by the critics. The fans, of course, loved it, and it made a huge profit for Columbia. George had also added another string to his bow, that of associate producer, for Vera Lynn, the Forces' Sweetheart, had invited him to work on her first film, *We'll Meet Again*.

CHAPTER SIX

I DID WHAT I COULD WITH MY GAS MASK

'I'm just a clown without the make-up, the circus clown who magnifies the reactions of ordinary people to the things that happen around them.' George Formby

In the summer of 1942, George became embroiled in an argument with the then highly-influential Lord's Day Observance Society, an organisation which had already filed several suits against the BBC for playing non-secular music on Sundays. In an act of what may only be regarded as sheer spite, the LDOS now focused their attention on the theatrical profession, declaring that it was 'unethical' for entertainers to work on the Sabbath, even if they *were* doing charity work. They even claimed support for their cause by dredging up a still-extant law of 1677 which had 'forbidden any manner of thespian activity' – one which some sixty top-line artists swallowed without question, announcing a sit-down strike!

George had been appearing in regular Sunday concerts since the beginning of the war, and saw no reason to heed what he dismissed as 'the eternal damnation warblings of a bunch of meddling Bible-bashers'. He was contacted by ENSA's Basil Dean and informed that whatever decision he made would affect the outcome of the strike on account of his high-standing. For five years running he had topped the *Motion Picture Herald*'s popularity poll – and though Gracie Fields, Leslie Howard and Robert Donat were not far behind him,

125

Dean told him that their opinion did not count because they were not in England at the time.

George opted to attack the LDOS head-on with what was for him an unusually hard-hitting statement, though there would be a good many more of these over the next few years, usually penned by the ubiquitous Beryl. 'I'll hang up my uke on Sundays only when our lads stop fighting and getting killed on Sundays,' he announced, adding, 'as far as the Lord's Day Observation Society are concerned, they can mind their own bloody business. And in any case, what have *they* done for the war effort except get on everybody's nerves?' The next day, the strike was called off.

At the end of the year George began shooting *Get Cracking*, regarded by many contemporary critics as one of his finest films. It has an interesting assortment of peripheral characters – including a bungling gay recruit, very daring for the time – and a definitive villainous rival in the form of the ever-reliable Ronald Shiner.

George's leading lady *should* have been Eileen Bennett, but Beryl quickly scuppered her chances of appearing opposite George for a second time, following the incident which had occurred at the trade showing of *Much Too Shy* when Bennett, wearing a low-cut gown, had swanned up to George and, in an act of genuine bravado, pecked him on the cheek! Beryl therefore informed director Marcel Varnel that this time she would be sitting in on the auditions – 'to ensure that he did not engage another tart'.

Beryl's power, in fact, went further than this, as the successful 'candidate', Dinah Sheridan – then employed as a secretary to Welwyn Council's Survey and Sanitary Inspector – divulged:

I walked into one of the large offices at Denham and saw a very big desk with one lady behind it – no sign of anyone else at all. She told me she was Beryl Formby and that she wished to ask me some questions. First, was I married? I was able to say with blushes that I was [to Jimmy Hanley] and had been for four months. Presumably she considered that in that case I was hardly likely to look at anyone else but my delightful new husband, and no other questions were asked at all. She just said that I was what she had been looking for, and I left. Then, after the film I went back to my council office job, hoping the stories that all George Formby's leading ladies went on to better things was true.

Like Pat Kirkwood, Phyllis Calvert and only a handful of others, Dinah Sheridan certainly did hit the big time, becoming one of the country's most distinguished and best-loved stars. Her newlywed status, however, from Beryl's insanely jealous and blinkered perspective, did not necessarily mean that the young woman could be trusted. George too, in a rare moment of allowing his guard to slip, confessed that life with Beryl may not always have been a bed of roses, as Dinah explained.

During the making of Get Gracking *I discovered that if I was on the nightly call-sheet, Beryl was also called. No 'leading lady', no Beryl! When I was working, our lunch was taken in the dining room – most artists together – though not George. He was given his meal in his dressing room, cooked by Beryl. I remember very little about the actual making of the film, except one remark which has stayed with me. Some of the other male artists were talking to George, and I was there too. The subject of girlfriends came up and George was asked whether he was a happily married man. I should have thought it was fairly obvious! His reply was, 'Oh yes, it's all right – but when you have chicken every day you get tired of it by Friday!'*

Unable to find fault with George's leading lady, Beryl vented her spleen on one of his co-stars, forty-two-year-old Irene

Handl – renowned for her charlady and generally bedraggled roles. In this instance, a furore erupted on the set because the actress invited George to accompany her to the studio canteen. As she explained a few years before her death, in 1987:

I'd heard a lot about Beryl, but I never expected her to be so bad. She was such a nasty, spiteful piece of work to just about everyone, including George. I don't know whether she was thinking that I wanted to borrow money off him, or take him to bed. She was so twisted and conniving that it was impossible to work out what was going on inside that head of hers. I suppose I could have told her that all I wanted to do was share a pot of tea with him and have a little chat, but she was so blooming arrogant that I didn't even give her the satisfaction of letting her know that some of we actresses don't have sex on the brain every minute of the day!

Get Cracking was considerably more than a film. In the darkest days of the war it was an inspiration for the ones left behind – those who, unable to enlist on account of age or infirmity, formed Local Defence Volunteers groups all across Britain. It begins as a documentary, wherein we learn of the rivalry between the LDV divisions of the adjoining villages of Major and Minor Wallop. These hold regular military exercises, with the men of the former, as the name suggests, usually emerging as victors. George Singleton, the local hero who leads his contingency to muster – all lustily singing and whistling the film's title-song – is not, however, held in similar regard by his superiors. Throughout the scenario he is persistently losing and winning back his corporal's stripe.

When an unlabelled machine-gun turns up at the railway station shared by both villages, both set out to claim it, though George – as his community's representative – is outwitted by Manley, who has been tipped off by the barmaid at George's local. Not to be outdone, and confident that Minor Wallop *will* win the next exercise, George builds his own secret weapon – a tank, the Mary Mk1 – assisted by his sweetheart and an evacuee apprentice. In the closing moments of the film the tank makes an assault on the 'enemy', also pursued by the Army after Manley has reported that there is a German tank in the vicinity. George outwits everyone, as usual, and Minor Wallop wins the day . . . and as *Sergeant* Singleton leans against the tank with his girl, after bashing his rival, it drops to bits.

Get Cracking, amazingly, was completed in less than a month. It also brought complaints from some filmgoers when in one scene George calls someone an 'old pillock', a term widely used today in Northern dramas such as *Coronation Street*, but in those days about as 'blue' as one could get. He actually told one reporter that he had not realised that the word was so offensive, but that in any case he had only been repeating what had been written in the script. True, perhaps, but in years to come George would often refer to *Get Cracking* as 'the pillock movie'. It went on general release in May 1943, by which time George had completed a tour of the Orkneys and other remote, off-coast British islands, *and* almost completed his next film, *Bell-Bottom George*.

George had also finally agreed to visit Canada, but the trip was again deferred when he was informed that Basil Dean had added his name to the ENSA party which would be leaving for the Middle East as soon as all the arrangements had been finalised. Marcel Varnel, the new film's director, was therefore told that he would be able to have George for a maximum of five weeks. And Harry Parr-Davies, on leave from the army where he was with the Irish Guards Orchestra, was given just ten days to supply the music and songs.

Bell-Bottom George starts off by combining fact with fiction – thus the on-screen character, George Blake, *and* the man portraying him are both exempted from military service for having 'flat feet and a groggy heart' – and again, as in real life, Blake is determined not to accept this rejection, insisting on doing his bit for his country. The film is also unique in that the majority of the cast and almost every one of the male extras were unashamedly gay. Charles Farrell, Peter Murray Hill, Charles Hawtrey, Reginald Purdell and Manning Whiley were referred to by Beryl as 'The Five Queens', and the scene in which George sings 'It Serves You Right', surrounded by a bevvy of well-proportioned, posing matelots, was a potent exercise in camp homoeroticism revered by George's surprisingly large, closeted gay following in wartime Britain – as indeed is the entire film.

The action takes place in Porthampton, a South Coast naval base where German agents led by the sneering Johnson (Elliot Makeham) are working from the cellar of his taxidermist's shop. They are transmitting wireless messages overseas and plotting to blow up a prototype warship, during its maiden voyage when all the Navy's top-notchers and engineers will be aboard.

George Blake, the clumsy but far from stupid bar-steward at the Navy's Senior Service Club, develops a crush on the admiral's pretty blonde chauffeur, Pat (Anne Firth), after she knocks him off his bicycle whilst he is showing off on his way to work. She gives him a piece of her mind – indeed, she rattles on for more than a minute without pausing for breath, and he is unable to get a word in edgeways. The admiral, meanwhile, takes pity on him and, as he too is on his way to the club, he offers George a lift. Any admiration he might feel is short-lived for George nearly wrecks the joint whilst putting up the blackouts. 'You'd make a *rotten* sailor,' says the admiral.

Fate intervenes, however, in the form of Jim Bennett (Farrell), an old boxer pal assigned to sail on HMS *Seaworthy*. When Jim's girlfriend invites him to a party, so that he will not be arrested by the 'crushers' – the Navy's equivalent of the Military Police – he sneaks into George's room and borrows his only suit, leaving his sailor's uniform in its place. George is forced to evacuate the building wearing this when, after he has serenaded Egbert, his goldfish, there is an air-raid . . . Egbert goes down the drain, the crushers get George, and he is dispatched to Jim's ship, where the other men give him a hard time until he wins them over with a song and a nifty hornpipe.

George's unexpected popularity earns him a place in the Navy's band – Pat is their unheard vocalist – and he is engaged for a broadcast with the BBC. Meanwhile, he takes Pat to dinner, during which the taxidermist's dog steals her cap. George chases the animal through the restaurant – more mayhem – and eventually into the shop, where he hears the radio transmitting Morse code. Sufficiently gullible to believe Johnson's explanation that the cellar is infested with crickets, George later hears the same sound coming from a studio at the BBC, where they are recording an espionage play, and the penny drops.

Johnson's plan to blow up the ship is now taking shape. His chief agent, Shapley (Murray Hill), has a rendezvous on a train with a beautiful female spy, but when George and Pat end up on the same train it is George and not Shapley who ends up with the envelope containing the sabotage plans pushed inside his shirt, resulting in him being pursued by both. 'Get away, you cheeky fast cat, you brazen hussy!' he yells at her, whilst the beefy Shapley gropes George's chest and opines, 'I'm feeling a bit queer myself!' Our hero, however, evades them both and eventually follows Shapley to the crooks' lair. This time, the dog steals *his* cap, and in chasing it a second time he is captured and stripped by Johnson's cronies, one of whom is a double-agent working for Naval Intelligence and helps him to get away.

Pursued by the crooks – and by Jim Bennett, who has re-entered the scenario – George meets up with Pat and they set off with a life-or-death message for the admiral, who by this time has already set sail on the doomed warship – which by way of a producer's *faux pas* has considerably reduced in size! Their journey begins in the admiral's car, with Pat driving like a maniac, and concludes in no better fashion when George attempts to navigate a motor-boat after the steering wheel has come off, crashing and flinging them both into the water. Then, whilst the spies are being rounded up, George tells his sweetheart to stop tickling him. The culprit, however, is Egbert, his missing goldfish, and the film ends with all three submerging beneath the briny after he has asked her, 'Pat, will you be my missus – and Egbert's mum?' Brilliant stuff!

The songs from this production, too, are exceptional, though special praise must go to two. 'Swim Little Fish', George later said, always made him feel sad because it was a child's song, and he would always regret that he and Beryl had not had children of their own. And who could possibly forget the beautiful pastiche which he croons to the woman he loves – one who, in this film, he has fallen for more quickly and more confidently than usual?

> *I'd never long for meals they'd ring a gong for,*
> *The shows they throng for, I would never view.*
> *I'd have pennies from heaven,*
> *I could live in a shoe,*
> *They could take my clothes coupons,*
> *If I had a girl like you!*

Most of the location shots for *Bell-Bottom George* were filmed in Fleetwood. The opening scene caused a problem when the director, Marcel Varnel, signed up a bit-part cyclist without asking him if he could ride a bicycle! He could not, so Varnel searched amongst the crowd which had gathered to watch the scene being filmed, and hired a fourteen-year-old local, Siv Joensen. The youngster's 'film' career, however, was short-lived when the original actor threatened to sue Varnel for duping him, and in an exercise of (in some prints) abysmal editing the editor was compelled to superimpose his head over Joensen's!

Whilst filming another scene, George was nearly seriously hurt one afternoon whilst piloting a speedboat, when the bottom of one leg of his flared trousers became caught in the open driving-shaft. George managed to drag himself free, leaving his mangled shoe and shredded trouser-leg trapped in the mechanism, but he had to have hospital treatment for a skinned foot. Once again questions were raised as to whether he should still be allowed to perform most of his own stunts.

Having suffered Beryl's machinations on the film-set first-hand, Basil Dean was anxious that she would not be accompanying George on his ENSA tour, declaring, 'Our boys out there have enough misery to contend with, without having to put up with her as well!' Dean, however, had not reckoned with George's inability to cope on his own, and when he insisted that it would have to be *both* Formbys or none at all, Dean gave in.

George was being very serious when he asked Basil Dean if he would be allowed to take his motorcycle with him on the tour. This way, he declared, he and Beryl would experience no difficulty keeping up with the Eighth Army. The request was refused, so George bought a huge customised 1939 Ford Mercury from Sir Malcolm Campbell – 17 feet by 6 – which Campbell had commissioned to convey his team of technicians during speed-trial events, which had subsequently been cancelled on account of the war.

George had the car refitted so that its five rear seats folded down into beds, and he bought a special lean-to tent to provide sleeping accommodation for his valet and pianist. The vehicle took some getting used to: for several weeks before the tour the Formbys could be seen driving around Singleton. Basil Dean agreed that it would be ideal for desert conditions, though he complained when ENSA, who were responsible for their artists' expenses, were sent a bill for the fuel. The car devoured petrol – the best George ever got out of it was 15 miles to the gallon.

Little is known of the Formbys' tour. Unlike Gracie Fields, who later spent several months visiting the more remote – and menacing – areas in the Pacific and kept a detailed diary of her activities, Beryl does not appear to have put pen to paper in all this time, other than a log-book of sorts detailing the distances between shows and their content . . . and George, of course, was never allowed to become involved in any aspect of his career but entertaining. We must therefore rely on witness accounts, which are few and sketchy.

The couple flew to Lisbon at the beginning of August, then on to Tunis and Algiers, where George opened one show for the great French chanteuse Damia, and shared top-billing in another with Josephine Baker, secretly employed by the French Resistance. He strolled on to the stage whilst the soldiers were still applauding her famous 'J'ai deux amours', and pointed at the desert, chirping, 'Ee, it's just like Blackpool sands!'

Some of George's comments after this show, however, to the Forces publication, *Union Jack*, caused a furore when made public back in England. Stars such as Damia, Baker, Gracie Fields and Arthur Askey had been risking their own lives entertaining and helping others less fortunate than themselves since the beginning of the war, and these artists all loathed what that other great fighter Marlene Dietrich had scathingly referred to as 'the lazy sunbathers' – those big stars who could have done much good, had they been interested in helping anyone but themselves. When a young reporter from *Union Jack* asked George, therefore, where all his contemporaries were, he could only reply honestly, 'Most of them are in the West End, where we left them, though one or two *would* be willing to put on show for the troops, I guess, providing the camps aren't too remote, and where there's no shortage of red carpets and cocktails.'

The press were wrong in accusing George of attacking certain members of his profession, for his criticisms were justified. For example, the musical-comedy star Florence Desmond had told him how much she would love to sing to the troops if only the dates did not clash with her new London season, and he knew of a young actor who had evaded being called up because he had agreed to work for ENSA, then refused to do so outside London.

George would not name names, even when threatened with action by the Variety Artists' Federation. Back in England, some fifty 'available' entertainers of varying fame petitioned Basil Dean to publish their names in the national press so that they might not suffer prejudice from their peers. Many of these, who were genuine 'lazy sunbathers', threatened to go on strike unless Dean also recalled the Formbys to face the music. Dean refused to submit to such pressure. Much as he disliked George and Beryl as individuals, he privately believed that George's comments had been justified, and was filled with admiration for the sterling job they were doing. In 53 days they would cover much of North Africa, Italy and Sicily, Malta, Gibraltar, Libya, Egypt, Lebanon and Palestine – thirteen countries, clocking up 25,000 miles and entertaining over 750,000 troops. George proved so popular that the Eighth Army made him their mascot, a well-deserved honour. The Formbys performed in burnt-out aircraft hangars, defunct opera houses, an ancient Roman amphitheatre, sitting on the backs of lorries, and once perched on an upturned dustbin. He would sometimes sing half a dozen songs if the going was tough, if not at least twenty before being forced off the stage by the heat. At most venues the troops drew lots for tickets, whilst letters for the soldiers' families were placed in a drum, and several pulled out at random by George, who countersigned them so that they could be posted upon his return to England.

There was nothing tactful about Beryl, however, when she learned what the Variety Artists' Federation were up to, and on 9 September her response came in the form of a telegram to the *Blackpool Gazette*'s Sylvia:

THOSE ARTISTS THREATENING TO STRIKE OVER IN ENGLAND OUGHT TO BE SHOT OR SENT OUT HERE TO HAVE A BASINFUL OF WHAT THE LADS HAVE HAD

The following week Beryl's telegram, together with a letter from her, appeared in the national press – alongside a defence sent in from Algiers by Squadron Leader Frank Ellis and countersigned by eight of the officers who had been present at the Formby-Damia-Baker concert, and at the *Union Jack* interview:

> *We had the pleasure of entertaining Mr and Mrs Formby in our humble desert mess, and on that occasion had the opportunity to share with them the absence of top-line artists in entertainments for the troops. They [and the others on the bill] were the first well-known stage personalities we had seen during the whole of the desert campaign, and we are glad someone has had the courage and gumption to explode the myth, apparently current in some quarters, that the lights of the theatre world are shining on the battle fronts. Only by the personal efforts and honesty of people like Mr Formby can we hope 'through trials to reach the stars'.*

In the wake of the invasion of Italy, the Formbys were refused permission to enter the country – until Beryl learned that the Eighth Army had already been entertained by Damia, Marlene Dietrich, Alice Delysia and Josephine Baker. Beryl kicked up a stink about this, and would not back down even when informed that each of these stars had opted to tour the Italian camp-circuit of their own volition, despite being advised not to do so by the authorities – and in any case none of them was connected with ENSA. Gracie Fields was, and when Beryl was told this – George had just performed in temperatures of 125 degrees F in Palermo, Sicily – she dashed off a letter to the

Daily Film Renter, in London, which fortunately never made it into print. Two years previously, the publication's 'Tatler' – his identity was never revealed – had signed his name to a piece which had actually been *written* by Beryl, attacking Gracie on account of her marriage to Monty Banks, at that time officially listed as 'an enemy alien'. In addition she had, as usual, blown all the facts out of proportion as far as George's benevolence towards his showbusiness contemporaries was concerned:

Here's poor old George Formby literally working his fingers to the bone – traipsing all over the country – giving concerts everywhere unstintingly and at his own expense – paying his fellow artists' hotel expenses, raising immense amounts of money and even better raising the morale of the people – and, blow me, George is slung into the background whilst an overwhelming amount of sob-stuff heralds the approach of the lil' lady who has been doing admirably similar work in Canada and America – but who, after all, has done it thousands of miles away and has been absent from this country for a year! Apart from which she took with her her mother, father, two sisters, sister-in-law, three nephews, one niece and an Italian-born husband . . . PLUS a considerable amount of dough!

Beryl's letter to 'Tatler', then, had concluded that although she had nothing against Gracie, 'This latest outburst of hysteria over her belated comeback rather makes me want to vomit.' Why she should have been so bitter towards this incredibly brave woman – who laid herself open to more dangers during the war years than almost any other entertainer – cannot be readily determined. It may well be, as Gracie's stepdaughter Irene Bevan pointed out, that in an essentially man's world, Beryl was jealous of any other woman possessed of the same mettle as herself. The fact that Gracie, like herself, had spent her entire life pulling herself up by the bootstraps and, despite her intense naivety, had never allowed any man to push her around may have irked Beryl, too. Neither is it known what was written in Beryl's second letter to 'Tatler', save that the *Daily Film Renter* refused to publish it for fear of being sued!

Unable to bear the thought of Gracie Fields being in Italy when George had been told to stay away, Beryl bribed a Sicilian fisherman to ferry them across the Strait of Messina to the port of Reggio, where they gave an impromptu show to 5,000 troops on the beach within minutes of landing.

Two days later, just outside Naples, the Formbys' convoy caught up with the Eighth Army, and the couple were invited to dine – on bully beef, canned fruit and ersatz coffee – with General Montgomery. En route, their escort jeep had accidentally forced a group of Italian soldiers off the road, and two of these had stepped on a landmine and been blown to bits. According to contemporary reports, neither the jeep nor George's car had stopped, though to be fair, to have done so would have been sheer folly. After their meal, the trio posed for photographs which would be wired home, then George and Beryl drove back down to Reggio. After several concerts they then returned to Syracuse, in Sicily, where they stayed for a few days before heading for Gozo and Malta.

George and Beryl had always wanted to visit the Holy Land, and on 26 September 1943 they gave the first of two shows at a base near Tel Aviv, one of which was attended by J H Dunn, a 23-year-old RASC driver. Dunn's letters home to his sister, Margaret, in Kent, have been preserved by the Imperial War Museum and make for fascinating reading. Of this first Formby concert, the young man quaintly observed:

I went to an ENSA show with George Formby heading the bill last night. I was one of the lucky ones to draw a ticket, and he sang a song about Mr Woo being an air-raid warden, and if you have a chink in your window you will have a chink at your door, get it, and others just as laughable. In fact he was great, and the funniest thing of all was, when he came on the stage in his shorts about ten sizes too big, and during his act with his wife, he was looking through his shorts and laughing and saying, 'Ee, I've never seen those through here before!' – and after playing about the stage and us laughing and thinking of course the obvious, he finished up with saying he could see his feet! He played three guitars [sic] and, singing about ten songs he spoke to us, saying he would meet us coming into Berlin, and that he had been in ten countries in thirty-one days – some travelling, nearly as fast as the 8th Army, and they are still going strong and George will have to get a move on if he is going to keep his appointment.

From Palestine, the Formby convoy drove further north towards Syria, where the weather posed an even bigger threat than the enemy. At Damascus and Zebdani temperatures were well into the hundreds, whereas at a fighter station high in the Lebanon Mountains it was below freezing. In Aleppo, a huge locust flew into George's mouth whilst he was singing 'It Serves You Right', to gales of laughter from the 10,000 soldiers. Then the next day he and Beryl went down with malaria, and their subsequent shows in Syria and Turkey had to be cancelled. They were back in shape – more or less – one week later for their tour of Egypt, though when Beryl appeared on stage in Cairo for their very last show in the Middle East, in spite of the intense heat she was wearing thick stockings to conceal dozens of bug-bites on her legs.

The Formbys arrived home during the first week of October 1943, thoroughly exhausted and each of them a stone lighter than when they had left. Yet within hours of reaching their London flat a representative from the Variety Artists' Federation was hammering upon their door demanding that George offer an explanation for his outburst to *Union Jack*, and that he disclose all the names in his supposed blacklist. Beryl's response was to tell the man, 'Bugger off!', before slamming the door in his face – the consequences of which would later prove dire, and come close to irreparably damaging George's reputation and career. In the meantime, the couple did consent to attending a press-conference a few days later at the Waldorf Hotel, to which they were accompanied by their manager, Ben Henry, and representatives from ATP and Columbia Pictures.

George thought of taking his ukulele with him, hoping that this might bring a little light relief to the proceedings, but Henry advised him not to. And it *was* a solemn affair, with Beryl bursting into tears whilst recalling the incident when their car was escorted across a minefield two young soldiers had been blown to bits in front of their eyes – and with George chain-smoking and looking very worried.

In order to extricate himself from the predicament which he had only put himself in in the first place by being honest, George explained that he had been chatting with several soldiers in Algiers, wholly unaware that one of them had been on *Union Jack*'s payroll. This was untrue, though the interrogating committee did not press; they wanted George to be more specific, and name names. A simple nod or shake of the head would suffice, he was told, after each name was read out from their list of 'suspects' – in other words, entertainers who must have had something to feel guilty about to have assumed that they had been blacklisted at all. George would have nothing to do with this. 'It's a classic case of "If the cap fits, wear it",' he told the gathering, before leaving.

A few weeks later, on 23 January 1944, having in the meantime received countless poison-pen letters and obscene telephone calls, George once more left his ukulele at home and gave a broadcast for the BBC, immediately after the nine o'clock news, describing his recent experiences in Europe and the Middle East. The broadcast would be George's last in Britain for another three years. 'With all respect to the many learned, expert and scientific broadcasts there have been about Middle East affairs,' commented the London *Evening Standard*, 'there has not been one which got home to the hearts of the listeners more than this.'

George told listeners that the most important aspects of the tour had been his long chats with the soldiers after each show, adding:

They wanted to talk to somebody from home. We used to sit around, always with mugs of tea, like a lot of old women gaffing . . . what was the beer like, was it getting stronger, how often does it rain, how are the food and cigarettes – are the people being looked after? They were worrying quite a lot about you folks at home, but we soon put them right about that. We told them that after four and a half years, Britain was still the best country to live in . . . We never met a grumble or a grouse. All you mothers and wives and sweethearts at home – don't worry about your boys. When they write home and tell you they're fit and well and happy, please believe them. They're telling the truth!

A few days later, George started work on his next film for Columbia, *Asking For Trouble*, a title which the Formbys considered inappropriate after their run-in with the Variety Agents' Federation. It was therefore changed to the even less apt, as shall be seen, *He Snoops To Conquer*. His co-stars were Elizabeth Allen and Robertson Hare.

Snoops, as it is affectionately known by the few Formby fans who have seen it – like George's other films it was not re-released for the cinema, and has not been seen on British television for more than thirty years – is a hugely entertaining tale of the fight between the 'little man' and bureaucratic corruption. Tanglewood is depicted as a small town representative of many in wartime Britain, where the civic powers cream off the fat of the land and live in the lap of luxury, whilst the ordinary citizens who are the lifeblood of industry are forced to eke out a miserable existence in poverty and sometimes appalling housing conditions. When reporters from a London newspaper visit the town to investigate this, the crooked council officials, headed by the odious Oxbold (Claude Bailey) plan to pull the wool over their eyes but do not reckon on the visitors encountering George Gribble, the town-hall factotum who innocuously shows them around. Thus the public are outraged to observe photographs of the massive Oxbold mansion, which houses just four people, next to the Gribbles' tiny terraced house on the pretentiously-named Paradise Row, which houses fourteen.

There is further skulduggery when a government scheme grants £200 to the council so that it may carry out a Public Opinion Investigation into housing conditions. The officials need £150 for a new road-sweeper, so they decide to appoint their own officer to conduct the survey, and pay him the remaining £50. 'Any idiot can do that, even Gribble,' one says, and when George is asked to name his own fee they get an even better bargain: all he wants is £27 10s to repay a loan-shark from whom he has borrowed the money to help out a friend.

George visits every house in Tanglewood save one – that belonging to the millionaire philanthropist, benefactor and eccentric inventor, Sir Timothy Strawbridge (Hare), whom hardly anyone in the town has ever seen, and who is so caught up in his own world that he is completely oblivious to the people's suffering. Oxbold is hoping that if Sir Timothy can be persuaded to stand for councillor, he and his fellow conspirators will be able to rake in more money from the government and line their own pockets. Oxbold also has another hold over them: as the local bank manager, he will continue giving them loans so long as they do as he says.

George fills in hundreds of survey forms, of which only those on behalf of householders who are content with the council's running of the town – in other words, the councillors themselves and the wealthy – are dispatched to Whitehall. The rest are wrapped in newspaper and given to George to be placed in the salvage bin. He does this, and accidentally meets Sir Timothy, just as the recently acquired road-sweeper passes by. When this breaks down, the pair lend a helping hand, resulting in the machine running amok through the town, drenching passers-by, billowing out clouds of dust . . . and regurgitating the survey forms.

Forced to hide in Sir Timothy's house, George familiarises himself with its multitude of gadgets – and meets the inventor's daughter, Jane (Allen). George also has to cope with his own financial problems, when Oxbold sacks him for speaking to the press: a bailiff moves into his room and vows that he will stay there until his debt to the loan-shark has been paid. He then suffers the wrath of the townspeople who, having seen their forms scattered throughout the streets, believe that it is *he* who has conned them. When he leaves the house they chase him back into it, and he ends up frozen stiff in Sir Timothy's newfangled refrigerator.

It is after this episode that Jane suggests that *George*, as one of the 'little people' who have been wronged, should stand against Oxbold at the next council elections. He is further persuaded by Sir Timothy, who opines, 'Don't need brains. Look at the Commons, the House of Lords. He knows one fool from another, can drive a road-sweeper backwards and sideways, he can dive through a window and didn't freeze solid at zero temperature. If he can stand all that, he can stand politics!'

The film ends with the big showdown between the corrupt officials and the public during his first election rally. The bailiff has seized George's goods, including the vase where he has hidden the survey forms which were dispatched to the salvage bin, and this has ended up in the canal. Sir Timothy, however, has recorded these on his latest patent – almost uncannily, a precursor to the modern microfiche – and after Oxbold has been exposed as a swindler and the inevitable brawl has taken place between the honest, hardworking folk of Tanglewood and the crooks, George emerges as the local hero . . . and he of course gets the girl.

George later said that working on *Snoops* was a nightmare, but never added *why*, or why he had always considered it his worst film, when it was anything but . . . leaving everyone to assume that any dissension must have been linked to on-set problems. This was not true. Both he and Beryl got on well with Elizabeth Allen, and Robertson Hare was just as dotty and as much fun to be with away from the camera as he was in front of them. The real reason for his unhappiness was therefore much more sinister.

One morning, George and Beryl were on the set – George had just completed his first scene with Elizabeth Allen – when they received a visit from Mr Madden, the Dance Music Supervisor with the DMPC (Dance Music Policy Committee). This was the body responsible for vetting songs, music and comedy routines, and for investigating artists' possible political and collaborationist leanings during wartime. The Formbys were told that though they themselves were not and never had been suspected of having Nazi sympathies, their names had been included on a list compiled by the DMPC because the committee had declared three of George's songs 'enemy-friendly'. These were all written by Harry Parr-Davies and came from *Bell-Bottom George*: 'Swim Little Fish', 'If I Had A Girl Like You', and the film's title-track.

The Formbys were horrified. Madden showed them a document drawn up by the BBC. French stars Mistinguett, Maurice Chevalier, Sacha Guitry, Charles Trenet, Lucienne Boyer and the pianist Alfred Cortot had all been denounced as collaborators, and the English performers Geraldo, Stella Ramon and George Elrick had their names included in a clause labelled 'PASSED BUT WATCH'. Madden concluded that a huge question mark would hang over the Formbys' future trips into France until their 'fate' had been decided at the DMPC's next monthly meeting, and left.

That same afternoon there was an emergency meeting with George and Beryl, their manager Ben Henry, a representative from ENSA and as many Columbia executives as could be mustered at such short notice. Incredibly, the press were kept away and never found out that the name of Britain's foremost entertainer had turned up on a DMPC document – in full, whereas his 'accusers' were represented only by their initials: AC, ADM, GD, PO, DV and DM. Only Madden's name appeared in full.

George had recorded the three songs in question, but the records were yet to be released, so he was instructed to perform them in front of the DMPC committee within the BBC's Criterion Music Room – by no means an easy task under such harrowing conditions – and his versions were checked against the sheet-music supplied by the Victoria Music Publishing Company. George was then told that the committee would come to a decision within seven days and that only then would he learn if he would get away with having to remove the numbers from his repertoire, if Columbia would have to withdraw the 'offending' film from cinemas, and if he would be allowed to entertain the troops again.

It must have been an agonising wait, and a totally unnecessary one. There was absolutely nothing seditious about the songs, and the only likely explanation for George's name appearing on the DMPC list seems to be that it had been put forward by someone from the Variety Artists' Federation – an act of revenge by one of those entertainers he had branded a 'lazy sunbather'. Lucienne Boyer had also complained about her name being included on the list, as had Mistinguett – both were actively engaged by the French Resistance, the former organising British parachutist drops in Normandy, whilst Mistinguett was raising money for French Food Aid. Nevertheless, George's sheet-music was re-examined at the next DMPC meeting on 1 February 1944, and the following morning George was informed by Mr Madden that the 'offending' songs had been re-categorised in a special document headed 'PASSED WITH PROVISOS'. 'Mr Formby may be permitted to perform these works,' the minutes of the meeting read, 'but no additional chorus may be added to them without reference to the Dance Music Supervisor.' The most ridiculous situation of George's career had been resolved, though it would leave an aftertaste of bitterness.

Throughout this latest ordeal, the Formbys had stayed in touch with General Montgomery's office – which had also been made aware of the DMPC list – and now that they had been 'cleared', Beryl told Marcel Varnel, the director of *Snoops*, that should the invasion of France begin before the film's completion, this would be abandoned until their return from France. 'Our boys over there are much more important than a few feet of celluloid,' she told him.

Only days after finishing the film, Beryl received a telephone call from Montgomery himself. George's services were required in France, the great man told her, though in view of the danger she was advised to stay at home. Beryl told him sharply that *she* would be the judge of that, and a few years later, in an impromptu radio interview in Melbourne, George's 'shadow' – as Beryl announced herself – spoke of her run-in with Monty:

We were having a meal with Monty in his tent one evening after we'd done a show for his boys, and he said, 'George, there are some boys who made the initial landing on D-Day, the paratroops over the other side of the Orme – and they haven't been relieved yet. It really would do them a world of good if they could only see your face for a few minutes.' So George said, 'All right, I'll go up and have a look at them.' Then Monty said, 'Of course, Beryl won't be able to go.' So I told him, 'In that case George doesn't go either!' So he said to me, 'All right, Beryl, if you want to risk your silly neck, go ahead and do it!'

George's first show in Normandy – following a dreadful four-day Channel crossing – was not given aboard HMS *Ambitious*, as has frequently been stated. Prior to this, he sang to a group of fifty soldiers in a Bayeux farmyard! Over the next four weeks, he and Beryl appeared in over seventy sometimes hastily-arranged shows, some lasting only minutes on account of the fighting, others running on for hours. At Caen they bumped into Gracie Fields. A few weeks previously she had crossed the Channel incognito to join up with the 53rd Welsh Division, who had just taken Carpiquet airport, two miles from one of the main German artillery lines. As far as is known, however, these two great British institutions did not get around to performing in the same show.

At some 'venues' George handed out sticks of Blackpool rock after singing that particular song – at others, mere yards from the enemy line, he was not allowed to sing at all and had to make do with crawling into the trenches and sharing a few jokes with the lads. In Amiens, when told that the Formbys were Catholic, a priest invited them to evening service, insisting that George take his uke along. When he arrived he realised why: part of the church, including the organ, had been damaged by a shell and he was asked to accompany the congregation whilst they sang hymns! And *only* George could have got away with singing the Hargreaves-Dammerell number, with its echoes of Fragson, which had appeared on the flipside of 'The Ghost' back in 1937:

> *I'm a Frenchie dirty-doggie . . .*
> *I'm a mais-song, a très-bong,*
> *Perhaps I can-can, I'm not sure.*
> *The shirt that I'm now wearing*
> *Is pomme-de-terre-ing,*
> *I'm a Froggie, I'm a Lancashire main-sewer!*

Before leaving for France, George had agreed upon his next

film for Columbia – very reluctantly, for he was the first to admit that these 'tiresome pictures' were starting to interfere with his war work. For this reason, only days after arriving home he renewed his ENSA permit, then informed Marcel Varnel that he had just eight weeks to complete the project.

I Didn't Do It, a tragi-comedy in the finest Grand Guignol tradition, within which the high-camp action is in the major whilst the songs are relegated to the minor key, contained the weirdest but most fascinating assemblage of characters in any Formby film. There are hammy actors, an Irish conman, a bungling magician, a psychopathic ex-circus performer, Siamese twins, and an alcoholic landlord. The setting is Ma Tubb's theatrical boarding house, to which Manchester millworker George Trotter arrives, aspiring to become an actor. Some years before he had met Terry O'Rourke (Jack Daly) who, after giving him his autograph, had told him to look him up the next time he was in London. O'Rourke has completely forgotten him, but he knows a soft touch when he sees one, so when George misleads him into thinking that he is rich, the actor coerces him into funding a West End cabaret revue wherein this gaggle of has-been thespians will make their comeback – something that the house's resident agent, Vance (Carl Jaffé), has thus far failed to effect.

An improbable but effective drama begins when one Tom Driscoll arrives on the scene – a wealthy, arrogant Australian trapezist who boasts that the troupe he is about to assemble will take the country by storm. Driscoll and Vance were once two-thirds of the famous Flying White Devils, a partnership which ended twenty years before when Driscoll had an affair with the act's third member, Vance's wife. During their last performance in Sydney, Driscoll deliberately allowed Vance to fall, leaving him crippled and disfigured in hospital, and running off with his wife. Because these injuries and the passage of time have greatly changed his appearance, and because he did not speak English at the time, Driscoll has not recognised him.

George's and Vance's rooms are next to each other, their exterior windows connected by a narrow ledge. Vance uses this to his advantage when he abseils down the side of the building into Driscoll's room, kills him, then swings along the ledge using his hands to plant the incriminating evidence in George's room: George's plimsolls which he has worn on his hands, his handkerchief and bloodstained gloves, the scouting-knife with which he stabbed his victim, and a wad of Australian banknotes which Vance hopes the police will assume to be George's motive for the crime.

The police arrest George, but soon release him when they realise that the killer has left *too* much evidence – they assume that now he is free, the real criminal will slip up.

For no apparent reason, a famous impresario turns up at Ma Tubbs' with a £2,000 cheque for George to finance his project, but he is waylaid by O'Rourke, who announces that he is George's agent. George, meanwhile, is in grave danger. Vance tells him that Driscoll also owned two valuable diamond rings, items not found by the police because *he* has hidden them in the eyes of the stuffed owl which George keeps in his room! When George finds these, Vance forces him at gunpoint to sign a confession that he murdered Driscoll, then orders him to swallow poison. He does, using a trick glass he has borrowed from a magician friend, and pretends to be dead. The film ends with a denouement straight out of Edgar Wallace. O'Rourke gets to put on his show, involving all the acts from the boarding house, but with a mysterious 'Mr X' topping the bill. Surrounded by mirrors so that the audience cannot differentiate between himself and his reflection, George sings 'The Daring Young Man', a number centred around the Driscoll-Vance saga, and the killer – exposed by him as 'Mr X' – is apprehended by the police after a shoot-out.

As usual, Beryl made her presence known on the set of *I Didn't Do It*, particularly when she heard a rumour that George's leading lady, Marjorie Browne, intended making a play for him. Browne had little to do in the film. She was neither pretty nor convincing in her role, and when Beryl saw her without her make-up – in her words, 'with a face like the back of a bus' – she did not feel it necessary to read the riot-act. The Boswell Twins, on the other hand, were the personification of glamour and had a bad but undeserved reputation. Born in Loughborough in 1920, Honor and Beryl Boswell had toured England as a song and dance act until the outbreak of the war, whereupon they had created their infamous 'Tassel Dance' and played some of the less reputable cabarets and halls. Although he claimed that it was impossible to tell the sisters apart, George did engage in a brief affair with Beryl Boswell. As had happened during the shooting of *I See Ice*, Beryl Formby found a suitable excuse for turning a blind eye, as Irene Bevan explained:

The Boswell Sisters were little more than strippers – 'naughty revue-dancers' they used to call them in those days. Gracie [Fields] knew them well, and she also knew Jack Daly, the young Irish comedian who had begun his career as a warm-up in one of her shows. During the thirties, Daly had had a brief but passionate affair with Gracie, since which time he had slept with more women than most of us have had hot dinners. It was as if he knew that he was going to die young, as if he was packing them in, so to speak, whilst there was still time. Beryl Formby was just another notch in his bedpost, something she must have known considering his dreadful reputation. I'm sure that, had this one got out – as opposed to her earlier fling with Gavin Gordon – despite George's own indiscretions it would have signalled the end of the Formby marriage. Not that George would have divorced Beryl, though I am certain that he would have left her.

Meanwhile, still incensed by the media's attitude towards George following the *Union Jack* fiasco, the Formbys pleaded with Columbia not to invite any critics to the premiere of *He Snoops To Conquer*, which took place on 8 January 1945 at the Strand's Tivoli Cinema. Initially, the studio objected to this – until Beryl supplied Columbia's chief with real proof of George's popularity . . . a list of the names of the 20,000-plus members of his fan club.

Ten days later, George and Beryl were amongst the first contingent of ninety ENSA artists who flew to Karachi, in Pakistan, where they stayed for four days before crossing the border into India. There were few concerts here, but on a 'day off' George and Beryl chartered a private plane to Imphal, the capital of the Manipur state, close to the Burmese border, which had been besieged the previous year when Japan had invaded Assam. No shows at all had been scheduled for this region – indeed, the Formbys were forbidden to make the trip by ENSA officials, to which Beryl had responded, 'It's our money we're spending and our necks we're risking. Mind your own business!'

It was only several weeks later that the Formbys' 'mysterious trip into the middle of nowhere' was fully explained, not to anyone of official status, but to their friend Sylvia, back in Blackpool. During their tour of Scotland in aid of the Shilling Fund, Beryl had shared a pot of tea with a Glasgow housewife. And here she had made a heartfelt promise, one which she had had every intention of keeping, no matter what it entailed:

She asked us to find the grave of her brother, who was killed fifteen miles from Imphal, and take a photograph of it. I never thought for one moment that I would be able to carry out her request. So I got in touch with the Graves Commission officer, helped him look through the files, and found what we wanted. The boy had been brought in from where he was buried, and re-buried in the Military Cemetery at Imphal. We found the grave, and George took the picture.

From India, the Formbys travelled to Ceylon and Burma. It was in Columbo, in the middle of a football field and in temperatures of 130 degrees F, that George had 15,000 soldiers in hysterics with the most recent episode in the saga of Mr Wu, whose talents were by now extended to putting out small fires – without using sand – for, having dispensed with the laundry *and* the window cleaning business, the honourable gentleman was helping the war-effort:

His cousin, Wun-Way-Hin, was one day helping him
To move a time-bomb from the shop, I know,
But it went off Bang! and there's no doubt,
Wun-Way-Hin flew one way out,
And Mr Wu's an air-raid warden now!

During this tour, George had flatly refused to speak to the press or be drawn into any arguments such as the one sparked off by his comments to *Union Jack*. No sooner had the couple arrived home, however, at the end of March, than they and a number of other artists found themselves in the firing line following remarks broadcast on All Air India by Basil Dean. Although her name had not actually been mentioned, Dean had obviously been referring to Beryl when, after praising his 'team' for their bravery and loyalty, he had confessed his disappointment upon hearing that, 'Certain parties had demanded privileges way and beyond the norm, including first-class hotel rooms, maids and batmen and the unnecessary chartering of special aircraft . . . and an expectation that the order of battle should be altered to suit their convenience.'

In the Formbys' case, much of this seems unlikely to have been true: one cannot imagine them risking their lives on what was, to be perfectly honest, a well-meaning but costly and some

(Above) George Formby (centre) during a Whit Monday fancy dress parade circa 1920. (Dennis Poulter)
(Below left) On the threshold of fame, aged 18, shortly after his father's death. (GFS)
(Below right) As George Carter in *Spare a Copper* in 1940. (GFS)

(Above) Looking glum whilst taking a break during the shooting of *No Lim it* in 1935. Next to George in the white shirt is director Monty Banks. The woman is Florence Desmond, his troublesome co-star. (Below) Publicity poster from *No Limit*. (GFS)

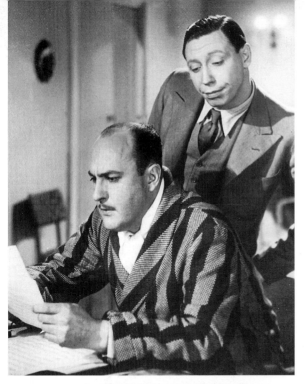

(Left) With Formby stalwart Gerry Marsh in *Let George Do It*, 1940. (GFS)

(Below) Scene from *Much Too Shy* with Eileen Bennett, 1942. (GFS)

(Above) A scene from *Get Cracking* with Dinah Sheridan, 1943. (GFS)

(Left) With Formby regular Ronald Shiner in *George In Civvy Street*, his final film, in 1946. (GFS)

George preparing for a show during the Second World War.
(Imperial War Museum)

Entertaining the troops in the War. (Imperial War Museum)

(Left) In his dressing-room.
(GFS)

(Below)With Barbara Perry
in *Zip Goes a Million.*

Best Wishes from
George Formby
+ Beryl 1950

With Beryl at Christmas in 1950. (GFS)

George preparing for a show in a spartan dressing-room. (GFS)

Towards the end of the run of *Zip Goes a Million* in London, 1952.
(GFS)

After his heart-attack forced him to pull out of *Zip Goes a Million*,
George visited sick children whilst recuperating in a London hospital.
(GFS)

(Above) Surrounded by a bevy of beauties during his final summer show in Blackpool in 1960. (GFS)

(Below) George with his co-stars in that show, from left to right, Jimmy Clitheroe; his last mistress, Yana and Tony Dali. (GFS)

(Above) The summer of 1959 launching of *Beryl II*. 'I hope I'm not paying for this,' Beryl said quite seriously as she smashed the bottle. (Jack Littlewood)

(Below) The party after the launch. Beryl was excluded and according to the director of Windboats, this was the first and last time George paid for a round of drinks. (Jack Littlewood)

George's final television appearance on *The Friday Show* in 1960. (GFS)

February 1960, the official engagement picture of George and Pat. (GFS)

George with Pat, in February 1961, just days before he died. (GFS)

would think futile expedition to photograph a soldier's grave, then suddenly beginning to lay the law down about hotel conditions and luxury flight arrangements. Even if they had, they would not have been the only ones. After all, the ENSA chiefs and military hierarchy were never expected to rough it, and unlike George and Beryl they were getting paid con-siderably more than £10 a week. Beryl was therefore justified in seeing red, and such was her anger that she was even prepared to mount a mini-insurrection with the comic Wee Georgie Wood, who was also the chairman of the hated Variety Artists' Federation, by penning a letter – signed by Wood and George – which was, equally bizarrely, published in the 3 April 1945 edition of *The Times* . . . the newspaper which George had once dismissed as, 'Only fit for wrapping fish and chips in.'

There is much criticism directed at the stars, that they prefer to work comfortably in the large base areas instead of going forward. The fact is, of course, that we have to go where ENSA sends us. The George Formby party played to over 250,000 troops, the Georgie Wood party played nineteen more shows than ENSA had scheduled for their tour. General Leese made it possible for Mr Formby to get to Burma. Air Marshal Joubert arranged for Mr Wood to go there. It is nonsense to suggest that they would pander to artists by making it possible for them to have special aircraft unless they saw good reasons for giving the actors such valuable transport . . . The suggestion that the stars expected the order of battle should be changed to suit their convenience is childish. We certainly have not suggested that our services were not wanted because we could not be accepted in the front line at a particular moment. We did suggest that our services were wanted in the forward areas and ENSA seemingly did not realise this.

The second section of the Formby/Wood letter does not make

sense. Basil Dean had not commented on this point in his broadcast, only on the inordinate demands of some of his artists – and Beryl *had* put her foot down about the Burma trip, declaring that unless she and George could be guaranteed their safety, in so far as this was possible – then they would not set foot in the country. But if the Formbys were expecting an apology from Dean, they were to be disappointed. The letter was ignored.

In July 1945, *I Didn't Do It* went on general release, though if it proved *almost* as popular with George's fans as his previous films, it did little to endear him to those critics who in the past had raved over his every gesture – cheerful, loveable old Formby, he of the toothy grin and bungling disposition simply was not convincing in the role of a murder suspect. The reviews upset George a great deal. His contract with Columbia Pictures was drawing to a close, with just one more production in the pipeline, and he announced that he was not in a hurry to renew it or solicit another. It would be far better, he declared, to go out riding the crest of a wave than to fade into celluloid obscurity . . . in which direction, according to Basil Dean, he was clearly heading, as the producer explained in a television interview of 1966:

> George wasn't an easy person to find the right vehicle for. His range was limited, though fortunately he had a very shrewd idea of his own capabilities, and was always determined never to step outside them. It was never a case of the comedian wanting to play Hamlet. Of course, the real secret of his success was personality. That wide grin of his seemed to spread right across the screen. George never acted gormless like some successful comedians. He was gormless as far as the audiences were concerned, and they took him to their hearts accordingly.

Irene Handl, on the other hand, strongly disagreed with Dean, believing that much of George's genius had been left untapped:

He was a sort of elemental that would have needed a very, very clever director, quite out of the class of the kind of film he did. And of course, those directors didn't direct his kind of film. But I think if you'd have got him with an ace director, they'd have got something really special out of him. He didn't know what he held in him. It was like a very frail glass with something very precious in it. And that thing would never come out because what people liked about him wasn't that.

After almost two decades at the top of his profession – six years of which he had been Britain's Number One draw – and still unable to work out *why* he was so popular, George had suddenly become convinced that he was losing his appeal. He had recently even been ousted from the top of the *Motion Picture Herald* poll by James Mason and David Niven. This was a relatively unimportant factor, for his records were still selling in vast quantities, even the older songs, which had been re-issued by Regal Zonophone. If the critics generally regarded his Columbia films as inferior to his Ealing comedies, the fans were just as ecstatic about them.

To ensure his and Beryl's future security, however – even though he had around £150,000 in the bank – George sold his Singleton home during the summer of 1945 and purchased Sullom End, a farmhouse just a few miles away at Barnacre, near Garstang. Beryl's elderly parents moved in with them. The main building comprised of six bedrooms, three reception rooms, and a servants' quarters. Annexed to it were two smaller houses and a pair of labourers' cottages. 'I intend to become a gentleman farmer and breed cows,' he told the press. 'That way Beryl and me need never starve!' To make a point, George posed for photographs with four beautiful Ayrshire calves he had bought at the Penrith cattle-market, the first of the proposed 'Beryldene' herd – Beryldene Beryl, Beryldene George, Beryldene John Willie and Beryldene Funny! His most important acquisition, however, was the new motorcycle he had bought for his and Beryl's shopping trips into Garstang and Fleetwood.

A few weeks after moving into Sullom End, George began shooting *George In Civvy Street* for Columbia. It enabled his film career to end on a high note. There were none of the over-worked routine gags and lines, the slapstick was sophisticated, the songs first-class. When one hears the big production number – 'We've Been A Long Time Gone' – at the *start* of the film and witnesses the spectacle of George doing the Argentinian Tango with Ronald Shiner, one instinctively knows that one is in for a treat. And *what* a treat!

Like *Bell-Bottom George*, this is a rip-roaring, hand-on-hips high-camp extravaganza. Indeed, the director Marcel Varnel brought in the 'lavender extras' from the earlier film, utilised many gay in-house jokes which must have sailed above the heads of George's straight fans, and even called one of the characters Lavender.

The war is over, and the boys are coming home to their wives and sweethearts. Amongst them are George Harper and his pickpocket pal, Fingers (Shiner). During his absence, George's father has died, bequeathing him the Unicorn, a run-down riverside pub which for months has only had one regular customer – Shadrack (Ian Fleming), an artist who donates his works to the establishment in exchange for board and lodgings. Across the river is the Lion, an up-market hostelry which used to be run by George's sweetheart Mary Colton (Rosalyn Boulter) and her father. Since the old man's death, however, it has been managed by the unscrupulous Jed Brindle (Frank Drew) and his domineering mother, who treat Mary like dirt.

Not long after George's return home, he is visited by a pair of crooks who try to con him into selling the property for less than its actual value. Their ploy fails, so they join forces with

Brindle and plot to have him relieved of his licence. First they tamper with the clock in the bar so that he can be charged with serving after hours, then they spike the beer with paraffin. None of these schemes work, but George does temporarily fall out with Mary, and to cheer him up Fingers sends for some of their old army chums. George, meanwhile, goes off to dream *Alice Through The Looking Glass* – he is the Mad March Hare to Mary's Alice and Fingers' Mad Hatter, and the dream takes on a symbolic theme when the Unicorn fights the Lion in the boxing-ring, emerging as victor and inspiring George to tackle his rivals head-on.

The Unicorn is closed for refurbishment: his pals all 'muck in' to get the place ready for its re-opening as a pantheon for the opulent river-trade. The big day arrives, and George hires the real-life bandleader, Johnny Claes – the only black actor to appear in a Formby film. His rivals, however, bring in their 'secret weapon' – a showgirl named Mitzi Montrose (Daphne Elphinstone), who tells George that she is a singer. She is actually a stripper – earning the film an 'A' certificate – and when she gets down to her undies, an all-out brawl erupts, whereupon the crooks get their come-uppance. Then into this confusion an art expert arrives from London. Mary, now reunited with George, has sent one of Shadrack's paintings (of George) to the Royal Academy, and it has caused a sensation. The rest of Shadrack's canvases, in effect George's property, are then bought for a small fortune . . . and as per usual the hero gets to live happily ever after with the girl – in this instance, literally – of his dreams.

CHAPTER SEVEN

SITTING PRETTY WITH MY FINGERS CROSSED

'George Formby's more obscure songs are so hilarious, the language so flat and Lancastrian, always focused on domestic things. Not academically funny, not witty, just morosely humorous. That really appeals to me.' Morrissey, singer.

George's career, certainly in Britain, did suffer a temporary slump in the first few years after the war. In March 1946 he was guest of honour at the very first *Daily Mail* Film Festival, held at the Leicester Square Theatre. This paid tribute to some of the British screen stars who had risen to international prominence during the war. One of these was James Mason, whose handsome, brooding looks and seductive voice had set hearts a-flutter – and not just female ones – as the calculating aristocrat in the 1943 film, *The Man In Grey*.

Mason had rocketed to the top of the *Motion Picture Herald*'s popularity poll, and along with contemporaries such as Stewart Granger, David Niven and Laurence Olivier was largely responsible for the declining screen careers of not just George, but those of Tommy Trinder, Will Hay and even Gracie Fields. To all intents and purposes, now that the bad times were no longer just around the corner, mirth was no longer the only order of the day. The public had begun clamouring for intrigue and suspense, and above all romance.

George, however, suffered celluloid rejection very badly, and a few weeks after the *Daily Mail* Film Festival, he became so chronically depressed that his doctor and Beryl genuinely believed that he was losing his mind. But whereas George's doctor merely suggested rest and lots of it, Beryl had him admitted – under the pseudonym Ingham, her maiden name – to a psychiatric hospital in York, where he remained for five weeks. The press and worried fans who turned up to see him at Sullom End were told that he was in bed, suffering from the flu. A hospital spokesman, who cannot be named for legal reasons, told me:

He suffered a complete nervous breakdown. For years, Formby had been one of the country's top box-office draws, and his insensitive wife had more or less convinced him that he was a has-been. According to our records he wasn't put into a strait-jacket or anything like that. He was given medication, and afforded a little peace and quiet. Certain aspects of the case are, however, very disturbing. Mrs Formby insisted that her husband remain here until he was fully recovered, and that in the event of failure in this respect he should be committed to a suitable institution. He stayed here for over a month – then one day, after Mrs Formby had signed an overseas contract, she came to collect him and she told the doctor that in her opinion he was well enough to go home. As the doctor refused to discharge him, Mr Formby signed the discharge papers himself.

The overseas contract was for a tour of Scandinavia, astonishing everyone because this was one part of the world where George was largely unknown. It came about as a result of his being 'spotted' by a Swedish variety agent. And not only this, the tour proved that even the usually impeccably organised Beryl, the undisputed queen of wheeling and dealing, could be taken for a ride.

The couple flew to Stockholm on 13 May, and Beryl's first tantrum took place in the lounge at the Bromma Flyfalt airport when one of the small contingency of reporters – seeing George in his dark glasses – rushed to his aid, thinking that he was blind! 'No, he isn't,' Beryl snarled, 'and neither is he as daft as you, thank God. Get out of our way!'

Beryl also lost her temper with the Swedish promoter – whose name has never been revealed – when he informed her that the auditorium where George's first show was to take place, at Nöjesfaltet – was a 12,000-seater . . . until he added that *all* the tickets had sold out in record-time. This was on account of the hype surrounding the Formbys' visit, for a sizeable portion of the audience had never heard the name George Formby until a few days previously, when a national radio station had played his records non-stop for several hours.

Neither did the show get off to a good start. Several artistes preceded George in the programme – he was in fact the *vedette-américaine*, which on the Continent is the artist secondary to the top of the bill who closes the first half of the show. So contrary to what has been said the public were not there solely to see him. Beryl had not minded this, though she had objected to the clause in George's contract dictating *how* he should perform. George had wanted to appear on the stage alone, with just his ukuleles, but the theatre's resident bandleader, a tetchy individual named Thor Jedderbys, had objected, claiming that his musicians would have to be paid for sitting around for more than an hour until the top of the bill came on. Beryl was therefore left with no option but to supply Jedderbys with a selection of George's records that she had borrowed from the radio station – there was absolutely no time for rehearsals – hoping that by listening to these, his musicians might have some idea how to accompany an artist with whom they were wholly unfamiliar.

The orchestra proved hopeless. George opened with 'When The Boys Of The Village Get Cracking', but was forced to abandon it halfway through. During his next number, 'I'm The Ukulele Man', he had to struggle whilst Jedderbys' musicians played the wrong tune! Matters were then made worse by the delayed appearance of the Master of Ceremonies – the actor Thor Modeen – who had been engaged to address the audience between songs and explain what each was about. Modeen ambled on to the stage drunk and started clowning around. Not without considerable difficulty, George pressed on and completed his set, but there were no encores – just a polite thank you before he walked off. In their dressing room Beryl was already on the telephone to the airport, trying to book seats on the next plane back to England.

The next morning, 15 May, in the breakfast room of Stockholm's Grand Hotel, the Formbys were shown a photograph of George on the front page of a national newspaper, and a fellow guest translated the accompanying feature. There were no references to the bungled orchestration, or Thor Modeen, and George was described as, 'The greatest British phenomenon of all time . . . a consummate professional who last evening overcame every adversity to entertain us.'

Beryl contacted the tour promoter at once, and within two hours he had found George a new set of musicians who *were* familiar with his work . . . which was just as well, for his next show was that very evening, again as *vedette-américaine*, at Malmö's vast Folkets Park in front of a crowd of 20,000. This time there were no problems, and two evenings later George gave a supplementary recital at the Bernsbee, Sweden's most prestigious music-hall. Because there was no continuity-robbing MC, some of his quick-fire numbers had to be slowed down and have many of their Northern colloquialisms removed. George still scored a huge success singing about his plus-fours, his horoscope and snapshot album, and the ubiquitous Mr Wu . . . and he had them rolling in the aisles with 'Believe It Or Not', another 'ghost' song which he had recorded back in 1934.

I whispered, 'My dear, don't give way to fright,
But, in the room you sleep a ghost appears every night.'

161

'No silly ghost,' said she, 'could ever frighten me!'
That night, at twelve o'clock,
Just as the light she turned out,
'Who's that in my room?' she cried, and started to shout.
I whispered, 'Shut up!
I'm the ghost I told you about!'

From Stockholm, George and Beryl flew to Copenhagen, where they spent two days sightseeing before getting down to the serious business of work. George was photographed with the Little Mermaid and could not resist pointing to the statue's breasts and cracking, 'Ee, I bet you don't get many of them to the pound!' He then went on to earn £1,200 for three appearances at the city's famous Tivoli Gardens – a record fee which would not be exceeded until Marlene Dietrich's season there some years later – before ending the tour with concerts at Odense and Aarhus.

Back in England, barring a handful of charity concerts to aid relatives of deceased servicemen, George spent much of his time at Sullom End, 'tending the herd' and tinkering with his motorcycles. It did not take him long to realise, however, that the life of a gentleman farmer was not for him. The expense by far swamped any income, so the farmstead was put on the market, along with the still four-strong Beryldene herd. It would eventually be sold to the Thompson family, then the proprietors of the Blackpool Pleasure Beach. In the December, the Formbys played their annual pantomime – *Dick Whittington* again, at the Liverpool Empire – and by the end of its run they had acquired a new property. The Spinney was set in two acres of landscaped gardens, near Knutsford in the Cheshire countryside. Again, Beryl's parents moved in with them, though sadly, a few days before Christmas, her father died.

On 24 June – the Formbys were appearing in a summer revue, *Starry Way*, at the Blackpool Opera House – George was awarded the OBE in the King's Birthday Honours List for all that he had done for his country during the war. Receiving similar accolades were fellow entertainers Elsie and Doris Waters, Doris Hare, and Wee Georgie Wood. Although obviously delighted by the award, George was unable to conceal his disappointment – and anger – that Beryl had been completely ignored. 'It should have been something the wife and me could have shared,' he told Sylvia, 'not that we ever expected anything for entertaining the lads overseas. Now, *that* was an honour.'

George's comments to his friend were very much of an understatement. Two skippers from Fleetwood had been awarded the MBE, and two local women the BEM: the latter pair had worked side by side with Beryl, raising money for her Jump Fund, and Beryl of course had been the brains behind every single one of George's charity drives. He firmly believed that she had not only been snubbed by 'the establishment', but deliberately insulted, and there seems to be no reason to believe that he was wrong. For her unselfish, tireless dedication, no one deserved to be recognised for her wartime efforts more than Beryl Formby.

In October 1946, the Formbys flew to South Africa for what would prove the most problematic tour of George's career – one which would be curtailed on account of Beryl's (and later George's) political views, and her strangely alternating fits of greed and intense compassion in a country torn apart by poverty and racial oppression.

Beryl had cabled ahead, as with every major series of engagements, to ensure that she and George be awarded maximum publicity, only to be told that if they were expecting this, they would have to foot the bill. The couple were, on the other hand, promised that a high-ranking delegation would meet their plane at Johannesburg's Palmietfintein airport, along with a limousine which would convey them to the railway station, where George's show was scheduled to take place . . . on the actual platform. Both the delegation and the car failed to turn up, but George's fans did not let him down: five hundred of these, some plucking ukuleles, mobbed the couple the instant they set foot on the tarmac, and *they* escorted them to the station. Many of these people had greeted Gracie Fields when she had first visited South Africa in 1935. Indeed, to capitalise on the publicity, the distributors of Gracie's films were showing them back-to-back with George's . . . and just in case anyone did *not* know who he was, he was actually billed in some cinemas as 'George Formby – The Male Gracie Fields With The Banjo'!

Such measures were obviously unnecessary. At each stop along the journey to Cape Town George was obliged to get off the train for an impromptu performance on the platform – once on top of the train itself – and between the railway station in Cape Town and his hotel there, over 20,000 fans lined the streets, chanting his name. The intense heat and this noisy welcome – though appreciated – did George no good at all. His health was just beginning to fail, though for a few years more he would often give a variety of excuses as to why he was feeling unwell, and whilst he and Beryl were being manhandled from their car into the foyer he tottered and very nearly collapsed.

George was back on form, however, for his performance that evening at the Alhambra Theatre, and after singing twenty of his best-loved songs he rewarded the enthusiastic audience with his own arrangement of 'Sare Maraise', which he sang phonetically in Afrikaans . . . halfway through he giggled, and announced, 'Ee, it's ever so funny when you don't know what you're singing about!'

The Formbys moved on to Pretoria, and a massive controversy when Beryl learned that the civic luncheon, arranged in their honour, was to be presided over by Daniel Francois Malan, the head of the National Party who, two years hence, would introduce apartheid. George was not in the least interested in politics, but even he disapproved of the man known as 'the Boers' back-veldt Moses' – a man who had already cautioned Beryl that she and her husband would not be permitted to perform to coloured audiences, even on station platforms.

Much has to be said in praise of Beryl's audacity and courage in ripping up Malan's message and telling the courier, 'If that man turns up at the do, George and I will be on the first plane back to England.' Astonishingly, Malan was 'replaced' by D P Van Heerden, the Mayor of Pretoria, who informed Beryl – as he had Gracie Fields, ten years previously – that, on account of the city's abject poverty, it had always been customary for visiting entertainers to pay for their own civic receptions. Beryl hit the roof, telling a press-conference, 'Imagine the cheek of the man. He invites over two hundred people to a slap-up lunch – people *we* don't know from Adam – then expects us to pay the bill. Well, he knows *exactly* what he can do!'

Beryl's outburst was certainly justified, though not so some of her mercenary demands. When George had been interviewed in the lobby of their four-star hotel – and photographed tipping a porter with English money! – he had commented that his room was 'champion', and that he and Beryl planned travelling around the city the same as everyone else, by taxi, or Shanks's pony. Beryl, however, complained to the tour organiser that their accommodation was not up to her expectations. Mayor Van Heerden therefore arranged for the couple to stay at the most expensive hotel in Pretoria, and supplied them with a limousine, a liveried chauffeur *and* a manservant. The cost came out of the City Council's already severely depleted funds.

Today it would doubtless be argued that words such as 'darkie', 'nigger' and 'Chink' are politically incorrect, and rightly so, though in George's day such terms were largely acceptable, even by those to whom the terms were applied. George's Chinese fans were never offended by Mr Wu, just as he remained unaffected by suggestions from some quarters that all Lancastrians wore flat caps and clogs, raced pigeons and thrived on hot-pot. The harsh prejudices of South Africa, however, affected him badly – until Beryl suggested, to her eternal credit, that they should defy Malan's instructions and put on a series of shows for blacks-only audiences, a move which resulted in the Formbys being virtually *ordered* to leave the country.

Most of these exclusively black venues were flea-pit cinemas in some of the city's most run-down districts, where anything could and did happen. Beryl was advised to dress down whilst they were being driven to them . . . not in a civic limousine, this time, but in an armoured police truck flanked by a fleet of motorcycles. George and Beryl bore the cost of this, the people were allowed in free of charge, and George did not accept one cent in salary for each of the twenty shows.

It was during one of these performances that Beryl inadvertently sparked off a massive row. George had just sung 'When I'm Cleaning Windows', and had called his wife on to the stage to join him for his curtain-call when a three-year-old girl toddled on to present Beryl with a box of chocolates. She instinctively picked the child up, gave her a big kiss, then passed her to George – a perfectly natural reaction, though something of a historic one for this part of the world.

Outside the theatre, a hundred or so of the most hardened thugs the couple had ever seen cheered and pelted them with flowers, and for almost an hour the Formbys chatted to these people and signed autographs. The next morning, at their hotel, a delegation arrived sent by Malan, warning Beryl that she must never pull such a 'despicable stunt' again. She reacted by slamming the door in their faces, and that same evening she overstepped the mark again, by handing out sweets, and more hugs, to a crowd of children who had gathered around the stage-door. This time she received a call from Malan personally and Beryl, almost always the lady even when laying into someone, quietly told him before putting the phone down, 'Why don't you piss off, you horrible little man?'

Within the hour, Malan had exacted his revenge. Throughout the tour there had been speculation that the Formbys might purchase a property in Pretoria or Cape Town where they could spend the winter months. George's doctor had told Beryl that there was every chance of his developing his father's chest complaint, and had advocated a warm climate. Now, however, they were told by Malan's office that, not only were they no longer welcome in South Africa – the tour still had a week to go, and the organisers had arranged for an extension – they would have to leave the country at once. There was no civic vehicle this time to convey them to the airport, and shortly before boarding their plane another message was delivered from Daniel Francois Malan – 'Never come here again!'

The Formbys returned to England and began rehearsals for their annual pantomime. *Dick Whittington*, at the Leeds Grand, was a resounding success and sold out every night for two months, a pleasing antidote to the dreadful reviews for *George In Civvy Street*, still playing to capacity audiences five months after its release. There would be no more Formby films, he vowed, even when approached with a possible Hollywood contract. Gregory Ratoff, the former actor who had just directed Gracie Fields in *Madame Pimpernel*, saw no reason why George could not be as big as Gracie, Stateside. George told Ratoff that he would mull over his offer – then promptly forgot about it when, in the February, Beryl suddenly fell ill.

The couple had rented a boat for the weekend on the Norfolk Broads, and were just outside Great Yarmouth when Beryl collapsed and was rushed to a private clinic. At first the doctors suspected she might have been anaemic, but tests revealed a small growth on the uterus. This proved benign, but it was worrying all the same and after surgery Beryl was hospitalised for almost three weeks. George only left her side once – Beryl's doctors had advised him that she would need plenty of fresh air, so he went out and, on impulse, bought a 48-foot boat, the *Maudau*, which over the coming weeks would be converted into a handsome, two-berth cruiser which George would relaunch as the *Lady Beryl*.

Following Beryl's brief recuperation, George played two weeks at the London Palladium, where he was supported by Billy Russell, the Birmingham comic, a precursor of Les Dawson, then renowned for his mother-in-law gags. Again, the season was a sell-out . . . again, George was hammered by the London critics. 'Formby is in such bad taste, and so mechanical,' observed *The Times*' Paul Dehn, a man who despised any artist hailing from 'North of Watford Gap', and who received dozens of poison-pen letters and even death-threats for his barbed remarks.

In July, George and Beryl travelled to Birmingham, where they appeared on the hugely popular radio show, *Workers' Playtime*. This particular edition was broadcast live from Norton's Motorcycle Factory, and although the event was to raise more money for charity, George was more than compensated when the managing director presented him with a prototype 490cc International, the first machine to roll off the company's production line since the end of the war. The couple posed for photographs, with Beryl perched pre-cariously on the pillion. George would hardly ever ride the bike, however, declaring that it was too powerful even for him, and a few months later he would sell it to a drinking pal from his local for £250, and donate the money to a children's home.

In September 1947, George and Beryl set off on a six-week tour of Australia – flying in what he termed 'arse-about face fashion', stopping off in New York, then Hollywood. George, with his easy-going mien, took an instant dislike to the rowdy, hectic pace of the film capital. He and Beryl were invited to several glitzy parties, one of which was attended by Marlene Dietrich, who told me:

He spent most of the evening looking very much like a fish out of water, and his wife never left his side for a minute. He was a friendly man – I would meet him a few years later, when he was doing a musical in London – but he seemed really scared of this woman, who scowled at him every time a pretty actress stopped by to chat. I remember him in Hollywood, not playing his [ukulele], but singing 'Remember Me'. But I don't think appearing in American films would have done his career any good. George Formby was too special to appear in anything that was not entirely English.

From Hollywood, the Formbys flew to Sydney, where within hours of their arrival George was invited to address a film convention. The actual tour kicked off in Melbourne, where on the morning of his first show he was asked by the organisers if he and Beryl would be doing comedy sketches, or just singing. When George replied that they would be doing both, he was told that in order to perform non-musical routines he would have to join Australian Equity – providing his application could be processed within the eight hours before curtain-up – otherwise he might not be allowed to perform at all!

George's initial reaction was to ask Beryl to book seats on the next plane back to London. Then he changed his mind, and with his penchant for saving pennies asked if there would be a discount if he joined the actors' union for just a few weeks, as opposed to the full year. This was not possible, and again George submitted to defeat – until Beryl stepped in, defiant as ever, telling a press-conference, 'We won't be submitting to petty bureaucracy, if that's what they're expecting. We don't make this much fuss when your people come to England, so Australian Equity can like us or lump us. We're off to New Zealand in the morning, so that'll give them a couple of days to decide whether they want us or not. We don't care either way!'

The couple arrived in Auckland during the afternoon of 24 September and there was another row when Beryl was told that George would not be permitted to sing 'When I'm Cleaning Windows' because the New Zealand authorities considered it too vulgar. 'If he can't do that one,' she told reporters outside the IZB Radio studios, 'Then he won't be doing any of the others. Bugger the lot of them!'

More sparks flew inside the actual studio when Beryl was shown the station's 'Not To Be Played' list, for this contained no fewer than twenty Formby songs, many of them his best known. And when Beryl saw the woman assigned to George's interview – a flirtatious pretty blonde named Alice – she declared that he would not be doing the broadcast. After a great deal of unpleasant wrangling, during which the object of everyone's attention sat in a corner, smoking, a compromise was reached. 'Mr Formby is very tired after his long journey here,' Alice told her listeners, somewhat haughtily, 'but Mrs Formby has kindly consented to address the nation this evening, when hopefully we'll be able to play some of Mr Formby's recordings after the 10 pm watershed.'

Again, Beryl hit the roof. Once she had left the building, she snarled at Alice that that would be it – and in any case, she added, she and George always went to bed before ten when they were overseas. The situation was saved by a technician and his assistant. George was escorted to an adjacent studio, where he recorded ten songs on to an acetate which could be aired and edited at the producer's discretion. Beryl likewise recorded her interview – but if she sounded pleasant and friendly towards Alice, she never stopped glaring at her throughout the conversation which, for the better part only touched on the Formbys' quest for food parcels, centring mostly around their fondness for the British royal family, and Beryl's tastes in fashion:

Several American women asked me about my clothes and said, 'My, what a lovely little suit you have on. We can see that you come from England by the cut of it.' I thought that was rather complimentary . . . I think our hats too are definitely smarter than anywhere in America. Our hats are mostly trimmed with feathers, now. We have lovely birds of paradise, ospreys, and of course the ostrich feathers which the Queen made so popular. And they do *look very smart and becoming . . .*

The biggest glare of all, according to the reporter who witnessed the scenario, came from Beryl when George walked into the studio – his own performance having been recorded without hitch – and pronounced, 'As usual, once two women start talking, you can't stop 'em!' His wife was also disapproving once her broadcast had been completed and they were leaving the building. Two-hundred fans had gathered in the forecourt to see them off, and when they began chanting his name, George grabbed a litter-bin, turned it upside-down so that he would have something to sit on, and reprised the ten songs he had just recorded.

Later that evening, George's recital was broadcast on the national network and IZB's switchboard received so many calls that it was repeated the following evening, along with some of Beryl's comments, not just on IZB but on most of the independent stations. At the end of Beryl's conversation with Alice, George had said that he would only be staying in Auckland for two weeks – meaning to say two *days*. This was just as well, for within hours of the broadcast so many offers came flooding in that the Formbys did indeed end up staying in New Zealand for over a fortnight, and as a result of this the Australian tour had to be extended.

Their success, however, had little effect on their problems with Australian Equity – they were hounded by the union throughout their tour, though the adverse publicity worked in their favour when theatres who had originally turned George down now clamoured for him – enabling the wily Beryl to demand a hefty increase in his fees, which in any case were handed straight back to charity. George did, however, refuse to perform at any Equity functions after its members picketed a Melbourne cinema where they were showing a short season of his films. The union hit back at him by putting out a statement that, when invited to participate in benefits concerts to raise money for the Food For Britain Fund – rationing was still taking place here – he had denounced his compatriots with a sharp, 'Don't talk to me about British workers. They're not even worth the effort!' This was ridiculous propaganda. George had never said such a thing, and a few weeks later the charity thanked the Formbys in the press for the staggering £35,000 they had raised, enabling 75,000 food parcels to be dispatched from Sydney.

In Sydney, in the middle of November, there was also an altercation between George and one of Australia's top jockeys, Derby Munro. The two men should have competed against each other in a one-mile race, with all the proceeds going to the Food For Britain Fund, but when George arrived at the course he was informed that the race had been cancelled because of an 'insurance matter'. He assumed that his tour-promoter had stepped in to prevent the stunt from taking place, as had happened with Basil Dean when he had arranged to climb Blackpool Tower. Munro then swaggered up to him in the bar and bellowed, for all to hear, 'Sorry sport, but I didn't want a little fella like you to get hurt!' and George rounded on him and yelled back, 'I was good enough to ride in races in England, *sport*, and I'll give you a run for your money any day!' Despite his protestations, however, the course committee refused to reschedule the race, and when the Formbys flew out of Australia a few days later, in view of all the problems they had encountered they must have been asking themselves why they had bothered going there in the first place.

Back in England, George was besieged with more film offers, all of which he turned down. 'When I look back on some of the films I've done in the past,' he said, 'it makes me want to cringe. I'm afraid the days of the clown are gone. From now on I'm only going to be doing variety.'

It was at around this time that the media began speculating about George's health. The reports in the British press about his South African and Australian tours had been second-hand. Now they could observe for themselves that he was looking more than a little peaky, though he laughed this off as fatigue, which was at least partly true. His doctors were treating him for a suspected gastric ulcer, and he had started to have breathing problems on account of his heavy smoking. He had certainly not begun hitting the bottle, as one of the tabloids suggested, though Beryl did nag him into booking himself into the same York psychiatric hospital where she had incarcerated him earlier. This time she stayed for just two weeks, and left when the *doctors* discharged him.

In December, George opened in *Cinderella*, playing his first Buttons to Beryl's Dandini at the Liverpool Empire. The production hit a snag when, two weeks into the run, the chorus elected to go on strike because Beryl had told the local press that the management had been lucky to acquire George for a 'snip' – he was on his usual £1,000 a week, plus a percentage of the profits – whereas most of them were struggling on £20 a week, if they were lucky. George, in a rare outburst which he later claimed had been only intended as a joke, called them 'a bunch of Communists', and threatened to fire his personal assistant, Harry Scott, for publicly declaring that they were probably justified in taking action. Scott saved him the trouble by storming out of his dressing room, yelling that he was going home to Blackpool. This upset George and Beryl more than the potential strike. With only a few hours to go before curtain-up, Beryl told the chorus that they could have the rise they so badly needed – without even checking with the management to see if this would be all right! – then she and George jumped into their Rolls Royce and sped off to Blackpool, where they discovered Scott drowning his sorrows in the Opera House Bar. Two hours later, the trio were back in Liverpool, still the best of friends.

Although they hung on to their Cheshire home for the time being, the Formbys were far from happy living out in the sticks, and in June 1949 George bought Linden Lea, a few miles outside Blackpool. The house, close to Fairhaven Lake and overlooking Grannie's Bay, cost £10,000.

On 24 September, George and Beryl celebrated their silver wedding anniversary during a long-awaited, much delayed tour of Canada. Indeed, they should have left England at the end of August, but George, with his flair for stepping into the breach, had replaced a laryngitic Donald Peers in *Buttons And Bows*, at Blackpool's Grand Theatre – in one of the revue's tableaux he sang a cod-opera duet with the Manchester-born tenor, Frederick Ferrari.

By now, the Formbys had become reduced to little more than a marriage in name only – not entirely loveless, but more a mutually respectful business partnership. Some, of course, were willing to swear that it had never been anything else, and that the pair had become institutionalised in each other's ways – Beryl, the bullying *patronne*, and George the underling provider – and that neither would have been capable of surviving without the other. 'Darby and Joan precursors to George and Mildred,' was how Irene Bevan described them, alluding to the characters from the Seventies' television sit-com.

Cynics too have often wondered why, if George had been dealt so hapless a hand in the marriage stakes, he did not just take advantage of his established reputation and vast wealth and walk out on her. This is not a difficult question to answer. In George's day, especially in Northern England, the adage still held strong that, as one make's one's bed so must one be prepared to lie on it . . . one which the Formbys would harness themselves to, forcibly or otherwise, until the end. And, of course, in 1949 the general public knew nothing of what transpired within the portals of the latest Beryldene. Whenever the Formbys put in an appearance, with Beryl linking George's arm with apparently genuine affection, usually gently chiding him whenever they were in proximity of an attractive younger woman, they gave a convincing display of marital harmony . . . as indeed happened in Ontario whilst cutting their cake, with George still joking that it was not too late to hear the patter of tiny feet!

The couple had flown into the country five days previously. Beryl caused an immediate furore by demanding a four-star hotel instead of the modest guest-house provided by the tour promoter – not an unreasonable request – and George told reporters, with a deadpan expression, that he had been unable to offer the airport porter a tip because he only had on him £4 17s 6d in English money, and he would need this for cigarettes when he arrived home! Beryl had also insisted that he be paid after each engagement in hard cash – $1,000 for each of the twenty shows, and $500 for his radio appearances, which she could convert into pounds at a time when the exchange rate was the highest it had been for many years.

The entire tour was a sell-out, with most of the tickets being snapped up within hours of the box-offices opening. Not all of the venues were legitimate theatres, either, enabling Beryl a better opportunity of bartering with the management. In Saskatoon George performed at the Kinsmen Club, a rowdy dance hall frequented by a largely gay clientele who must have wondered what was in store for them when he strolled on to the stage and opened his set with 'Dare Devil Dick'. In Brandon, he discovered that he had been booked to appear at the local ice-rink – on the same evening the establishment were holding a cattle auction in the car-park. George could not resist opening with 'I Wish I Was Back On The Farm', which he sang in an almost incomprehensible Devonshire brogue!

In Toronto, George strolled on to the stage at the Royal

Alexandra Theatre, and before launching into his opening number pointed to a middle-aged man in the front row and shouted, 'Ee, Walter, is that really you?' The fan was Walter Nicholson, a Blackpool man who had emigrated to Canada some years before with his wife. After the show the couple dined with the Formbys at their hotel and George explained that this was his first decent meal in two days. He had been so worked up about his first appearance in a Canadian theatre that he had been virtually unable to keep anything down.

Another fan, however, was not so lucky. Dennis Poulter, the son of the Middleham shoemaker who had befriended George thirty years previously, was now living in Canada. He told me:

I wrote to George, relating the association of himself and my father, but all I got was a very curt letter from Beryl which more or less suggested that if I wanted to see her husband, tickets were available at the box-office. Needless to say, I didn't bother . . .

The show business reporter with the *Toronto Star* readily appreciated the Formby genius:

George Formby is one of those fortunate theatrical personalities who can stand in the middle of a bare stage and carry a show on his own – like Jolson, or Cantor, or Gracie Fields. His infectious personality ricochets across the footlights and makes everybody feel at home. Here he was, thousands of miles from his Blackpool in a strange country among strange people who say 'street car' instead of 'tram', 'elevator' instead of 'lift', and talk of dimes instead of sixpences. He wasn't even sure they'd know who he was, or if they'd enjoy his songs. Yet after that first split second of jitters, it was roses, roses all the way!

George and Beryl arrived back in Liverpool on 25 November.

Both looked unwell, having spent much of the crossing in their cabin on the *Empress of France*, suffering from flu. Three weeks later they opened in *Cinderella* at Leeds' Grand Theatre. As had happened earlier in Liverpool, the chorus and bit-parts complained about George's massive salary, and Beryl's demands that he should not be stared at whilst working his way through the wings towards the footlights . . . an exercise described by his former co-star, Garry Marsh, as 'the parting of the Red Sea'. George only added fuel to the flames by telling a reporter from the *Yorkshire Post*, 'I always say the managers should pay everybody what they think they're worth so don't go blaming everything on me!' Again, a strike was narrowly averted, and for four weeks the show played to packed houses. Then, a few days before Christmas, during the interval, George collapsed in his dressing room. The theatre manager, terrified that he was having a heart attack exacerbated by all the in-house problems, called for an ambulance, but before this arrived George had been examined by an off-duty doctor who had been sitting in the audience. He diagnosed a simple dose of food-poisoning, and George was driven back to his hotel. The next afternoon he was back on stage for the matinee performance, looking a little green but still bubbling over with the inimitable Formby magic. What the audience did not know was that only minutes before curtain-up his own doctor, summoned from Blackpool, had administered a shot of morphine . . . to which he would soon, but thankfully only temporarily, become addicted.

On 21 January 1950, unsteady on his feet and his face bloated on account of the drugs he was taking, George entered the Decca studios in London and in single takes re-recorded three of his old hits – 'When I'm Cleaning Windows', 'Auntie Maggie's Remedy' and 'Leaning On A Lamp Post' – and a new song, Max Miller's 'Come Hither With Your Zither'. The comic known as 'The Cheekie Chappie' stayed with him throughout the session, which would be George's last for almost two years.

Although still only forty-five, in these recordings George sounds much older, though this mellow timbre befits him inordinately well and gives one cause to rue that his health and his heavy schedule did not permit him to spend more time in the studio. Then on 7 March he was taken ill again at his home, and this time his doctor *thought* he was suffering from dysentery, a condition which had plagued him on and off since his return from North Africa. In absolute agony, he was rushed to Blackpool's Victoria Hospital, where surgeons performed an emergency appendectomy. He very nearly died, and his daily dosage of morphine was increased, affecting his features to such an extent that when he left the hospital, the photographers waiting outside respected Beryl's request not to take any pictures – a far cry from what would have happened today. For a month he recuperated aboard the *Lady Beryl*, cruising the Norfolk Broads and spotting a cottage which was for sale at Wroxham, a tiny, quaint residence with a thatched roof and no amenities. The price was just £2,000. George bought it on impulse, then arranged for it to be renovated. Over the next six months he spent another £2,000 and turned it into a riverside showpiece, but he spent little time there, preferring to recover his investment by renting the place out to friends. By April, however, he was suitably recovered to top the bill in a Lifeguards Variety Show at Windsor Castle, before virtually the entire royal family. Princess Margaret met him beforehand and asked him to do 'Leaning On A Lamp Post'. He obliged, dedicating it to her.

One week later, the Formbys embarked on their second tour of Scandinavia. There were two concerts at the Tivoli Gardens in aid of the wartime resistance movement, another at the Berasbee, and part of George's 90-minute show at the Stockholm Pleasure Ground was televised. Also in Stockholm there was a meeting with the film director, Alf Sjöberg, whose screen version of August Strindberg's novel, *Fröken Julie*, had recently been released to huge critical acclaim – the following year it would be awarded the Grand Prix at the Cannes Film Festival.

Sjöberg's intention was to make a film in Sweden with each scene shot twice – in English, then Swedish – teaming George with Anita Björk, the voluptuous blonde star of *Fröken Julie*. The Formbys were invited to sit through a screening of the un-subtitled film. There was little doubt that Björk was more appealing to the eye than any of George's previous leading ladies, but the stark reality of this particular film frightened the life out of him – it ends with Miss Julie grabbing her lover's cut-throat razor and slashing her throat! Beryl was naturally extremely apprehensive about leaving her husband alone for two minutes with an actress who also, inexplicably, had taken a shine to him. The Formbys, Sjöberg and the young woman spent several days discussing the project, which would follow a similar theme to Marcel Carné's *Les Enfants du Paradis*, made in 1945 and generally regarded as the greatest French film of all time.

Sjöberg had observed the immense similarities between the type of character George had played in most of his films and Carné's tragic mime, Baptiste, immortalised by Jean-Louis Barrault. George's role in the new film was therefore to be a largely silent one, though his singing voice would be used over the opening-closing credits. George called Eddie Latta from Stockholm and commissioned him to write two songs, one which would see him duetting with Björk, and even made a screen-test. This, however, was quickly consigned to a vault after Beryl put a very firm damper on the proceedings . . . having discovered that one of the secrets of Sjöberg's success in producing sparkling comedies and atmospheric dramas was that outsiders were never allowed on to the set, no matter who they were. The next morning, the Formbys left for London.

In May 1950, Beryl received a cable from a Canadian entrepreneur, inviting George to participate in a gala performance at Toronto's Maple Leaf Gardens in aid of the

Winnipeg Flood Relief Fund. The other artists had all agreed to pay their own expenses, and Beryl saw no problem with this, though she was initially far from happy with George travelling such a long way for a one-off engagement, particularly as he had been so unwell of late. 'Better that I send you a cheque to cover what George might have earned,' she cabled back. The sponsors, however, would not take No for an answer for they, like George's transatlantic record companies, stood to make a lot of money out of his appearance. Beryl swallowed the bait when told that the entire three-hour show was to be broadcast to 40 million listeners on 730 radio stations right across the North American continent – ironically, on 26 May, George's forty-sixth birthday – and that in view of this Decca Canada and Canadian Columbia were anticipating a sudden rush for George's records.

George performed just six songs, before a hypercritical audience of 20,000 – his largest ever, apart from his overseas wartime shows – but he caused a sensation. He walked on to the stage to chants of 'Happy Birthday', and afterwards he and Beryl were presented with a huge horseshoe of one-thousand red roses . . . which they sold for a dollar each to fans, the money augmenting the £30,000 already raised by the event.

The next day, George was inundated with offers to tour the United States, including $10,000 for an eight-day stint in Chicago, and $5,000 for a single performance at the pantheon of American entertainment, Carnegie Hall. Beryl was all for accepting, but this time George put his foot down. The 'Yanks', he declared, would never understand him; they would laugh *at*, not with him. He did, however, agree to a compromise: a full-length tour of Canada at the end of the year.

The summer of 1950 was spent quietly at home. Between recurring bouts of dysentery and chronic depression George worked little – a handful of variety engagements, and the switching on of Morecambe's illuminations. There were two more trips to the hospital in York and several discreet visits to

Dublin where the Formbys hoped to find a property. 'I'm sick to death of the tax-man robbing me of ninety per cent of my earnings,' George complained to a reporter who had trailed them to an estate agent's office. For this reason too, he announced, he and Beryl would not be appearing in a pantomime that year.

There was a little light relief, not to mention what George called 'handbags at fifty paces', on 4 August when he participated in the second 'Petit Prix', the Blackpool theatrical set's annual one-mile charity horse race between Squires Gate and St Annes. Over 5,000 holidaymakers jostled along the promenade to watch the event, whose 'jockeys' included the handlebar-moustached comedian Jimmy Edwards, Terry-Thomas, and that other infamous exponent of the uke, Tessie O'Shea.

The trouble began when Terry Thomas complained that George should never have been allowed in the race because he had formerly been a professional jockey, and as such would have a distinct advantage over everyone else. At this, 'Two-Ton' Tessie, a great admirer of George, yelled out that she hoped Terry Thomas' mount would throw him so that *he* would be barred from the race for having a broken neck! There then followed a fierce argument between Jimmy Edwards and the actor-stooge Jerry Desmonde, a pal of Terry Thomas' from his Sid Field era, who had won the race the previous year. Edwards' *horse*, Desmonde declared, was too good for him, he really ought to be riding an ass! Upon this, the comic dismounted, left his horse in the middle of the promenade, and strode off in a huff. A few minutes later the race took place, with George emerging victor by eight lengths – Desmonde came last. Then the squabbling resumed . . . until Beryl silenced everyone by bellowing, 'Grow up, for heaven's sake. The whole damn lot of you are worse than a load of bloody schoolkids!'

At the end of August, George and Beryl boarded the *Empress*

181

of France for Montreal and the first leg of their Canadian tour – seven weeks which would be extended to ten, mostly one-off shows in different towns and cities – for which George was paid up to $4,000 a time, often with a hefty percentage of the profits. Asked *why* he had elected to do one-night stands as opposed to week-long stints at selected venues he cracked, in a statement which the press would misconstrue, 'Because most of the time I can only stand one night in the flipping place!'

At one show, the couple were presented with traditional, multi-striped Hudson Bay coats, and George was given a ten-gallon Stetson to match the one at home. After another, on Vancouver Island, a Kwakiutl Indian chief handed Beryl a miniature totem-pole fertility symbol!

George was inundated with offers to do radio shows, but accepted only one – a short spot on Norm Pringle's *Midnight Merry-go-Round* in Alberta, where he sang the number most requested by Canadian fans, 'It's No Use Looking At Me'. George had introduced this back in 1934, and one can well imagine him having a crack at the Bard and sending up Hamlet!

> *I got rather muddled when I dressed for the part,*
> *The audience were full of grins.*
> *I shouted out, 'Odds-boddikins!' . . .*
> *I was feeling a draught around my anatomy,*
> *I must have looked the sight of sights!*
> *I shouted, 'Ee, turn out the lights!'*
> *'Cause I'd only got one leg in me tights . . .*

In all, the tour earned George around $200,000, of which $68,000 was paid back in Canadian taxes, and some 90 per cent of the balance collected by the British Inland Revenue. As he had been working almost exclusively for charity, George was well justified in telling reporters, upon his return to England, 'That's it. So long as this government keeps bleeding me dry, I shan't be in much of a hurry to work again!'

For almost six months, barring a charity show in Dublin in February 1951, George was as good as his word, and many of his fans truly believed that they had seen the last of him. Much of this time was spent on the Norfolk Broads, where the *Lady Beryl* was moored at Potter Heigham, between Great Yarmouth and Hoveton. Here, his eccentricities – and some might say roguish fondness for making a fast buck out of absolutely any situation – reached a new level. After he had guided a fellow yachtsman through a tricky bridge the man had asked for his autograph and joked that if George ever gave up the stage, then at least he would be able to get a job as a lock-keeper. The next day George put on a sailor's cap and dark glasses so that no one would recognise him, and began charging for his services! It has to be said, however, that he did give every penny of his 'salary' to a local children's hospital.

And then, just as he was beginning to enjoy his 'dotage' – at the age of forty-seven – he received an offer to appear in his very first West End musical, a wholly unexpected volte-face which would see him catapulted back into the limelight after almost five years in the virtual wilderness.

CHAPTER EIGHT

LIKE THE BIG POTS DO!

'It wasn't the songs, so much as how George Formby sang them. He could have an audience in the palm of his hand more quickly than any other entertainer I've ever seen.' Harry Scott, personal assistant.

Brewster's Millions had had a chequered history. Based on the novel by George Barr-McCutcheon, it had been adapted for the stage by the author and Winchell Smith and first produced in 1907. Jack Buchanan had starred in the film version of 1935, and ten years later there had been a Hollywood remake with Dennis O'Keefe. More recently the rights had been acquired by Emile Littler – famed for his recent London production of *Annie Get Your Gun* – who had commissioned a libretto from Eric Maschwitz, renowned for his screenplays for *Balalaika* and *Goodbye Mr Chips*.

Both Littler and Maschwitz later said that the musical version of the story of Percy Piggott, the man who has to dispense with one fortune in order to inherit an even bigger legacy, had not been created with any specific actor in mind – though it had not taken them long to figure out that the role could have been tailor-made for George Formby. Beryl, on the other hand, began telling everyone that she had been wanting George to *film Brewster's Millions* for twenty years. Having been disappointed with the play and the Buchanan film, she told the press, she was certain that George would have turned it into his biggest hit ever, if only one of the better directors she had approached had listened to her. Truth or wishful thinking, it did not take Beryl long to sign the pre-contract with Littler – *before* telling George, who fortunately would be just as excited about the project as she was.

It was only after the actual contract had been argued over and signed – and the piece's title changed to *Zip Goes A Million* – that both George and Beryl began having serious misgivings about what they were letting themselves in for. The West End of London, with the exception of the Palladium, had never really been Formby-friendly, and George had done himself few favours by once denouncing its producers and clientele as, 'A bunch of snobs who know nowt about real life.' Emile Littler reminded him of this comment before rehearsals got under way, adding that he was taking an enormous risk by staging a musical at the imposing Palace Theatre with a Northern comedian playing the lead . . . and that as such George should not anticipate the £1,000 a week he had been paid in the past for his pantomimes. For once, Beryl was justified in jumping down the producer's throat. Littler was told that the so-called common North had just as much talent as anywhere else in England, if not more, and that if he could not pay George what she and every other producer in the country obviously thought he was worth, then he would be quite happy to *stick* to pantomimes. Littler knew that she was right and George's salary was set at an unprecedented £1,500 a week, plus a share of the box-office.

Eric Maschwitz's libretto, scored by George Posford – who had also worked with him on *Balalaika* – differed from the original play in that it was set in the United States. Percy Piggot, a Newton-le-Willows window cleaner – a last minute change of occupation, Maschwitz later confessed – inherits $1 million from his uncle in Piggotsville, Texas. There is a coda attached to the old man's will: Percy must spend every last cent of this within four months in order to inherit another $7 million – moreover, he must not divulge to anyone why he is doing this, especially his sweetheart Sally, who was played by the Australian singer-dancer, Sara Gregory. The piece contained several fine songs, four of which constituted George's penultimate visit to the recording studio on 5 November 1951, and that same evening he repeated them all on the BBC Light Programme's *Henry Hall's Guest Night* before dashing off to the theatre. Three were new, but Gifford and Cliffe's 'The Pleasure Cruise' had been in his repertoire since 1935.

As George was extremely apprehensive about opening in London with such a vast change of direction, *Zip Goes A Million* received its premiere at the Coventry Hippodrome on 4 September 1951 . . . and there were just as many backstage squabbles at these try-outs as there had been on the sets of George's films.

Emile Littler, himself gay, objected virulently to the middle-aged Wallace Eaton's pursuit of rough trade – young male prostitutes who would often hang around the stage-door, or even be sneaked into the actor's dressing room. When Eaton became amorously interested in Ward Donovan, the show's adagio dancer, Littler threatened to fire him unless he behaved himself. Eaton compromised by getting his lovers to wait for him in a local pub, though by the time the production hit the West End of London, Littler had relaxed this ruling – actually *accompanying* Wallace Eaton to well known pick-up spots around Piccadilly and Waterloo.

The production's most threatening dilemma, however, was at the time said to have been instigated by the second female lead, Barbara Perry, a voluptuous but volatile blonde already known to British audiences. Having played bit-parts and walk-ons in several Hollywood films, she had appeared on the London stage – perhaps most noticeably in *Starlight Roof* with Pat Kirkwood – before being snapped up by Emile Littler for the *lead* in *Zip Goes A Million*. It is now known, however, that most of the backstage problems were caused by Littler himself,

Perry's mother who chaperoned her everywhere . . . and by Beryl.

Littler had originally wanted Perry to play the part of Sally, for which he had agreed a salary of £100 a week. However, when he realised before rehearsals got under way that Sara Gregory was by far the better singer she was promoted on the proviso that she retain her salary of around £50 a week, whilst Perry was expected to take a cut in pay! Not unexpectedly, her mother objected to this, but rather than tell her the truth Littler informed Mrs Perry that her daughter had been moved down the cast because she was not a member of Equity. This had not hindered her in the past, for the young woman was a fully paid-up member of the Variety Artists' Federation and had actually been warned by Littler that *if* she joined Equity, she would be fired from the production!

Simon Blumenfeld – writing then as now for the *Stage*, and one of the most respected journalists in show business who rarely has a bad word to say about anyone – told me:

Emile Littler was an absolute martinet, a thoroughly nasty piece of work who would stop at nothing to get his own way. He would do this sort of thing often – hire someone for a certain fee, then try to get rid of them once he'd found someone else who could do the job for less money. Hardly anybody in show business liked him, yet working for him was such a bonus because his productions were always so phenomenally successful.

Barbara Perry's mother had also done her homework as far as the Formbys were concerned. When Beryl quietly pointed out that it was the 'done thing' for visiting thespians to temporarily join the actors' union, Mrs Perry pointed accusingly at George and levelled, 'He didn't when he went to Australia!' Henceforth, he and Beryl would *publicly* declare that the dispute between Barbara Perry and Equity had nothing to do with them – then in true Machiavellian style work behind the scenes to ensure that the rest of the cast snubbed her, whilst Equity instructed its members to disrupt or boycott rehearsals. 'It seemed a bit daft sending somebody to Coventry when they were there already,' George said afterwards, 'but it had to be done.'

Barbara Perry submitted to the pressure. Only hours before the dress-rehearsal she handed Eric Maschwitz a receipt which proved she had joined Equity. This was shown to the press, though Perry herself refused to speak to reporters. Almost half a century on, however, she did break her silence, to Peter Holland and Dennis Taylor of the George Formby Society. And, *still* unaware of the Formbys' machinations she recalled them with great reverence:

I've got to tell you the nice things about Beryl because you'll hear plenty of the other. I was the oldest virgin in captivity, so she trusted me, though the fact that she took me under her wing was the worst thing that could have happened so far as the rest of the cast were concerned. She told me, 'You know, people don't like me. They're inclined to say that North Country women are dumb, and I made up my mind years ago to show them that North Country women are smarter than any men in this business.' When she told me that, tears came to my eyes. As for George, he had magnetism, a charm which never stopped. I only saw one of his films, No Limit, I never saw his vaudeville act, so I can only judge him on that one show. But to me he was a lovely actor.

Perry had, however, nurtured one big regret:

I'd had rave reviews, everybody loved my dancing. I got second revues to George even though I couldn't sing a song with him. That was terrible. There could at least have been a reprise of 'Ordinary People' somewhere in the show . . .

Barbara Perry would find herself persistently rubbed up the wrong way – albeit inadvertently, so far as George was concerned – throughout the run of the play. Though undoubtedly a talented all-rounder, this was *George's* triumph. The audiences were interested *only* in him, so much so that sometimes when he was not on the stage they chatted noisily and ignored whatever else was happening. Declaring the plot secondary to the songs and the infectious Formby grin, the *Coventry Evening Telegraph* dubbed him, 'The one-man pantomime that never palls.' Indeed, every time George produced his ukulele – as in his films, at the most inopportune or silliest moments – the audience became hysterical, so much so that he contributed an additional line to the script which was repeated every evening – 'Ee, you're not supposed to do *that*. You're holding up the play!' And, milking the situation for all it was worth – it is no understatement that George was having a similar effect on his admittedly smaller fan base as the Beatles would have in the next decade – Emile Littler made room for more Formby songs by cutting some of the other parts, including Barbara Perry's.

By the time *Zip Goes A Million* reached the Manchester Palace at the end of the month – the next stop before London – Perry's part had been so reduced, on top of hardly any of the cast speaking to her, that she was close to throwing in the towel. Matters were made far worse when the BBC announced that they were to broadcast excerpts from the first night – Beryl 'persuaded' the producer to record only George's numbers, and was not surprised when he informed her that this had been his intention in any case. After the show, Perry marched into Littler's office and demanded that he release her from her contract. This, however, was not possible and on 20 October the play opened in London.

Because this was ostensibly a showcase for George's spellbinding on-stage antics, standards, and lousy jokes, critics who were non-fans and who had never fully understood his appeal did not know what to make of a middle-aged man – now portly, and looking older than he actually was – whose every gesture brought him screams of approval and endless standing ovations. *The Times* did not like him at all, declaring that he lacked any vestige of finesse, and Kenneth Tynan positively loathed the way a tedious plot had been woven around George's lack-lustre personality:

> *It is only when the music stops that I start raising provisos like a palisade around my liking for him. I cannot laugh as he fidgets, gapes and fusses flat-footed across the stage . . . and I am unable to accept the theory that a banality or catchphrase acquires wit or philosophy when delivered in a North Country accent. Simplicity and unaffectedness can be carried to extremes. Mr Formby works with what Henry James called 'great economy of means and – oh – effect'.*

George pretended not to be offended by Tynan's scathing attack on his roots, but he was deeply hurt. Even Cecil Wilson's otherwise enthusiastic euphemism in the *Daily Mail*, that he was 'Lancashire hot-pot served on a silver platter' did not detract from the fact that, from these people's point of view, he would never be anything but common. 'I wish I'd have stayed in bloody Manchester,' he told Gracie Fields over the telephone. 'At least up there folk know what I'm all about!' Neither was he impressed when he read in the press that Oscar Hammerstein had called him 'Britain's most characteristic comedian' . . . until earlier in the week, Hammerstein later confessed, he had never heard of George Formby, and he had only attended one of the performances because Emile Littler had persuaded him to do so – hoping that the great man might just 'see his way' into writing something for George which would tempt him into crossing the Atlantic. 'If that's his game, he's just wasting his time,' was George's response.

Beryl also left herself wide open to sarcastic criticism when she compiled the notes for the second edition of the *Zip Goes A Million* programme. Writing in the third person, she spoke of how she and George had met in Castleford, how devoted they were towards each other, how happy their marriage had always been. Critics who were already aware of Beryl's well-intentioned machinations must have cringed when reading such ace quotes as, 'The general opinion of all concerned is that his wife is conscientiously carrying out a good job,' and, 'As an established actress in her own right Beryl Formby possesses her own vivid personality, on stage and off.' She was most criticised, however, for stating that *she* had written some of George's songs, and for including what she said was the play's best revue: 'The zippiest, snappiest and happiest musical comedy that's happened in a long while!' . . . for this had come not from a showbusiness column, but from the *Weekly Sporting Revue*!

What most of the critics thought or said, of course, was immaterial. Not one performance of *Zip Goes A Million* played to a less than 100 per cent capacity house, though after the first few weeks George's own enthusiasm for the production started to wane. Emile Littler had told him to expect a very long run, and this he did not want. He had proved the cynics and the 'anti-North brigade' wrong by triumphing in the West End, now he wanted his life to resume normality, at least as far as his failing health would allow.

The biggest threat of all, hanging over George's head like the Sword of Domocles, *was* his state of health, one aspect which Emile Littler had apparently chosen to ignore whilst attempting to insure George for the show. Prior to rehearsals, George had undergone a medical examination and been pronounced unfit to perform in a production which, having set Littler back a cool £40,000 before the first curtain-up, would *have* to have a long run in order for him to recover his investment. George had shrugged at this, genuinely believing that the show would prove a flop and that in next to no time he would be heading home, or back to the *Lady Beryl,* on the Norfolk Broads. Littler too had chosen to break the law by completely ignoring the insurance report and hoping for the best.

The best was not to be. Early in April, on the Thursday before *Zip Goes A Million* broke off for the Easter weekend, the Formbys set off for Potter Heigham. George was driving. That morning he had made up his mind to tell Emile Littler that, come Whitsuntide, he would be dropping out of the production – this would give the producer ample time to find a replacement. The couple were twenty miles outside London when George felt a sudden bolt of pain shoot through his chest. Nevertheless he still managed to bring the car to a halt at the side of the road before passing out. Beryl flagged down a motorist, and between them they moved George into the passenger seat. However, instead of calling for an ambulance, Beryl drove back to London, put George to bed in their flat, and summoned a doctor. Why on earth *he* did not admit George into a hospital is not known: all he did was inform Beryl that George was displaying the symptoms of a duodenal ulcer, and advise her to get him to drink plenty of fresh milk.

The show, of course, had to go on. Absolutely no statement was given as to why George would not be returning to the Palace Theatre. All the seats for the next two weeks' performances had been sold, and Emile Littler announced that there would be no refunds. George's understudy, Geoffrey Piddock, made a valiant attempt to bridge the gap. Unfortunately, he was hopeless in the role of Percy Piggott, though in retrospect it is extremely difficult to imagine *anyone* stepping into George's shoes, and was eventually replaced by Reg Dixon, the Coventry-born comedian who at least restored a little life and dignity to the party.

Dixon would carry the show to the end of its London run. It closed in February 1953 after 544 performances, toured for two years, and finally ground to halt with Charlie Chester in the coveted but by now over-worked role of Percy Piggott.

Meanwhile, an interview which George had given to a reporter from the *Sunday People* halfway through the Palace run – ostensibly to complain about all the begging letters he was being pestered with – now surfaced, giving many people who knew nothing about George's health problems cause to believe that he had abandoned *Zip Goes A Million* because of an argument over his salary. If this particular interview was anything to go by, George was not just interested in making money, he was obsessed by it. The interviewee, of course, had been Beryl:

The gossips forget our old friend the income-tax man. He stung me for nearly £800,000 during the war years even though I spent most of that time entertaining the troops all over the world for £10 a week, singing in shelters and war factories. Nowadays, with surtax higher than Mount Everest, I have to earn a pound before I can afford two packets of potato crisps, and seven more for a packet of fags! Even when I earned $100,000 for Britain during my Canada tours, all I had left after tax and expenses was $800 . . . I think I can claim to have made a lot of people happy, and in return they made me both happy and rich. Their appreciation totted up to around £84,000 a year . . . I have made two pictures a year – that's £50,000. My percentage of the takings added another £10,000. I earned more than £500 a week in pantomimes – the BBC and commercial radio forked up another £8,000. If you add on my income from gramophone records and 'George Formby' ukuleles it makes a grand – and I do mean grand – total of £84,000. On top of all the rest, I earned about £20,000 a year for charity . . . unfortunately, today I am taxed at 19s6d for every pound I give to charity, which makes it difficult. I hope the begging-letter merchants will take note of that. Last week they asked me for a cool £4,000.

It took George's doctor an incredible five *days* to realise that something was seriously wrong, and that he had in fact suffered a coronary. On 4 May he was admitted to the London Clinic where he was tended by the King's physician, Sir Horace Evans, who told him that he was lucky to be alive. Here, George was finally weaned off his morphine addiction, and when Beryl issued a public statement explaining to George's fans *why* he had had to drop out of *Zip Goes A Million*, over the next few days he received thousands of get-well messages and cards, including several from the royal family. Meanwhile Beryl kept unwelcome visitors, reporters and irksome press-photographers at bay. And George once again announced his retirement . . . not that anyone believed him.

On 4 June, having spent almost nine weeks in hospital, George returned to his Fairhaven home. Suffering from acute depression, his features bloated once more, he insisted upon inviting old pal Sylvia for tea. This interview was a grim one, for by and large he was only interested in speaking about his death, which he believed to be imminent, and his ubiquitous tax problems:

The doctor will only let me walk to the garden gate and back once a day. It'll be nine or twelve months before – if – I'm all right. Still, I've had a grand life and I'm sorry it's had to end like this. I've topped the bill for nearly thirty years and I hate to have to give up now. But what can you do? We're not wealthy, but we're all right. We've enough to live on. We're also thinking about selling this house. We've never spent much time here, and now there doesn't seem to be any point in keeping it on.

Two evenings later, George and Beryl turned up at Max Wall's Blackpool Palace Theatre revue, but so as not to create too much of a fuss watched the show from the wings. The manager, however, asked George if he would not mind stepping on to the stage, just to surprise the audience and prove to everyone that he was back in circulation. George obliged – halfway through Wall's patter – and as he made his entrance, leaning heavily on Beryl's arm, the orchestra struck up 'Chinese Laundry Blues'. He looked so ill that at first many people failed to recognise him – but when he approached the microphone and muttered, 'Ee, this *is* a grand tonic!' the audience went mad.

During George's illness, the Formbys' other house in Cheshire had been put on the market, and Ben Henry had bought another, on George's behalf – one of several the couple had looked over several months previously. The move, George declared, would get him away from the taxman, besides which he still wanted to breed horses. Aldon was a 24-roomed mansion near Foxrock, just outside Dublin, which had originally been built as a club, but subsequently refused a liquor licence. George paid £20,000 for it, and like the others it was rebaptised Beryldene.

Whilst the move was taking place, the Formbys had planned to spend several weeks on the Norfolk Broads. In the middle of September, however, George fell ill with gastro-enteritis and a suspected bloodclot on the lung. This time he refused to go into hospital, so he was confined to his bed whilst the removal men crated up his belongings. 'The furniture's being whisked away under our very noses,' he told Sylvia over the telephone, 'and I'm expecting them to remove the bed any minute, with me in it!'

The Formbys, however, would spend little time in Ireland. Away from his beloved Lancashire, George was like the proverbial fish out of water. By January 1953 *this* house would have been put up for sale, along with the one in Fairhaven, enabling George to buy a six-bedroomed residence but a stone's throw from the latter. It was an astute move. The house, Cintra, belonged to the popular Irish tenor, Josef Locke, a massive star in Britain at this time, but who was experiencing severe financial difficulties and needed the money fast. Soon afterwards he would flee England for tax evasion. Beryl, therefore, did not have to bargain too strongly to get Locke to drop the price to just £15,000 – though only on condition that if George ever sold the house, he would be able to buy it back at the same price, providing of course he had any money. The papers were signed on 22 February. This particular Beryldene would remain George's favourite, the one within whose walls he would achieve eventual peace of mind.

Meanwhile, in the middle of September 1952 there was another drama when George choked on a fish-bone which pierced and became lodged in his oesophagus. He was taken to Blackpool's Victoria Hospital in considerable pain, but the surgeons were terrified of operating on him on account of his heart condition. Eventually, after forty-eight hours and with the threat of serious infection, they were left with no choice. It took him several hours to come out of the anaesthetic, and his first visitors were Beryl and Sylvia. His first words, according to the journalist, were, 'Ee, everything seems to happen to me. And they *still* can't keep a good man down!' He was right. The doctors told him that he would have to stay in hospital for at least a week, but George discharged himself after just four days because, he said, he had a 'pressing engagement' – the judging of a beauty contest at the Middleton Towers Holiday Camp, in Morecambe!

In March 1953, the Formbys were spotted by the *Daily Express*'s Michael Walsh at what was for them an unusual location – a West End nightclub where they were offering moral support to an obscure comic named Arthur Riscoe, making his cabaret debut. Walsh observed how George had put on weight, and that he looked sun-tanned and healthy. 'I'm going to plunge in and work again,' he told the journalist, 'I think I can make it in another musical. The winter in Dublin did it – eating Irish steak and drinking Scotch. My doctor's orders were a daily ration of six doubles and a single. Relaxes the arteries, they say!'

In April, looking far from well, but claiming that his doctor had given him permission to travel, George and Beryl flew to Bulawayo, Southern Rhodesia, for a series of seventeen shows which formed part of the Rhodes Centenary Exhibition. At the end of August – billed as 'A Formby Come-Back Special' – he topped the bill at Southport's Garrick Theatre. A few weeks later he switched on the 21st Blackpool Illuminations – kissing Beryl on the cheek after crooning 'Leaning On A Lamp Post' to her, he told the crowd, 'It's the old woman's birthday today. Twenty-one summers, but I won't tell you how many winters!' Beryl is said to have been far from pleased.

In October, after a great deal of wrestling with his 'inner demons', as he called them – and after consulting Sir Horace Evans – George returned to the West End. There had been talk of his replacing Reg Dixon in *Zip Goes A Million*, still raking in the money but now only playing to 75 per cent audiences . . . but in George's eyes a jinxed piece all the same. He had therefore opted for his only 'lucky' London theatre, the Palladium, and opened in Val Parnell's revue, *Fun And The Fair*. With him were Terry-Thomas, the Deep River Boys, Audrey Jeans, and Billy Cotton and his Band. Parnell, who had never been a Formby fan – George did not like him at all – had initially instructed George to come up with a set of brand new songs. He, however, was far less interested in learning new material than he was in giving fans what they really wanted – the standards he had made his own – and Parnell gave in. Having Formby in any revue was enough to guarantee standing-room only, besides which, Beryl had confided in him that these performances could well be her husband's last.

Strictly speaking, *Fun And The Fair* had not started out as a Formby vehicle. It had originally been put together by producer Charles Henry to showcase the then limited talents of Terry-Thomas. Though their names appeared side by side and in same-sized letters on the playbills, Terry-Thomas was being paid £1,400 a week – £400 more than George – and he was closing the show. George had been relegated to *vedette-américaine*, the spot immediately before the interval. Beryl had complained to the producer about this during rehearsals, for George's sketches – one a spoof on the television programme, *What's My Line* – were weak, and she did not believe that the seven numbers he had chosen for his solo spot would placate the fans. In fact, it was only when the curtain had fallen on what the audience took to be the close of the first half, that the real magic began. The first time this happened, an announcement over the theatre tannoy urged the audience, 'Ladies and gentlemen, you are requested, keep your seats please!' The curtain then rose on a pitch-black stage, and a few seconds later a spotlight picked out a small couch upon which were three ukuleles, and the orchestra struck up 'Chinese Laundry Blues' as George materialised, stage-left. This was Beryl's *coup de grâce* . . . not seven, as arranged, but fifteen songs, beginning with 'I Wonder Who's Under Her Balcony Now?', each one greeted with hysterical cheers and the stomping of feet. 'He's back!' screamed the *Sunday Express*, 'George Formby is back, in good health and spirit. Last night at the premiere we were one big happy family rejoicing at the return of the prodigal!'

Terry-Thomas, who like Audrey Jeans had risen to prominence in *Piccadilly Hayride*, the Sid Field extravaganza of 1946, was not amused, as he later confessed:

I closed the show with my impression of a sergeant-major impersonating Noël Coward. The trouble was, George Formby put the audience in a certain mood which made them non-receptive to whoever followed . . . Even though the closing act was the star spot, I felt on this occasion that being there was an anti-climax. I told Charles Henry, 'George Formby is really the star of the show. He should go on last. Put him where he belongs and make it easier for me.' But Charles liked my work and wasn't keen on Formby's. 'What?' he said, 'put him on last with all those fucking awful parrot stories?'

In fact, Terry-Thomas had asked Charles Henry to *remove* George from the show because he was stealing all his thunder, and when Henry refused, the comic threatened to take up the matter with Equity – not that they could have done anything. This brought a sharp response from Beryl, who cornered Terry-Thomas in his dressing room and told him, 'It's no use complaining to the union. The fans have clearly decided who *they* prefer. So why not just pack your bags and go to America. They're used to your brand of rubbish over there!'

The Palladium run should have lasted for six weeks, but on account of George's popularity it was extended to nine. It was also a tremendous triumph of mind over matter for him. For the first time since his debut in 1921 he had started to suffer from stage fright, and between performances often endured lengthy bouts of depression, aggravated by recurrent stomach problems, themselves brought about by worrying about his heart condition.

Towards the end of 1953, on the strength of his *What's My Line?* skit, George made two appearances on the programme – first as the week's 'mystery' guest, then replacing the indisposed Gilbert Harding in the Christmas edition. The latter reunited him with Pat Kirkwood, his co-star from *Come On George* who later sympathised with him for having to tolerate Beryl's interference – mouthing the responses to his questions – in the Shepherd's Bush television studio in full view of contestants and audience. To be honest, he should never have been asked to do the show. Gilbert Harding was noted for his acerbic, sometimes cruel sense of humour, and George was far too naive to realise that the other team members were taking him for a ride, certainly whilst the programme was on air. He did have a run-in off the set with regular panellist Lady Isabel Barnett, whom he accused of looking down her nose at him and of demanding that George should not be allowed to crack gags.

For six months, George did little. His annual pantomime – *Dick Whittington*, in Manchester – had been cancelled after his doctor had warned him that the strain might prove fatal, and his place had been taken by the *PC 49* actor, Brian Reece. In February George's car was involved in an accident on the Great North Road, just outside Peterborough. Overtaking a lorry on a bend he crashed into the side of an oncoming saloon. No one was injured, but the other car was a write-off. The police were summoned, but the driver, one Owen Aveling, did not press charges when George agreed to buy him a new car. Had the matter gone to court, George would almost certainly have had his licence taken from him, for he clearly should not have been driving in his state of health. 'He's been so ill, I'd feel awful adding to the poor man's problems,' Aveling told local reporters, whilst George quipped, 'Oh, well. I suppose it was just one of those things, as they say in the song!'

The accident, however, affected George badly. Within the week, without even bothering to have it repaired, he had sold his car and even talked about *burning* his driving licence – until Beryl persuaded him otherwise and, at the end of May, he bought another Rolls Royce. The first time he took it out, he parked it opposite Blackpool Tower and was walking away when another vehicle backed into it – not only this, the driver stuck his head out of the window, yelled an obscenity, and drove off. George took the man's number, and he was later arrested and fined.

During the first half of 1954 there were a few shows here and there, the rejection of another film script, and a cancelled recording session with His Master's Voice. He also turned down another season in the West End, choosing instead a summer show in Blackpool where he shared top-billing with Josef Locke; though Beryl insisted that the title of the revue should be named after George's catchphrase and not after one of the tenor's songs.

Turned Out Nice Again, produced by Jack Taylor and premiered at the recently refurbished Hippodrome on 25 June, should have run for thirteen weeks. It closed after just six when George again fell ill with dysentery and depression. This time his doctors *ordered* him to take things easy. George was pushing himself so hard he was slowly but surely killing himself.

Again, George announced his retirement, and a few days after pulling out of the show he and Beryl drove down to Wroxham, where over the next few months they moved between their cottage and long, relaxing outings on the *Lady Beryl*. It was at Heronby, on the August Bank Holiday Monday, that the Formbys organised a tea-party for the Howsons, a family of friends who were holidaying on the Norfolk Broads. Fred Howson was the general manager of a motor firm in Penwortham, near Preston, and the Formbys had known him and his wife, Kathleen, since the early Thirties, often spending time with the family whilst having their cars serviced or repaired.

Over the years, George had become particularly fond of the Howsons' daughter, Pat, always calling her his 'sweetheart' and occasionally taking her little gifts. Now, the little girl had blossomed into a pretty, vivacious brunette, still unattached at twenty-nine and working as a schoolteacher. And, that afternoon in Wroxham – right under Beryl's nose – George promptly fell in love with her, though it would take him a little longer to actually *do* anything about his feelings.

Meanwhile, incapable of just sitting around twiddling his thumbs – 'I've *got* to pick up my knitting again,' he told Sylvia, using the expression he had borrowed from Gracie Fields, 'otherwise what else have I got to do with my time?' – George made his 'comeback' on New Year's Eve, performing a medley of his hits on *Ask Pickles*. This was followed, on 9 January 1955, by a longer television slot headlining the BBC's *Top Of The Town*. He performed two sketches, sang 'The Pleasure

Cruise' from *Zip Goes A Million*, and duetted – very much against his will – with Terry-Thomas on 'Leaning On A Lamp Post'. The broadcast was so popular that George was asked to make another appearance in the programme's 20 February edition, along with singing star Eve Boswell. This had to be cancelled, however, when six-foot snowdrifts prevented the Formbys from leaving their home.

At the beginning of March, George and Beryl made their second trip to South Africa for a series of engagements which would raise £15,000 for the National Cancer Fund. Daniel Francois Malan, the country's prime minister since 1948 and Beryl's sworn enemy, had recently resigned, so she was hoping that this visit would prove less troublesome than the last.

Once again, the Formbys were instructed not to perform in the townships at exclusively black venues, though this time Beryl got around the problem a little more diplomatically, telling the private secretary of Malan's equally austere, whites-only pulpiteering successor, Johannes Strijdom, 'The deal is this. George sings to whom he likes, *where* he likes, and we hand over all the money to a charity of your choosing.'

Strijdom very reluctantly agreed. From their Johannesburg base the couple toured the whole Witwatersrand region, culminating with a show at Witwatersrand University – the very first appearance there of a European entertainer – which George was advised to cancel at the last moment because of Beryl's anti-apartheid comments at an earlier press-conference. She had stupefied journalists by proclaiming, 'All this racial stuff is just rubbish. We're all the same colour inside, so why pick on people just because they're a different colour on the outside? Black, white or sky-blue pink with yellow dots on, they're just as good as you!'

The concert went ahead, despite the death-threat received by Beryl one hour before curtain-up which necessitated the pair being guarded, from the wings, by armed police. George was on stage for over two hours, and at the end of the performance the organisers presented him with the establishment's most prestigious accolade, a Kruger half-sovereign medallion. Then, after wiping the tears from his eyes, George rewarded the 5,000-strong audience with 'Sare Maraise', which he recorded a few days later in Cape Town, but which was not commercially released until after his death. His British admirers heard the song for the first time on 16 April 1955 when he sang it on the BBC Light Programme's *In Town Tonight*.

Prior to this, on 13 April, George appeared in the Royal Variety Performance, at Blackpool Opera House – only the second time this famous event had taken place outside of London, the other being at Knowsley Hall in 1913, when George's father had topped the bill. George actually replaced Gracie Fields, who a few weeks previously had been taken ill in America and undergone an emergency operation for gallstones. Amongst the top names sharing the bill with him were The Crazy Gang, Morecambe and Wise, Arthur Askey, Joan Regan and the American singing sensation, Eddie Fisher. George brought the house down with 'Sitting At The Top Of Blackpool Tower'. Copyrighted under this title in 1943, until now George had always performed it as '*Spotting* On The Top Of Blackpool Tower' – the spotting not alluding to seagull droppings, as he often joked, but to wartime 'fire-spotting'.

The impromptu command performance did wonders for George's flagging career, which in the past had always been successfully resuscitated by Beryl's persuasive nagging and unfailing faith in his abilities. Now, however, indolence had been tragically superseded by rapidly failing health. For George, time was running out and, well aware of this, he embarked on a reckless, near-suicidal binge of events which he knew could quite possibly end up killing him. In May, he embarked on a gruelling ten-day tour of Canada, raising $50,000 for the Variety Club of Canada, for which he was presented with a Gold Life-Time Membership card.

Zigzagging back and forth across the country, he only found time to relax during the homeward journey aboard the *Empress of Scotland* . . . and was laid low with an attack of bronchial pneumonia. Yet no sooner had he recovered from this than he was back in the spotlight, starring in his first straight, virtually non-musical play.

Too Young To Marry had been written by Martin Flavin and first produced at the Liverpool Playhouse in 1935, with Michael Redgrave playing the central character, a hen-pecked Scotsman who stands up to his carping wife – but only when drunk. Cynics might have agreed that such a scenario was a little *too* apt as far as the Formbys were concerned, except that for once George was the one doing all the nagging, because Beryl had started hitting the bottle. And with good cause.

For months, Beryl had complained of feeling tired and ill, only to blame her condition on overwork, and the stress of having recently lost both her parents. In August 1955, however, she was admitted to a Norfolk hospital for tests – the same one that had cared for her in 1947 – and this time the results were devastating. She was found to have incurable cancer of the uterus, and the doctors told her that at best she would have just two more years to live.

CHAPTER NINE

GOODNIGHT, LITTLE FELLOW, GOODNIGHT ...

'I thought to myself, "What a charming man," and I hoped that he would eventually find a nice girl. But I never dreamt it would be me.' Pat Howson, fiancée.

George coped with the devastating news about Beryl the only way he knew how – by working. His own doctors had warned him that by stretching himself to the limit, he was well on target for another heart-attack, and that this one could be fatal. With this in mind, George began to take stock of his life. His wife was dying, and hastening the end by a daily bottle of whisky. For as long as he cared to remember, his marriage had been sexless, something which had never perturbed him because in this respect there had never been any shortage of offers. Cynics had persistently made fun of George's looks. He himself had mused about the potent pulling powers of unattractive men in albeit fictitious songs such as 'Why Don't Women Like Me?' . . . yet to be truthful, *he* did not fit into this category. In his youth he had been extremely athletic, and even now, in his early fifties, many much younger women still found him appealing. George was a man with a warm, outgoing streak which had been forcibly cooled by an overlong union with a woman who, in spite of being his anchor and saving grace, had always treated him like an errant schoolboy and never offered him the normality of a conjugal bed.

205

And now, George Formby was standing at the crossroads. Behind him, a glorious career – constructed and nurtured by the very same beautiful tyrant who, in turning him into an international icon, had for not intentionally selfish reasons, robbed him of so many of life's pleasures – not least the opportunity to become a father. And for what? So that she could predecease him and leave him alone in a world within which he had depended upon her for so long? For all that he had given to this world, George deserved at least some happiness before he left it.

'If only God could procure some tiny miracle,' he told Sylvia over the telephone, 'wouldn't that be nice?'

The miracle occurred in July 1955, when George bumped into Pat Howson again – for this time he told the pretty young schoolma'am just how miserable his life had become, and for the first time in years, Beryl was not breathing down his neck.

George Formby and Pat Howson became soul-mates during the summer of 1955, of this there is no doubt. Just how far their relationship progressed beyond the platonic is not known, though on the face of it this would seem unlikely. George was a very sick man who had already taken far too many risks with his health to jeopardise it any further by extraneous sexual activity. He was also, despite his occasional meanderings from the sanctity of his marriage vows, a moral man who, though he may have begun to hate his wife and thus long for a release from the invisible prison she had built around him, would not have wished to hurt her feelings and create a public and ecumenical scandal by letting the world know that he had found a 'replacement' whilst she was still alive. For this reason, even his friendship with Pat had to remain a closely-guarded secret – by no means an easy task, for over the coming years, whilst Beryl's life slowly ebbed away, necessitating sometimes lengthy periods when she could not be with her husband, George's movements would be carefully monitored by the eagle-eyed Beryl-worshipping factotum, Harry Scott.

Too Young To Marry was completely revamped by Emile Littler, to bring the main character into line with George's homely, cheerful mien. One song was added: 'If You Don't Want The Goods Don't Maul 'Em', which he had recorded with Jack Hylton back in 1932. The play toured spasmodically between September 1955 and November 1956, though for once not always to packed, enthusiastic audiences and to generally poor reviews. Several performances were recorded and subsequently issued on 'bootleg' tapes, notably the one in Glasgow where George was booed on account of his dreadful Scottish accent, and that at the Golders Green Hippodrome on 4 September 1956. Between venues, there were concert appearances, some forcibly shorter than they had been during George's heyday, and during the winter of 1955, George's annual pantomime – *Babes In The Wood* at the Liverpool Empire.

For the very first time, George appeared on stage without Beryl. 'I have quite enough to do, looking after George backstage,' she told the press, 'and I'm up like the proverbial lark every morning, getting all the correspondence out of the way before he gets up. I think I'm entitled to a rest, don't you?' It was, of course, her progressively worsening condition which was tiring her – and the fact that in order to cope with her pain, Beryl had begun drinking heavily. This, in addition to the cortisone she was taking, had bloated her features considerably and she, like her husband, had piled on the pounds.

George's first West End pantomime opened at the Palace Theatre in December 1956. The *Dick Whittington* premiere was attended by the Queen and Princess Margaret, Prince Charles and Princess Anne, and the royal party shared a 'pot of tea' with George and Beryl during the interval. Later in the season, part of the show was televised by the BBC. But again, the London critics were nothing less than severe, sometimes unduly so. 'If George Formby were long absent from the stage, he would not be missed,' *The Times* observed . . . two days before George was forced to drop out of the production with a throat and lung infection, to be replaced by Gracie's brother, Tommy Fields.

The year 1957 saw George doing virtually nothing. He and Beryl attended the premiere of the re-released *Keep Fit* in London, following this with a visit to the TT Races on the Isle of Man. In June, he hosted his own television spectacular, with guests David Niven, Petula Clark, and opera star Tito Gobbi. At the end of the year he appeared on ABC Television's *Top Of The Bill*, where at the last minute he replaced 'When I'm Cleaning Windows' with the rarely performed 'Trailing Around In A Trailer' as a tribute to Fred E Cliffe, who had recently died. On the strength of this performance he was offered a tour with Leslie Sands' musical-comedy, *Beside The Seaside*.

Subtitled *A Holiday Romp*, and already well-played on the repertory circuit before George took over, the play opened in Hull on 10 March 1958. After a short season in Blackpool it moved to Birmingham's Alexandra Theatre. Its audiences began dwindling until the promoter, Derek Salberg, finally pulled the plug in May, while it was playing at half-capacity at the Brighton Hippodrome. The critics – and the public – in this part of the country were simply not interested in witnessing the exploits of 'a boring family of Northerners' whose only pleasure in life appeared to be spending a rowdy week in Blackpool, engaged in a full-scale battle with a battleaxe landlady.

Blackpool theatregoers, on the other hand, had loved the play, and every house had been a sell-out. 'It may not be true, but it is funny,' declared the *Gazette*'s Brian Hargreaves, though he was not so sure that it would do the guesthouse trade much good:

One imagines that the only thing likely to stop its success would be a picket of landladies around the theatre. The place in which it is set is a shocker and the landlady, Mrs Austin, a terrible termagant, a cruel but comic caricature. She meets her match, though, in Wilf Pearson, a cheerful, naturally easy-going chap. The clashes between the landlady with the face as long as a fiddle, and the boarder with the face as round and beaming as a ukulele are formidable and funny. Stock characters certainly, but they have been written with acute and good-humoured insight . . . George has a part which fits him as well as his suit (surely too smart a piece of tailoring for a Wakes week visitor?). He gathers the guffaws in easy, accomplished fashion, and can be most touching at times, too. It really has turned out nice again!

George did not even care that the people of Brighton had rejected him as a dismal failure. Blackpool was his *home*, his second heart, and all that really mattered were the opinions of *its* public. He therefore told the producer, Maxwell Wray, that the production would more than recuperate its losses if he allowed him to add a few more songs and return with it to the Blackpool Grand, or even the Opera House. Wray would not hear of this, and George lost his temper, vowing that he would never appear in another stage musical. This time he would keep his word.

1958 was the leanest year of George's career. Friends stated at the time that he was closer to Beryl than ever – perhaps as much through unnecessary guilt that he would soon lose her, as through genuine affection – and that he wanted to spend as much time with her as he could. Her certainly experienced immense difficulties staying at the helm when, on bad days, Beryl was unable to leave their Fairhaven home – not just turning down a film appearance, by now a regular occurrence, but also cancelling several radio broadcasts and a recording session with His Master's Voice, who reciprocated by informing him that he would never be offered another. There were three television dates: an appearance on *The Frankie Vaughan Show*, another on ABC's *Second Birthday Show*, and his rock 'n' roll debut with the Deep River Boys, performing 'Rock Around The Clock' and a medley of his hits.

In October, convinced that this would be their last holiday together, George arranged to take Beryl on a Mediterranean cruise. Stubborn almost to the end, *she* cancelled this and booked them a cabin on the *Empress of Britain*, about to embark on a twelve-week cruise to the United States and Canada . . . having negotiated a crafty means of getting back most of the £3,000 she had forked out for the trip. The entrepreneur Hughie Green was shooting a television spectacular, *Atlantic Showboat*, aboard the vessel. David Whitfield, Shirley Bassey and Duke Ellington had already been signed up, and George now completed the line-up.

The couple spent much of the time they were at sea below deck, emerging only to do the show. George performed four songs, only two of which were left in Green's film – 'The Pleasure Cruise' and 'Hello Canada!' – which was screened by ABC on 13 December.

It has often been stated that George was suffering from stress at this time, on account of having to hide the fact from Beryl that she was terminally ill. This is not true. Not only had Beryl been told the truth by her doctors, she in turn had confided the grim news to her friend, Sylvia, now in her early seventies and herself ailing:

I first became ill two years ago, after a fall in a Liverpool theatre. I broke two ribs and a thumb, but evidently the worst result of it all was the shock to my nervous system. I got to such a pitch that I could scarcely walk downstairs as I had no sense of balance. The crisis seemed to come when I had to be helped up the gangplank for this last visit to Canada. On board, the ship's doctor looked at me and he said to George, 'Your wife is a very sick woman, you know.' He told me that I had pernicious anaemia, and straight away started me on a course of injections. After five days, even though it was a very rough crossing, I was able to walk back and forth across our cabin with perfect ease. I feel a different person, now. We're even planning another cruise to Africa, or to one of the sunshine countries.

The doctor had administered cortisone, and it was this that had contributed to Beryl's lulled feeling of well-being, along with her gradual addiction to alcohol. As far as her drinking was concerned, George was much more of a companion than a moderator, matching her glass for glass and quietly getting smashed within the privacy of their cabin. Only once did Beryl's secret almost become public knowledge – this was when the *Empress of Britain* stopped off in Montreal, and she was too drunk to go ashore and George had to announce that she was suffering from the flu.

In public, however, Beryl handled herself well, grimacing every now and then when a fresh wave of pain shot through her body, and steadily getting plumper on account of her medication. Like some latter-day Christian martyr, she refused to go into hospital and in April 1959 when she accompanied George to the BBC studios, in London, for the filming of *Steppin' Out With Formby*, she could hardly walk. George, too, kept having to sit down on account of dizzy spells, though his performance was just as bouncy as ever. He sang seven songs, including two new ones which should have been recorded during the aborted session with His Master's Voice: 'Piccolo Pete' and 'It Ain't No Sin To Take Off Your Skin'.

Two months later, however, when George opened in summer season at Great Yarmouth's Windmill Theatre, Beryl's condition had deteriorated to such an extent that even on better days she was unable to appear on stage with him. She was replaced, as George's stooge, by Bettina Richman – with her husband John Jackson a minor but popular comedy duo at this time – though this did not prevent her from ruling over the proceedings, from an armchair within the wings.

One afternoon Beryl was well enough to accompany George to the Windboats boatyard for the launching of his new yacht, *Lady Beryl II*. The old vessel had been traded in for a superior model, though George had taken his wife's advice *not* to pay the £500 difference, as James Spencer, a former Windboats employee – seventeen at the time and bought his first pint of beer, albeit illegally, by his idol – explained:

> *Beryl told us that a public appearance by the Formbys would be worth much more than £500 – you know, a good advertisement for business. She also complained about the champagne, declaring how she hoped she was not paying for an expensive vintage to be smashed against the side of a boat. And she absolutely hit the roof when George disobeyed her most explicit instructions not to go into the men-only bar and left her standing outside! I remember my boss telling me that it was probably the first time in his life that George Formby had dipped his hand in his pocket to buy a round of drinks. Then he concluded, 'If that was* my *wife, showing me up in public like that, I'd throw her into the water!' She really was a pain in the arse . . .*

Great Yarmouth was George's penultimate triumph. Every night was a sell-out, and no two shows were ever the same. 'Lamp Post' and 'Windows' had to be there, of course, but as the season progressed the sketches became shorter as George made way for more songs – the pauses between which may have been noticeably longer, allowing him to savour the rapturous applause, and to regain the breath to continue. Sometimes – purposely, it would appear – he would forget the words so that the audience would prompt him. No matter how obscure the song, they always seemed to know the lyrics, turning each evening into a wondrous singalong experience. 'I only wish it could go on for ever,' George told Sylvia over the telephone, 'but all good things have to come to an end, don't they?'

This particular 'thing' almost ended prematurely at the beginning of August when, on their way back to Great Yarmouth following a lightning visit to Fairhaven, George's Jaguar was involved in a collision with another car just outside Norfolk. Neither vehicle was badly damaged, and the other driver suffered only minor cuts and bruises. Beryl, who was in the back of their car, slept through the whole thing. George, however, went into a cataleptic shock, and the doctor who tended him at the scene of the crash was so convinced that he was about to have a coronary that he drove him, and the still-groggy Beryl, to the hospital at King's Lynn rather than risk waiting until the ambulance arrived. Tommy Trinder, holidaying in the region, heard what had happened on the mid-day news. He had bought tickets for George's show that evening – now he kindly stood in for him.

When the doctors in King's Lynn examined George, they declared it a miracle that he had been able to survive this long. His blood pressure was sky-high, his lungs were irreparably damaged through smoking upwards of forty cigarettes a day since the age of twelve – so called 'coffin-nail' brands such as Capstan Full Strength and Woodbine – he was three stone overweight, and his heart was in such a pitiful state that they did not expect him to last the night. Yet all he could tell a reporter who suggested that he at least ought to try and stop smoking was, 'Ee, lad. What good would that do me now?'

After three days in intensive care, followed by a week in a private ward, George discharged himself from the hospital and returned to the Windmill Theatre, picking up where he had left off as if nothing had happened. When the season ended, early in October, he learned that he had broken the theatre's all-time attendance record. 'Proof, if ever proof were needed, that George Formby is *still* Britain's greatest entertainer,' observed a local newspaper.

During this second run in Great Yarmouth the offers poured in: a tour of British provincial theatres spearheaded by Harold

Fielding, a recording contract with Pye International, yet another film, a summer season in Blackpool, and a twenty-week tour of Australia.

George's spirit was willing enough, but he was terrified of straying too far from Blackpool in case anything happened to him. 'I'd never forgive myself if I died abroad,' he told Sylvia, half-joking, whilst Beryl told the Australian promoter, quite seriously, 'Our real problem isn't George's health, this time, but that of our dog, Willie Waterbucket. He'll be fifteen this October, and we'd hate anything to happen to him whilst we were away. So I'm afraid George and I won't be coming to Australia just yet.'

The Blackpool season George accepted without hesitation, along with the two-session record deal at the beginning of May. The executives at Pye were hoping that even in this limited time George would tape enough of his old material to cover at least two album sides, though he soon made it clear that he had no intention of reviving any of his former hits.

This in itself presented George with a major problem. Fred E Cliffe was dead, and Harry Gifford had died whilst George had been negotiating the Pye contract. Such was George's reputation for insisting that his name be added to the songwriting credits, so that he could rake in the lion's share of the royalties, that no established composers wanted anything to do with him. Neither did he do himself any favours by lashing out at the mediocrity of modern 'pop-song' writers, and telling *Melody Maker*, when asked to explain why he had been as popular in his heyday as Tommy Steele and Cliff Richard were now, 'I don't know. I suppose I used to be what Cliff Richard is now – not very good, but what the public wanted.'

The two songs which George chose for his studio comeback, but which ended up being his last were, in comparison with his *grandes oeuvres*, no better than the pop ditties he had condemned. Indeed, their importance in the immensely rich and varied Formby catalogue may be determined by the *manner* in which they were recorded – in just ten minutes, with George not even bothering to remove his hat and coat, and leaving the studio without waiting to hear if the takes were of an acceptable standard. Of the two, 'Banjo Boy' is perhaps the more passable, with a jaunty ambience faintly reminiscent of the unsurpassable Formby style. 'Happy Go Lucky Me', on the other hand, is a contradiction of terms if ever there was one, for George sounds anything but. Every chuckle in the voice, an integral and natural element prevalent in his work for over three decades, is not simply contrived, but embarrassing – a pathetic, uninspired swansong to a mighty recording legacy. 'I would rather never work again and let people remember me the way I was, than disappoint them now,' he told the press after the record had been released, and many of his fans believe that he should have applied this maxim *before* cutting this final disc.

On 4 June 1960, George opened in *The Time Of Your Life* at the Queen's Theatre, Blackpool. He should have been sharing top-billing with Jimmy Clitheroe, but Beryl complained about this to the producer, Ross Taylor. The pipe-voiced little comic therefore had his part in the revue cropped to make way for George's infamous but horrendous parrot jokes, and the tenor Toni Dalli was brought in at the last moment. Glamour came in the shapely form of Yana, a busty, sultry-voiced chanteuse famous for her fish-tail dresses, whose hits in England included 'I Need You' and 'Mr Wonderful', both of which were incorporated into the flimsy plot.

George fell for Yana in a big way. She performed her showpiece number, 'Climb Up The Garden Wall', sitting on a swing surrounded by an ocean of artificial flowers. Blatantly lesbian and with a huge gay following, she was living at the time with an American actress, though George did not know this. Neither did he realise, until it was almost too late, that Yana was deliberately leading him on – interested not in the

215

tired, prematurely aged man who was making a last desperate attempt to recapture his lost youth, but in his very healthy bank-balance.

Despite the hefty £1,500 a week fee, George insisted that he would only sing for twenty minutes, immediately before the interval. After some arguing with Ross Taylor, he then agreed that he would appear in some sketches with the other artists, and that his spot could be moved to the end of the show. The latter change came after an objection from Yana, who claimed that if George closed the first half, the audience would simply begin vacating the theatre. George then threatened to pull out of the show altogether when told that, in keeping with BBC tradition, the audience would be admitted free for the performance of 14 July, which was to be televised. 'It's not that I object to people getting summat for nowt,' he told the *Blackpool Gazette*'s Brian Hargreaves, a young man who had replaced the recently deceased Sylvia as his most preferred journalist, 'but I am against all those civic dignitaries and scroungers who wouldn't normally give me light of day if they had to pay to get in.' He then upset the rest of the cast by refusing to turn up for rehearsals, declaring that these would only overtire him, which of course was true, and that in any case he had been singing most of the songs in his programme for so long that there was no need. 'Just stick a lamp post on the stage, and I'll do the rest when the time comes,' he told the producer.

Several people *did* storm out of the theatre, however, during George's second performance when, between 'Lamp Post' and 'Happy Go Lucky Me', he pointed to a young woman sitting in the front row and announced that he would like to dedicate a limerick to her:

> *There was a young man called Vickers,*
> *Who took his girlfriend to the flickers,*
> *He saw some white wool and he started to pull,*
> *And that's how the girl lost her – hankie!*

The Time Of Your Life broke all box-office records at the Queen's Theatre, and instead of closing in September it was extended by two months. The entrepreneur Jimmy Brennan, who had booked George for this show, had no trouble at all signing him up for a repeat season for the summer of 1961 . . . Beryl was not around to complicate matters. He also consented to an in-depth interview with Brian Hargreaves – the first *ever* when Beryl would not be present to vet his answers or reply on his behalf. At the last moment Hargreaves fell ill, but George was just as candid with his stand-in, Michael Berry:

BERRY: *No other British comedian has topped the bill for as long as you have. Why have you managed to remain an established star for such a long time?*

GEORGE: *Because I've never overworked myself and let the public see too much of me. It's foolish how some of these newer comics are on television so often. No matter how good you are, the public don't want to see your face every time they switch on the television.*

BERRY: *Would you call yourself an artist of inter-national appeal?*

GEORGE: *[laughs] I've performed in every country but Russia and China and I haven't had any eggs thrown at me yet!*

BERRY: *You have a reputation for being an extremely rich man . . .*

GEORGE: *I usually say 'I'm comfortably off' to that question, but I'll tell you this. During my career I've earned over £1 million . . . and I've paid out £300,000 in income tax.*

BERRY: *How would you describe your type of comedy?*

GEORGE: *Natural. I never have to be anything but myself when I go on stage . . .*

BERRY: *And what type of comedian appeals to you the most?*

GEORGE: *Straightforward, uncomplicated stuff. Jimmy James. Morecambe and Wise . . .*

BERRY: *And no blue jokes. Why is this?*

GEORGE: *Because it's not necessary. If you can't make people laugh without being vulgar, then it's about time you packed it in.*

BERRY: *Which is your favourite medium – films, television, or the stage?*

GEORGE: *The stage every time. You can get another chance the next night if you make a mistake – you only get once chance on television. And when I see myself in my old films, I always think I'd like to have another go at them and do them better.*

BERRY: *George, do you smoke or drink?*

GEORGE: *[cigarette in one hand, tumbler of whisky in the other] Both, but not a great deal, ha-ha!*

BERRY: *Throughout your career, your wife Beryl has accompanied you everywhere and managed your affairs. Has this been one of the contributory factors to your success?*

GEORGE: *Beryl and I have always been a team. As far as my career is concerned, I would not be where I am today if it had not been for her help.*

This latter observation, of course, cannot be reiterated often enough, though by now George and Beryl were no longer the team they had once been. She missed more of the Blackpool performances than she attended – initially through illness, but later on account of her unacceptable behaviour, which saw her actually being banned from entering the theatre. Beryl fell into drunken, violent rages more often than not sparked off by the latest reports on George's amorous activities from resident

'spy', Harry Scott. 'For almost thirty years, George's lackey –
and that's *all* he was, *never* a friend – had been waiting too
jump into bed with Beryl,' Irene Bevan said, 'and the mere
thought of George doing the same thing when *he* never
achieved his own goal drove the pathetic little man half out of
his head with jealousy.'

George's relationship with Yana cannot be denied. The
couple were observed checking into hotels not just in Blackpool, on his doorstep, but in Manchester and later in Bristol.
There is however some doubt as to how long they had been an
item. Though Scott does not refer to Yana by name in his
heavily ghosted memoirs – she was still alive at the time – he
leaves us with no doubts about her identity, and also states that
the affair had been going strong for two *years*:

> *When Beryl wasn't around she used to go to his dressing-room
> and cheer him up, but she never went near George when Beryl
> was there. While they were playing together at one particular
> theatre during the time that Beryl's health started to fail, after
> the evening's show George used to take this lady back to the
> flat she had rented. Beryl knew that he had struck up this
> friendship with this girl, whose talent and youthful beauty
> had captured his imagination. George told her so himself. Yet
> all Beryl had said was, 'Let him play, he's only like a big boy,
> really!' And she forgave him. Mrs Formby was, I think,
> tempering her fierce love and jealousy with unexpected
> tolerance. Her ill health was making 'Our Beryl' an even
> sweeter and more understanding person than before.*

If the latter part of Scott's diatribe *was* true – not an easy
conclusion to reach when one considers his almost manic
affection for Beryl – then George had exacted the ultimate
revenge on his wife, flaunting in her face his affair with a much
younger, much prettier woman, and doing so whilst the person
to whom he owed absolutely everything was virtually on her

deathbed. Taking into consideration George's track-record for being British show-business's archetypal 'easy-going chap', one cannot begin to imagine that he could have acted with such calculating cruelty . . . or indeed that, if he had confessed all to Beryl, she would have forgiven him, given her own jaundiced temperament. On the other hand, one must also consider the fact that for thirty-six years this indomitable woman had ruled the Formby roost like a Spartan tyrant – granting George neither his freedom to enjoy the fruit of his labours, nor the requisites of a normal and healthy marriage. It may well be that he had had no alternative but to seize upon this final moment of weakness to burst free of his chains. Perhaps one can come to this conclusion: Beryl had been pushing George towards taking his revenge for years, and despite the bad timing she should have counted her blessings that this had not happened much sooner.

Michael Berry is thought to have asked George about his 'friendship' with Yana, but to have been requested not to print the reply. Another subject touched upon in his interview for the *Gazette* was the rumour that a film was about to be made about George's rise to fame, with Tommy Steele, already a big star at twenty-three, in the title role. 'And why not?' George had posed, 'he can be made to look like me. He's got the same mouth – though whether he can master a Northern accent's another matter, of course.' The venture is said to have been scuppered by a statement from Beryl, 'If George does make the film, it will be properly handled because *I'll* be on the set at all times to make sure the project runs smoothly.' Ill or not, Beryl's name was still a by-word for terror in show-business circles.

George saw quite a lot of Pat Howson during these anxious months when he had absolutely no one else to turn to. In September, Beryl was rushed to the La Sagesse Convent Hospital, where she lay at death's door for a week. By the end of the month, however, she had discharged herself. The doctors had told her the truth – that she would be lucky to live beyond the end of the year – and her greatest wish was that she should die, 'religion-free', in her own bed at home.

In November 1960, George sang in public for the last time at the Grand Order of Water Rats Ball, at London's Dorchester Hotel. Afterwards he spoke to reporters about his enthusiasm for the future. The film-project with Tommy Steele had been cancelled, but he had received another offer, and he was also looking forward to his pantomime season in Bristol. Having failed to secure him for the tour circuit, Harold Fielding had persuaded George to star in *Aladdin*, playing Mr Wu, at the Hippodrome. At the ABC studios in Manchester, George had also filmed three short introductions to 'I See Ice', 'Spare A Copper' and 'Turned Out Nice Again'. These would be used during the *Formby Festival*, a retrospective of his films to be screened by the BBC during the winter.

On 16 December what is generally regarded as George's greatest performance – it was certainly his most sincere – was broadcast on BBC Television's acclaimed *Friday Show* . . . effectively, a virtual tête-à-tête containing the laughter, and the tears, of the finest singing clown Britain had ever produced. Like a sad, tired old man reliving his life whilst drowning in a sea of nostalgia, he summed up his whole existence in just thirty-five minutes, and sang nine songs in what we now know he intended to be his farewell performance.

The show is in some ways reminiscent of the later *Elvis 68 Special*, and the autobiographical recitals which Marlene Dietrich had just begun giving around the world. The backdrop is simple but effective: the door, surrounded by lights and surmounted with the massive 'Mr Formby' logo, through which George enters in silhouette to sing several songs and tell a few anecdotes, before transferring to the intimacy of a mock sitting-room, then lastly the inevitable street scene complete with lamp post.

George ambles on, looking a little plumper and occasion-ally sounding breathless, instantly creating an ambience of

radiant sincerity. 'No girls, no dancers, no acrobats, no con-
jurers, not even a guest star,' he says. 'Just me and the uke.
But I'm going to tell you a few home truths I've never told in
public before.'

And he does. Coughing every now and then, George cheer-
fully recalls his first film, and its world premiere – at Burslem,
near Stoke-on-Trent:

> *Oo, and it was a lousy picture! It was so dark in places you
> had to strike matches to see it. The courting couples liked it,
> though!*

He speaks of his roots:

> *Of course, most people know that I was born in Wigan. And
> don't say 'It serves you right!' because I'm very proud of
> Wigan. Every time I drive through it in the car I raise my
> hand and say, 'Thanks very much, Wigan!'*

He bemoans his lack of education and urges youngsters
watching him not to follow his example. Then before singing
'Goodnight Little Fellows Goodnight', he ruefully confesses
that this particular number always makes him feel sad, because
he has never been blessed with children of his own. He
dismisses his first stage appearance: 'Three minutes, died the
death of a dog!' Then he jokes about his inability to write music
or tune his ukes, and about failing his wartime medical:

> *That was the biggest laugh I ever got in my life. When I
> stripped off, I never knew I'd flat feet. And the doctor looked
> at me: he gave me a shilling, and he gave me a card which
> said I was Grade Four. I didn't even get in the first three!*

He praises Beryl . . .

> *I married her, and that was when my luck turned . . . I shall*

always be grateful to Beryl for doing all the business for me. Of course it'd take me a month to tell you all the things Beryl's done for me. Some other time, probably.

. . . but most especially his father, wiping away a tear whilst in the background we hear Formby Sr's 1907 recording of 'Standing At The Corner Of The Street'.

I think he went the way he wanted to do . . . in harness. He was a great fella, you know . . . he certainly was a great star. I don't think I'll ever be as good as him.

And finally he defines his impression of stardom:

People say to me, 'How did you become a star?' Huh, that's a daft question! I mean, what do we do? We don't do anything. We don't become stars. You people make us stars. We wouldn't be any good without you. And our present stars today, if they believe anything different, they're crazy! I shall always be grateful to the public for what they've done for me . . .

Beryl watched the programme with Harry Scott and his wife, on a bedside television set in her room. Scott cloyingly recalled an improbable scenario, how Beryl had treated the occasion like a gala premiere, taking half an hour to put on her make-up, saying, 'I must make myself up nice for George,' then selecting her best pink satin bed-jacket and most expensive jewels:

Gone, at least for the time being, were those heavy shadows under Beryl's eyes. Gone too was the pallor . . . the trans- formation, the excitement bubbling away like champagne, and the light sparkling in her eyes made me forget for a moment or two that she was so tragically ill. The scene was George's. The star was Beryl, for I will never forget the gentle

*smile on her face as she shared with her husband his quips
and his seriousness . . . She was always George's severest
critic, but back in those eyes that refused to mirror the pain of
her suffering came the unswerving admiration, understanding
and love she had always had for George.*

Again, one finds it impossible to imagine that Beryl could have
shown such demonstrativeness for a husband who, only weeks
before, had told her to her face that he had a mistress. Equally,
George seems to have made a Herculean effort *not* to be at
Fairhaven when the end came. For the last three years he had
refused to do pantomime, claiming that he was following his
doctor's instructions and that the medium would prove far too
strenuous for his own failing health. During his last Blackpool
season, he had been offered his usual £1,000 a week, plus a cut
of the profits, for a 'stress-free' pantomime season in Liverpool,
within easy driving distance of his home . . . only to turn this
down and *accept* the one in Bristol for just £600 a week. And it
was here, during rehearsals on 21 December – minutes after
singing the ironically appropriate 'Why Don't Women Like
Me?' to Yana, who was standing in the wings – that he received
a call from Fairhaven, informing him that Beryl had lapsed into
the coma from which she would never emerge.

The *Alladin* premiere went ahead, even though two hours
before curtain-up George had received a second call, from
Beryl's doctor, stating that she might not make it through the
night. After the performance, he spent several minutes signing
autographs in his dressing room. Then, instead of attending the
party in the theatre's Green Room, he climbed into his car –
despite being urged not to do so by Yana, who was terrified that
the stress of driving over such a long distance, so soon after his
performance, might bring about another coronary – and
headed *not* for his own home, but to the Warrington home of
Fred and Jessica Bailey, two old friends who owned a grocer's
shop in the town. It was here, at just after two in the morning

– Christmas Day – that he was informed that Beryl had passed away half an hour earlier.

George's reaction to his wife's death may be gathered from the business-like expediency with which he, who had hardly ever had to organise anything in his life, consciously mapped out the next few days. The news was included in radio and television bulletins throughout Christmas Day, and the next morning Harry Scott and George's London agent, Henry Foster, spent several hours calling friends and colleagues. Beryl's funeral, astonishingly, had been arranged to take place the next day and it emerged that she, an agnostic, had requested not only that there should be no religious service and no spot should mark her final resting-place.

George would not agree to the former, but he saw to the latter by having Beryl cremated, and insisted that her ashes be scattered 'with everybody else's' in the rose garden at Lytham St Annes Park Crematorium. George's wreath was simply inscribed, 'Goodbye, pal'.

Just one hour after leaving the crematorium, George returned to Bristol for the next afternoon's matinee of *Aladdin*. 'He's missed four performances already,' Henry Foster told the *Daily Express*'s show-business editor, Michael Walsh. 'He can't afford to miss any more!' George himself was asked by Walsh, who called him that evening at the theatre, why there had been no show-business personalities at Beryl's funeral. His excuse was a muttered, 'Because there were no newspapers to publish that she'd died, and because they all had commitments up and down the country.' This of course was untrue. Such was the dislike that this woman had inspired amongst virtually every-one who had come into contact with George that not one of these people had wished to be accused of hypocrisy by attending her funeral – or by sending flowers.

George soldiered on with *Aladdin* until 14 January, when he was forced to pull out of the production with a heavy cold which, he was warned, could easily develop into pneumonia.

He left Bristol – and Yana – early the next morning and drove the five hours back to Fairhaven, where he immediately contacted Pat Howson. Two days later, when his condition remained unchanged, she called his doctor and he was admitted to Blackpool's Victoria Hospital, where he stayed until the end of the month. He was so desperately ill that at one stage the hospital priest, Father Lakeham, thought of administering the last rites.

George's first visitors, once he had started to rally a little, were two small boys who had walked all the way from Preston, they said, to bring him chocolates. He was touched by the gesture. What he never knew was that the boys had stolen the money for the gift from a charity collection-box. Not only this, when the pair were brought before the Juvenile Panel a few days later, they were further charged with breaking into a number of shops and warehouses, and sent to a remand home.

During George's hospitalisation, Pat visited him every day, and the switchboard was instructed not to put any calls through to his room from Yana. The singer confessed to friends that her romance with George had been but a 'sugar-daddy fill-in' during the temporary rift with her female lover, and that she did not wish to be held responsible for him 'fucking himself towards another heart attack'. She was now also saying that George had proposed to her in Bristol, and that he was about to take steps to remove all memories of his late wife from his life by putting his house on the market and getting rid of Beryl's things. She added that George had 'cursed himself for being too good a Catholic', in that he had never tried to escape his living hell of the last two years by leaving Beryl, an atheist who had always mocked his faith.

The marriage proposal could have been pure invention, though the rest of Yana's statement was only too true. George actually discharged himself from the hospital, telling the nurse, 'I'm off home, lass, for a decent cup of tea!', so that he could organise the sale of Beryldene. And the next day, accompanied by Pat, he began searching for somewhere else to live. He settled on Clock House, a run-down property in Lea Town, near Preston – not far from the Howsons – and immediately brought in a team of builders to get the place renovated.

On 13 February, almost certainly on the rebound after dumping Yana, George called his journalist friend Brian Hargreaves, and announced that he was going to marry Pat Howson:

I was too shy to ask Pat herself, so I popped the question to her dad instead. A chap like me needs company. I don't think it's strange me proposing like this, and I don't think the public will begrudge me a little happiness late in life. I'm hopeless in the house and I can't leave everything to my valet, Harry Scott. And Pat and me are *already the best of friends!*

The engagement was announced to the public the next morning – St Valentine's Day, and Pat's thirty-sixth birthday – when pictures of the happy couple appeared on the front pages of most of the national newspapers. George had not had the time to buy his fiancée an engagement ring, so he had given her the one which had belonged to his grandmother. The wedding, he said, would take place in May, and would be followed by a Mediterranean cruise. 'It's a fairytale come true,' he told the *Daily Mirror*'s Arthur Brooks, 'I really *do* feel like singing "Happy Go Lucky Me"!'

Yana, on the other hand, appears to have taken rejection badly, in spite of having been reunited with her lover. According to Harry Scott, the telephone at Beryldene had not stopped ringing that morning. 'In replying to one of the many calls,' Scott recalled, 'I heard George say, quite distinctly and with an unusually firm voice, "Well, you've had your chance, now you've had your chips!"'

In choosing Pat Howson for his future bride, George was of course clutching at straws. Beryl had kept him on a leash for so long that he had hardly ever enjoyed *any* kind of female company for as long as he could remember – towards the end she had even been jealous of his affection for the moribund Sylvia – so George was not in any position to discern between the gentler refinements of courtship and the slobberings of lust. The latter was probably the only thing that had attracted him to Yana, and would have been quite out of the question with the young schoolma'am from a decent family which upheld all the moral sensibilities of the Catholic church . . . and who therefore almost certainly would not have made herself available for what George often referred to as 'hanky-panky' until after they were married.

George's greatest enemy, too, even more than the wife he had loathed in latter years, was the one commodity he now knew he had so little of – time. On many occasions he had dismissed his family – in particular his mother – as 'bloody scroungers', and as he had explained to Brian Hargreaves, he appeared to have developed a paranoia that his fortune would very soon end up in undeserving hands. And who else was there to lean upon but this wholly unselfish woman to whom he had confided so many of his most pressing problems – the only person who had been allowed to visit him in hospital, apart from the two boy fans, when he had truly thought himself at death's door?

Pat was sitting next to George a few days later when he offloaded his ultimate *mea culpa* on the *Daily Express*'s Michael Walsh. For the first time the *public* learned that his marriage to Beryl had been little more than a charade. 'For the last fifteen years we did not live as man and wife,' he told Walsh. 'We tried to keep drink away from her, but the damage was done. The public had built up a certain picture of us and I had no wish to spoil the illusion of that.' Adding that Beryl's atheism had clashed with his faith, and that each time he had wanted to go to church there had been a tremendous row, he concluded, 'My life with Beryl was hell.'

The excitement caused by his engagement, followed by the repercussions of this last confession, proved too much for George. On 22 February he suffered a heart attack whilst having dinner with the Howsons at their Penwortham home. The fact that a doctor lived only three doors away and that he was able to administer emergency treatment whilst an ambulance was on its way saved George's life, but only just. For the second time in weeks he was given the last rites, and his solicitor, John Crowther, was summoned to his bedside at Preston's St Joseph's RC Hospital.

George's main concern was that his house at Fairhaven be sold as quickly as possible, even at a loss, before he died. He had no intention, he vowed, of leaving this world whilst even the slightest vestige of Beryl's existence remained in his life. Pat, however, instructed Crowther *not* to inform anyone that the Great Formby was dying, as George wanted him to do. As a result a simple statement was issued to the press: 'Mr Formby is poorly, but he is in more need of a good long rest than anything. There is nothing to worry about.'

It did not take George's family, nor Harry Scott, very long to work out that the end was fast approaching, and as had happened with Yana, the nursing staff at the hospital received strict instructions to keep these people away from him. 'They're nothing but a load of money-grabbers,' he told John Crowther, who would soon prove just as grasping as they were. 'If it's left to them they'll pinch my shroud before my body's cold. I want nothing to do with any of them.'

On Saturday morning, three days after George's heart attack, and still clinging to a decidedly flimsy precognitive dream – the fact that all really will turn out well in the end, as long as this is what one wishes – Pat, assisted by the matron, the Reverend Mother Ignatius, granted a press-conference at the hospital, and the reporters who turned up agreed unanimously that *this* sincere, warm-hearted young woman was anything but a gold-digger, as the Booths had branded her.

'I'm happier about his condition today than at any time since he came in here,' she announced. 'George is very cheerful. He's now sitting up and can enjoy radio or TV if he so wishes. He's not likely to leave hospital in the immediate future – we expect him to be here for another two weeks at least. After that we'll be going somewhere where it's reasonably peaceful. And after our wedding in May – no exact details yet, I'm afraid – we'll probably be going for a long sea cruise. George has been told that he must rest for nine months.'

The end came peacefully, nine days later, during the late afternoon of Monday 6 March 1961. Pat was at his bedside, holding his hand. That morning she had gone out and bought her wedding-ring . . . we now know that the couple had decided to bring the ceremony forward to 8 March, so that it could take place before news of it leaked out to George's family. A hospital spokeswoman described George's last moments:

> *Mr Formby had asked to be married on the Wednesday and the hospital priest, Father Lakeham, had agreed to conduct the bedside ceremony. Mr Formby had especially demanded that no one else be told. It was whilst the couple were discussing this – Mr Formby's voice was raised and angry – that he suddenly began coughing. Then his head fell forwards. Father Lakeham, attending a patient in a nearby ward, was summoned at once, whilst Reverend Mother Ignatius and the [chest] specialist, Doctor Geake, attempted but failed to revive him. A moment later, Father Lakeham administered the Last Rites.*

It seems sadly but inevitably apt that a man who had spent the better part of his life sheltered from a rapacious family by a wife most of them had disliked – simply because she had been sufficiently astute to see through them and keep them at bay – should have died criticising them, and in such a hurry to divorce himself, financially, from them by wedding the woman he loved. Had he lived but two more days, the wedding would have taken place and saved Pat from a great deal of unnecessary pain and strife.

'All he ever wanted was for us to be happy,' Pat would say a few years later, in a radio interview. 'I can understand why the people jumped to all the wrong conclusions, but I never understood why they never gave us the benefit of the doubt. Ours *could* have been a nice story. Strange circumstances do occur with people, but we were just the *victims* of circumstance.'

The obituaries were legion, though George was perhaps best summed up by his friend, the *Blackpool Gazette*'s Brian Hargreaves:

The sudden death of George Formby is the more tragic because most people had the idea that he was over the worst. But the heart is a strange and unpredictable organ, and in spite of all possible medical care he went out like a candle in a sudden wind. So the last chord is strummed, and the last song sung. Blackpool, Lancashire and Britain as a whole are sad at the passing of a native comedian who came up the hard way and, in spite of his success and wealth, never had an easy life. Yet he was still, in essence, an unspoilt Lancashire lad.

BUNKUM'S TRAVELLING SHOW

'The tragedy is that a man who gave so much pleasure to others was not allowed the time to taste a little himself.'
David Nathan, film critic, *Daily Herald*.

For those who genuinely cared about George, mourning him was marred by a greedy family squabbling over his not in-considerable fortune. Just two *hours* after George died, his mother, now eighty-two and almost blind, called the *Blackpool Gazette* from her Liverpool home and announced, 'I don't care what *she* says. *We'll* be bringing George home here tomorrow, and he'll be buried in the family grave at Warrington.'

This attack was wholly unnecessary, and of course an exercise in supremacy on Eliza's part. George had always expressed a wish to be buried with his father, and Pat had known this. What she did not expect, either, was a call from his mother warning her to stay away from George's funeral.

Pat ignored the threat, assuming that Eliza's grief had affected her sensibility. When she turned up at the Booth House in Sefton Park, however, she realised that Eliza had meant every word. The undertaker Bruce Williams (aka the songwriter, Eddie Latta) had been given explicit instructions not to allow 'George's floosie' to ride in any of the limousines paid for by the family. She subsequently travelled in her parents' car, a dozen or so vehicles behind the main cortège. She was also requested, very loudly by George's sister, Ethel, not to sit on the same side as the family in the church. What the Booths could not prevent, though, was Pat's cross of deep red roses laying next to the family's one of pink and white carnations on top of George's simple oak coffin. It was inscribed, 'Now and always – Pat.'

George's funeral, on 10 March remains the largest there has ever been in Britain for a show-business personality. Over 150,000 people lined the two-mile route from the chapel of rest to St Charles' Roman Catholic Church, where the Requiem Mass was officiated by Monsignor Francis Chaloner. Traffic was reduced to a virtual crawl as the cortège set off on the twenty-mile journey to Warrington. Eliza Booth was so overcome with emotion that she had to be supported much of the time by her sons, Ted and Frank, who had seen little if anything of George in recent years. Most eyes were focused not on them, however – or Pat, who had been rudely shoved to the back of the crowd clustered around the graveside – but on George's sixteen-year-old Lakeland terrier, Willie Waterbucket, who had accompanied his master on his last journey sitting on Harry Scott's knee, and who whined inconsolably whilst the coffin was being lowered into the ground.

The entertainment world was represented by Ronnie Hilton, Jimmy Clitheroe, and Billy Matchett, who was there on behalf of the Grand Order of Water Rats. Eric Dobell represented the Variety Artists' Federation, the body which had caused George and Beryl such anguish during the war. There were wreaths from Yana, Beryl Reid, Arthur Askey, Gracie Fields, Tommy Trinder and a host of others.

Just forty minutes after George had been laid to rest the Booths – having first ensured that Pat was *en route* for Preston – convened an emergency meeting with George's solicitor, John Crowther, in a Warrington café, and demanded to know the contents of his will. Shortly afterwards, having learned that, aside from a £5,000 bequest to Harry Scott, Pat Howson had been made George's sole beneficiary – but not yet wishing for this to be made public – Ted Booth issued a statement through the *Blackpool Gazette*:

> *We cannot officially say what is in the will until I get a copy from the solicitor tomorrow. But if the will is disadvantageous to our family, we shall certainly contest it. My main consideration is that Mother should be well-provided for. We did hear that George had revoked his first will not very long before he died. George was a very sick man.*

This closing phrase, 'George was a very sick man', intimating more, of course, than mere physical illness, would be bandied about courtrooms and solicitors' offices for several years.

On the evening of Saturday 11 March, the day after George's funeral, Pat and Father Lakeham, the priest who had been present at his deathbed, organised a remembrance for his soul at Preston's St Wilfrid's Catholic Church . . . and despite their appalling treatment of her, George's family were invited. Not one of them turned up. That morning the contents of Beryl's will had been published and it was revealed that John Crowther had been holding on to this information since two weeks *before* George's death. It now appeared that the £25,000 left by George's wife would be going straight to Pat Howson.

Matters were further complicated when Crowther revealed that George had made *three* wills in as many months:

> *Will No. 1:* Dated 19 December 1960, the same day as Beryl's, wherein the couple bequeathed their entire estate to each other.
>
> *Will No. 2:* Dated 18 January 1961, wherein George bequeathed £5,000 each to Eliza Booth and Harold Scothron (Harry Scott), £1,000 to Lily Ashton (Beryl's last private nurse), and the 'residue' to his three sisters.

Will No. 3: Dated 23 February 1961, wherein George bequeathed £5,000 to Harry Scott, and the 'residue' to Ada Patricia Howson.

Two days later, on Monday morning Eliza, accompanied by her daughters Ethel, Louisa and Mary, went to see her lawyer, John Cowper and announced that she would be contesting George's third will. She added that she was doing so only very reluctantly, having been outraged because her son had snubbed his sisters. Ethel then told Cowper that, as the family's spokeswoman, she too was 'devastated' that George had shown such disdain towards the woman who had brought him into the world. Nothing whatsoever was mentioned about George's brothers. Within the hour, Cowper had applied for a caveat to be filed with the London High Court which would prevent probate from being released from George's estate until an agreement had been reached between Pat Howson and the Booths. Both parties were subsequently given until 25 August to settle their differences and prevent the matter from being brought before a judge.

Pat tried her utmost to placate the angry relatives, though she was neither legally nor morally obliged to do so. She attempted to call Eliza to arrange an informal meeting, only to be rewarded with a torrent of abuse. Her solicitor then advised the Booths that though she was not obliged to do so, his client would be willing to pay Eliza the £5,000 which George had obviously intended her to have at the time he had signed his second will, in addition to which *she* would personally ensure that his sisters would be generously provided for by giving them £2,000 each.

Eliza neither accepted nor rejected Pat's offer, but when John Cowper's caveat expired on 25 August she applied for a seven day extension. 'I need to think the matter over,' she told the press. This was refused by Pat, who told the same reporter – George's pal, Brian Hargreaves, 'The family have already had three months to consider my offer, and seeing as they don't appear to be able to make up their minds, the offer's been withdrawn. I've done my best to avoid a lot of trouble, and this is something of a bombshell. I suppose that it will mean court action and no doubt some unpleasantness, but otherwise I'm not in the least worried.'

Upon hearing this, Eliza at once announced that she had *every* intention of suing George's fiancée for every penny he had left her, even when told that it might take another year for the case to reach the courts. The fact that she could well be dead by this time did not perturb her in the least, she declared, because her daughters would still fight 'that fucking little floosie schoolma'am with their last breath'.

The sale of George's effects, ordered by John Crowther in his capacity as the executor of his estate, opened at Fairhaven on 20 June 1961, and went on for three days. A huge marquee was erected in the garden and a catalogue was printed detailing 1,007 items, much of this household furnishings and bric-á-brac of little value save that it had formerly belonged to George Formby. One lot comprised 'a walking stick, toilet-brush and holder, two truncheons and a shillelagh', another an empty oil drum upon which he had carved his initials, and a wine-bin filled with coal which fetched £200. There was a huge collection of clothes, jewellery, glassware, china and furs which had belonged to Beryl, and over a thousand articles of George's clothing, mostly unworn, several original paintings, and George's most recent Bentley which only had 2,200 miles on the clock.

For many, of course, the most important – and touching – items to come under the hammer were fifteen of George's ukuleles, several of which had been autographed by him and labelled with song-titles he had recorded with them, such as the 'Mr Wu' and the 'Windows'. Two were purchased on behalf of George's brother, Frank, by his wife, who outbid the skiffle-singer, Lonnie Donegan. 'They need to be cherished by us, his loved ones,' she told the *Blackpool Gazette*. What she did not add was that George had not spoken to her or her husband for over twenty years, and that like most of his family they had never been welcomed at the various Beryldenes.

Prior to the auction, Beryldene was thrown open to the public, and amongst the first to arrive were George's sisters, accompanied by Harry Scott, each of whom asked for 'a little something to remember him by'. Pat told them, sharply and quite rightly, that if anything caught their eye they would be at liberty to put in a bid the same as anyone else. Ethel would eventually pay £380 for a Jacobean dining-suite and a bedroom suite, telling the press. 'We had to borrow the money from friends, but we wanted to keep *some* of George's things in the family.' Scott bought Beryl's television and the bed she had died in.

Another interested party, of little consequence at the time but immensely so, today, was the George Formby Society, formed just two weeks previously by a fan, Bill Logan, who had travelled down from Carlisle hoping to buy ukuleles, photographs and other memorabilia so that his 50-strong group might perpetuate their idol's memory. Logan purchased six ukes, a gold-topped walking cane, and several other items.

The house itself was sold for £9,000 – less than George had paid for it to Josef Locke – to a female buyer who asked not to be named, but who was later revealed to be a Mrs Murray. George's yacht, *Lady Beryl II*, was sold back to Windboats, in Norfolk, for £5,500, the same amount paid for his Bentley by an Isle of Man hotelier. In all, the sale realised £22,430. Pat had not, however, allowed John Crowther to sell everything. £20,000 worth of Beryl's jewellery and George's four favourite ukuleles were set aside to be sold separately because, she claimed, George had wanted her to have them. She kept the ukes, but sold the jewellery at Sotheby's and placed the money in a 'kitty' which she had opened to pay for the court case.

The hearing opened on 13 May 1963 at the London High

Court, and was presided over by Justice Ormrod. Eliza and her daughters – described by one newspaper as 'acting and looking like a quartet of rowdy old washerwomen' – were publicly objecting to George's third will and about to gain themselves reputations for being not merely greedy, but downright nasty towards their kinsman's memory. John Cowper, their lawyer, told the court:

> *The substance of my clients' plea is that the testator, Mr Formby, was not of sound mind, memory or understanding at the time he executed his will. The previous day Mr Formby had suffered a coronary thrombosis. He was treated with drugs and therefore in consequence unable to understand the nature of the act of making a will or the extent of his property, or the claims upon his testamentary bounty to which he ought to give effect. Therefore the will of 18 January must stand.*

John Crowther, George's solicitor and now Pat's representative, strongly opposed this statement when he took the stand. 'I myself was present when he signed his third will,' he told the court, pausing to glare at Eliza Booth. 'Mr Formby was bright, cheerful and alert. There is no doubt in my mind that he knew what he was doing. I'm Mr Formby's sole executor, I receive no benefit under this will, but I still intend to prove its validity by way of my counsel, Mr James Fitzhugh.'

Fitzhugh's testimony was much more hard-hitting. He had been reminded beforehand to take into consideration Eliza Booth's age and infirmity, but he flatly ignored Justice Ormrod's instructions in this respect. To his way of thinking – not just in his capacity as counsel, but a Formby fan – if Eliza Booth could desecrate her son's memory by virtually implying that he had been insane towards the end of his life, she would have to be capable of withstanding the consequences:

> *It is of my opinion that the third will should stand. When the*

second will was made, Mr Crowther suggested to Mr Formby that the mother should share residue with the sisters, but Mr Formby replied that he had well-provided for her and had bought her a block of flats. About this time, Mr Formby was trying to persuade Miss Howson to marry him. He even took her to a doctor, who felt able to tell Miss Howson she would not be marrying an invalid. Mr Formby told Mr Crowther that he intended to marry Miss Howson soon, even if he was still in hospital, and wanted to leave everything to her. After some hesitation Mr Formby said, 'Let Harry have his £5,000 – if he's still in my employment.' But he said he had provided for his mother in her lifetime, and that he did not want his sisters to have anything. He made certain disparaging remarks – describing the family as a set of scroungers. Mr Crowther then asked if Miss Howson should receive the money only if they married. Mr Formby's response to this was most emphatic. If he were to die tomorrow, he wanted Pat to have everything. She had brought him more happiness than he had ever known before.

Fitzhugh's diatribe upset Eliza and her daughters so much that Justice Ormrod was forced to adjourn the hearing for an hour whilst they were treated for shock. Many of the press simply put this down to play-acting, particularly when Eliza used the period to tell reporters that George had never bought her anything in his life, let alone a block of flats – these, she declared, she had purchased herself with the money from her husband's estate, though she had unfortunately lost the documents to prove it. Strangely, her lawyer did not bring up this point when the hearing resumed, though he did ask the court to question what James Fitzhugh had meant by the term 'well-provided for' – arguing that upon his rise to fame during the early Twenties George had begun paying his mother a weekly allowance of 50 shillings, and that she had still been receiving the same amount at the time of his death. Fitzhugh's response was that George *would* have increased his mother's allowance had it not been for her 'persistent greed and insistence that, as she had brought him into the world, so he should continue paying her for the privilege. Fitzhugh again used the term, 'set of scroungers', the headline which was splashed across the *Daily Mail* the next day. And to add weight to his argument, he held aloft a bundle of letters – for once composed in George's handwriting and not Beryl's – and concluded:

> *I am not suggesting for one moment that these letters show that the description of scroungers is applied to Mr Formby's family. What they do show is that some members of the family sought help from him and that he had a certain resentment that greater demands were made upon him than ought to have been . . .*

Upon hearing this, Justice Ormrod declared that the proceedings should be adjourned yet again owing to 'the distressed state of Mrs Booth'. Before the hearing resumed the next morning, however, he agreed to a private meeting in his chambers with Pat Howson and John Crowther, during which the pair proposed a compromise. Should the Booths publicly renounce their offensive earlier statement that George had not been of sound mind when signing his final will, Pat would grant Eliza a non-negotiable, one off payment of £5,000 – the amount George had left her in his earlier will – and she would pay her daughters £2,000 each, itself a considerable gesture, she concluded, bearing in mind that George had not wanted them to have anything at all. Pat also agreed that the legal costs for both parties would be paid out of the Formby estate.

Eliza accepted the deal without hesitation, but her daughters initially elected to continue with their action against Pat. Justice Ormrod, however, instructed them that this was a 'take it or leave it' offer, that Pat's attitude throughout the hearing had been 'right and proper' whilst theirs had been anything but, and that if they did decide to pursue the case, they would be responsible for their own costs – indeed, that a further hearing might order them to reimburse the Formby estate for the costs of this one. As with Eliza, all three accepted the deal.

Outside the court, Eliza and her daughters posed for the press – one photographer yelled, 'Which one of you is Ena Sharples?' – referring to the *Coronation Street* battleaxe – but all four declined to give interviews. Pat, linking arms with Sister Marie Burnard, a nun from the hospital where George had died, offered a brief statement to a reporter from the *Daily Mail*, telling him how she had been impressed by the previous day's headline, and adding, 'I'm not sure what I'm going to do with my life. I'll probably go back to teaching. I certainly shall never marry. I'll never find anyone like George. Everyone loved him. He was the most wonderful man I've ever met.' Pat also defended her decision to sell more of Beryl's jewellery – a heart-shaped diamond brooch, and a ruby and diamond bracelet which went under the hammer at Sotheby's for £15,000, money which she had immediately handed over to her lawyer. 'I still haven't received the whole of my inheritance,' she said, 'and the jewellery was of no use to anyone lying in a bank vault. This is the best way to find the cash to meet the fantastic costs of the lawsuit over George's will. It's what he would have wanted me to do.'

For another two years, George's mother and sisters – knowing that *they* would not be contributing to the legal costs – fought to have Justice Ormrod's decision over-ruled, and the matter was only conclusively settled, in Pat's favour, in September 1965 upon the intervention of the Solicitor-General, Sir Dingle Foot.

After this unpleasant, wholly unnecessary business, whilst the Booths continued in their attempts to impress a disbelieving world how much they had loved George – adding the far less likely theory that he also had loved them – Pat

241

Howson retired gracefully to her house in Preston, emerging only rarely from her enforced solitude for the odd media interview. On 10 March 1969, on the eve of a television tribute broadcast by Granada, she stringently denied the latest rumour cooked up by George's sister, Ethel – that, not only had she been sleeping with George whilst Beryl had been alive, she had been doing so since the age of fifteen. 'George didn't even *like* this particular sister,' Pat told the *Blackpool Gazette*. 'And if she adored him the way she says she did, then she ought to be ashamed of herself for trying to blacken his reputation in such a despicable manner. George told me that she had always been such a disgusting woman. Now can you see why he didn't want any of them to have his money?'

In the actual television programme, Pat paid the ultimate tribute to the man she loved. When asked by the presenter, Brian McGregor, *what* it was about George that she had fallen in love with, she replied:

> *First of all, it was tremendous sympathy. But above all it was his wonderful warmth, his tremendous humility, and his honesty. I don't just mean being humble. He must have known of his own greatness, but he did not spout about it. He just took himself for granted and he was so wonderful in his relations with other people . . . I have no regrets. Materially, I would have been saved a great deal of trouble if we had been married, but that is the only regret. I have no personal regrets at all.*

On 22 November 1971, Pat Howson died of cancer, aged just forty-six, in a Lytham nursing home. Almost at once a legal row blew up over *her* will – instigated by her estranged father and Ethel Booth, who told the *Daily Mail*'s Sydney Brennan, 'George's money had a jinx on it, I'm sure of that. If the fortune is restored to its rightful place, back to our family, this jinx will be lifted.'

In fact, there was not a great deal of George's bequest left to be argued over. The bulk of the original £135,000 had been swallowed up in legal costs and death duties, and Pat had bequeathed the remaining £20,000 to two close friends, Marjory Butler and Mary Rawcliffe, who both lived locally. The royalty rights from George's songs – which he and Beryl had purloined from their composers – were to be shared amongst these same friends, and the Prioress Carmelite Convent, near Wigan. Effectively, anyone wishing to contest *this* aspect of Pat's will would, her solicitor declared, be running the risk of putting personal greed before the needs of the Catholic Church who had cared so much about her. Shortly before her death, Pat had announced that she intended returning this devotion by becoming a nun.

Fred Howson was so convinced that he would succeed where others had failed that he pleaded his case through the newspapers, and announced how he would spend his inheritance. 'I'll get myself a small bungalow, then delight in buying things for the poor and the needy who have had a tough life but never grumbled,' he told the *Sunday Express*.

In recent years, Howson really had fallen on hard times. His marriage had collapsed on account of his womanising, and soon after George's death he had moved out of the family home and into digs. His wife had died in 1970, and by this time he had been eking out an existence on £6 a week in State benefits and living in a filthy caravan, parked in a field in Garstang. His and Ethel's pleas fell on deaf ears, however, and Pat's will was not over-ruled.

Eliza Booth would plead poverty for another ten years. In 1979, she invited a *Sunday Mirror* journalist to her terraced house in Warrington – she had moved there eight years previously, she said, after selling her block of flats because she could not afford to keep them on, though she did not say what she had done with the money. Her plight was highlighted under the heading, 'ELIZA HAVE-LITTLE: FORMBY'S

MOTHER FACES HARD TIMES'. Now aged ninety-nine and totally blind, Eliza was living in near-squalor with another daughter, Louisa. Their home was infested with vermin, squatters had moved in next door, and for months the pair had been pestered by vandals. These deplorable living conditions had, however, been self-inflicted, for it later emerged that Eliza had rejected numerous offers from Warrington's council to be rehoused. Eliza lived on until the age of 102, dying in August 1981.

Louisa Formby had followed George on to the stage, forming a successful tap-dancing act with her brother Frank, before the war, then a comedy duo with Bob Hall. Off and on, Frank worked as a solo performer, imitating his brother and reworking his songs, but he never amounted to much and died completely forgotten.

The retainers – friends and foes alike – are mostly gone: virtually every member of his family, Harry Scott, the colleagues and many of the co-stars. Each played a part in his success, or failed to contribute to the besmirchment of his memory. Imitators, at best mediocre in comparison to the superb artist that he was, fail to capture his magic and will always be relegated to walking in the shadow of his sun. Thora Hird, who *almost* appeared in one of his films, once hailed him, 'A legend sent by God.'

Legends, of course, never die and George Formby's name and his unique legacy live on.

APPENDIX I

GEORGE FORMBY: DISCOGRAPHY

The following represents George Formby's recorded output between 1924 and 1960 on 78rpm shellac singles, and on 33rpm and 45rpm vinyl. Alternative and rejected takes, more numerous at the beginning of his career, are not included unless they were not released on 78rpm. The original recordings are as they were issued in the UK – the frequently differing B-sides which accompanied overseas A-sides are not included. More details of these can be found in Brendan Ryan's exhaustive, *George Formby: A Catalogue of His Work*, published in 1986 by the George Formby Society.

1924 (HMV)
Matrix: Rolling Around Piccadilly (Hargreaves-Dammerell)
   Audition.
Bb 4164 – 1/2 Piano: Mme Adani. Formby Sr song (1916).
   UNRELEASED.

1926 (EDISON-BELL WINNER) ALL FORMBY SR SONGS.
4409 John Willie Come On (Formby Sr, 1908)
      I Was Always A Willing Young Lad (Hargreaves-
      Dammerell c.1915)
4418 John Willie's Jazz-Band (Hargreaves-Dammerell 1913)
      Since I Parted My Hair In The Middle (David-Murphy,
      1914)
4437 The Man Was A Stranger To Me (Connor, 1915)
      Rolling Around Piccadilly. All acoustic recordings.

1929 (DOMINION)
C 347 All Going Back (Formby)
       In The Congo (Cobb-Lutzen)

1932 (DECCA)
Matrix T620-1 Our House Is Haunted (Hargreaves-Dammerell)
              I Told My Baby With My Ukulele (Formby-
              Gifford-Cliffe)
              Both auditions, pianist unknown.
              UNRELEASED.
Matrix GB 5028 – 1/2 Yo, Yo, Men of England Part One
       GB 5029 – 1/2 Ditto, Part Two. No other details.
F3079 Do De O Do (Hargreaves-Dammerell-Formby)*
       Chinese (Laundry) Blues (Cottrell)*
F3219 I Told My Baby With My Ukulele*
       If You Don't Want The Goods Don't Maul 'Em
       (Cottrell)*
F3222 The Old Kitchen Kettle (Woods-Campbell-
       Connelly)* Note: the B-side of this recording was an
       instrumental, The Baked Potato Man (Sarony).
       *Orchestra Jack Hylton.
F3259 John Willie At The Licence Office (Cottrell).
       Both sides, with Beryl Formby & Co. Formby Sr
       Sketch which is labelled George Formby Jr.
F3377 I Could Make A Living At That (Cottrell-Lawton)**
       Let's All Go To Reno (Cottrell) Piano: Claude Ivy.
       **From the film *Boots, Boots*.

1933 (DECCA)
F3458 Sitting On The Ice In The Ice Rink (Cottrell)*
       Levi's Monkey Mike (Cottrell-Rick)
F3254 Why Don't Women Like Me? (Cottrell-Bennett-
       Formby)*
       Running Round The Fountains In Trafalgar Square
       (Cottrell)

F3615 With My Little Ukulele In My Hand (Version 1:
Cottrell-Formby)**
As The Hours And The Days . . . (Gifford-Cliffe)
F3615 Sunbathing In The Park (Gifford-Cliffe-Kendall)
As The Hours And The Days . . .
Note: This ** version of With My Little Ukulele In My
Hand was deemed too offensive for release after
copies had been sent out to the media. The A-side
was therefore replaced with Sunbathing In The Park.
F3666 She's Never Been Seen Since Then (Cottrell)
Swimmin' With The Wimmin (Cottrell)***
F3752 My Ukulele (Cottrell-Formby)†
I Went All Hot And Cold (Cottrell-Formby)
†'Cleaned-up' version of With My Little Ukulele In
My Hand
F3800 The Wedding Of Mr Wu (Cottrell)
Baby (Cottrell)*
All songs marked * from the film *Boots, Boots*
*** Later included in stage play *Beside The Seaside.*

1934 (DECCA)
F3950 Believe It Or Not (Gifford-Cliffe)
In A Little Wigan Garden (Gifford-Cliffe)*
*From the film, *No Limit*
F5183 You Can't Keep A Growing Lad Down (Gifford-Cliffe)
It's No Use Looking At Me (Cottrell-Gifford-Cliffe)
F5232 John Willie's Jazz-Band. Second version.
There's Nothing Proud About Me (Gifford-Cliffe)
F5287 The Best Of Schemes (Gifford-Cliffe)
Madam Moscovitch (Gifford-Cliffe)
F5303 John Willie Goes Carolling (Gifford-Cliffe) Both sides.

1935 (DECCA)
F5569 Fanlight Fanny (Formby-Gifford-Cliffe)*
Share And Share Alike (Cliffe)

*From the film, *Trouble Brewing*.
F5699 The Fiddler Kept On Fiddling (Gifford-Cliffe)
I Do Do Things I Do (Gibson-Long)

1935 (REGAL ZONOPHONE)
MR 1932 Riding In The TT Races (Gifford-Cliffe)*
The Isle Of Man (Gifford-Cliffe)*
*From the film, *No Limit*.
**Written for the above film, but not included.
MR 1952 Pleasure Cruise (Gifford-Cliffe)
The Wash-house At The Back (Gifford-Cliffe)
I'm Going To Stick To My Mother (Mertz-Stansbury)
I Promised To Be Home By Nine O'Clock (Mertz-Stansbury)
Isn't Love A Very Funny Thing? (Mertz)*
Surely There's No Harm In A Kiss? (Mertz)**
Note: The above four songs were included in the film *Off The Dole*. **Duets with Beryl Formby.

1936 (REGAL ZONOPHONE)
MR 2033 A Farmer's Boy (Gifford-Cliffe)
Radio Bungalow Town (Gifford-Cliffe)
R 2060 Gallant Dick Turpin (Gifford-Cliffe)
Sketch, both sides. With Beryl Formby & Co.
Includes ditty, 'Gallant Dick Turpentine'.
MR 2083 *George Formby Medley*: Sitting On The Ice In The Ice Rink; Do De O Do; Chinese Laundry Blues; Madam Moscovitch; My Ukulele; Fanlight Fanny.
MR 2162 Ring Your Little Bell (Wallace)
Quick-Fire Medley: It Ain't Nobody's Business What I Do; Goody-Goody; I Like Bananas.
MR 2199 When I'm Cleaning Windows (Formby-Gifford-Cliffe)*
Keep Your Seats Please! (Formby-Gifford-Cliffe)*

*From the film *Keep Your Seats Please*. This version of the former song was banned by the BBC.

MR 2232 Sitting On The Sands All Night (Formby-Gifford-Cliffe)
Five And Twenty Years (Gifford-Cliffe)

MR 2270 I'm A Froggie (Hargreaves-Dammerell)
The Ghost (Hargreaves-Dammerell)*
*Updated version of Our House I Haunted (1922).

MR 2295 Bunkum's Travelling Show (Gifford-Cliffe)
Dare Devil Dick (Gifford-Cliffe)
Riding Around On A Rainbow (Formby-Gifford)*
Your Way Is My Way (Parr-Davies) Sung With Florence Desmond.* These songs were included in the soundtrack of the film *No Limit*, but not recorded.

1937 (REGAL ZONOPHONE)

MR 2368 Hindoo Man (Formby-Gifford-Cliffe)
My Little Goat And Me (Gifford-Cliffe)

MR 2399 The Window Cleaner (No 2) (Formby-Gifford-Cliffe)
The Lancashire Toreador (Gifford-Cliffe)

MR 2430 When We Feather Our Nest (Formby-Gifford-Cliffe)*
You're A Li-a-ty! (Formby-Gifford-Cliffe)**
*From the film *Feather Your Nest*.
**Written for the above film but not included.

MR 2431 Oh, Dear Mother (Formby-Gifford-Cliffe)
With My Little Stick Of Blackpool Rock (Gifford-Cliffe)

MR 2469 Trailing Around In A Trailer (Gifford-Cliffe)
Said The Little Brown Hen (Formby-Gifford-Cliffe)

MR 2490 Leaning On A Lamp Post (Version 1)(Gay)*
Hi-Tiddley-Hi-Ti Island (1922) (Stanley-Alleyn)
*From the film *Feather Your Nest*. Also later used

in the play *Beside The Seaside*.

MR 2506 Somebody's Wedding Day (Formby-Cliffe)
Easy Going Chap (Formby-Gifford-Cliffe)

MR 2570 Biceps, Muscle and Brawn (Formby-Gifford-Cliffe)*
Keep Fit [Whatever You Do!] (Formby-Gifford-Cliffe)*
*From the film *Keep Fit*.

MR 2571 I Don't Like (Formby-Gifford-Cliffe)
My Plus-Fours (Formby-Gifford-Cliffe)

MR 2616 Remember Me (Dubin-Warren)
Maybe I'll Find Somebody Else*
*Sung by the boxer Tommy Farr, with Formby
spoken intro/uke solo.

MR 2628 You Can't Stop Me From Dreaming (Friend-
Franklyn)
She Can't Say No (Bryan-Meyer)

IR-51 [Matrix: 4448-1] Keep Your Seats Please*
IR-52 [Matrix: 4657-1] Keep Fit*
*These were film-trailers issued to cinemas purely for
promotional purposes and not issued commercially.
Formby speaks about the film, followed by musical
extract.
– – – I'm As Happy As A Sandboy (Sarony-Holmes)*
*From the film *Feather Your Nest* but not recorded.

1938 (REGAL ZONOPHONE)

MR 2684 Does Your Dream Book Tell You That? (Formby-
Gifford-Cliffe)*
Like The Big Pots Do (Long) A Gracie Fields
creation of 1928.
*Duet with Beryl Formby.

MR 2709 Have You Heard This One? (Sullivan-Gilbert)
Wunga Bunga Boo (Stanley-Alleyn)

MR 2735 Springtime's Here Again (Formby-Gifford-Cliffe)
The Joo Jah Tree (Box-Cox-Butler)

MR 2752 Mother What'll I Do Now? (Formby-Cliffe)*
Noughts And Crosses (Hunter-Parr-Davies)*
*From the film *I See Ice*.

MR 2753 I Blew A Little Blast On My Whistle (Formby)
In My Little Snapshot Album (Formby-Gifford-
Cliffe)*
*From the film *I See Ice*.

MR 2890 Our Sergeant Major (Formby-Gifford-Cliffe)
Rhythm of the Alphabet (Lisbona-Steller)

MR 2891 It's In The Air (Parr-Davies)*
They Can't Fool Me (Formby-Gifford-Cliffe)*
*From the film *It's In The Air*.

MR 2925 I Wonder Who's Under Her Balcony Now?
(Formby-Gifford-Cliffe)
Tan-Tan-Tivvy-Tally-Ho (LeClerq)

MR 2947 Sitting Pretty With My Fingers Crossed (Formby-
Gifford-Cliffe)
MR 2969 Frigid Air Fanny (Formby-Gifford-Cliffe)
My Little Wooden Tool Shed In The Garden
(Steeles-Stevens-Wilmott)

1939 (REGAL ZONOPHONE)

MR 3022 It's Turned Out Nice Again (Formby-Gifford-
Cliffe)
Hill Billy Willie (Formby-Gifford-Cliffe)*
*From the film *He Snoops To Conquer*

MR 3039 Hitting The High Spots Now (Formby-Gifford-
Cliffe)*
I Can Tell It By My Horoscope (Formby-Gifford-
Cliffe)*
*From the film *Trouble Brewing*.

MR 3081 It's A Grand And Healthy Life (Formby-Gifford-
Cliffe)
I'm The Husband Of The Wife Of Mr Wu
(Formby-Gifford-Cliffe)

MR 3103 *Swing It George Medley*: Some Of The Days; Hard-Hearted Hannah; Sweet Georgia Brown; Sweet Sue; Dinah; Tiger Rag.

MR 3121 Dan The Dairy Man (Formby-Gifford-Cliffe)
The Blue-Eyed Blonde Next Door (Formby-Gifford-Cliffe)

MR 3147 With My Little Stick Of Rock*
Lancashire Hot Pot Swingers (Formby-Gifford-Cliffe)
*This song replaced the suppressed Low Down Lazy Turk. See G-23917 below.

MR 3160 Goodnight 'Little Fellow' Goodnight (Formby-Gifford-Cliffe)*†
Pardon Me (Formby-Frame-Allan & Patricia Nicholson)*
*From the film *Come On George*.
†First performed in the 1925 revue *Formby Seeing Life*.

MR 3161 I'm Making Headway Now (Formby-Gifford-Cliffe)*
I Couldn't Let The Stable Down (Formby-Gifford-Cliffe)*
*From the film *Come On George*.

MR 3026 Swinging Along Singing A Song (Formby)
A Lad From Lancashire (Formby-Godfrey)

MR 3233 Imagine Me On The Maginot Line (Formby-Gifford-Cliffe)
A Lancashire Romeo (Formby-Gifford-Cliffe)

MR 3301 Grandad's Flannelette Nightshirt (Formby-Latta)*
Mr Wu's A Window Cleaner Now (Formby-Gifford-Cliffe)*
*From the film *Let George Do It*.

G-23917 Low Down Lazy Turk (Formby-Gifford-Cliffe)*
Lancashire Hot Pot Swingers
*Suppressed in Britain, released only in Australasia.

1940 (REGAL ZONOPHONE)

MR 3316 Count Your Blessings And Smile (Formby-Gifford-Cliffe)

Oh, Don't The Wind Blow Cold? (Formby-Gifford-Cliffe)*

*From the film *Let George Do It*.

MR 3324 I Always Get To Bed By Half-Past Nine (Formby-Gifford-Cliffe)

You've Got Something There (Formby-Gifford-Cliffe)

MR 3325 Down The Old Coal Hole (Formby-Gifford-Cliffe)

On The Wigan Boat Express (Formby-Gifford-Cliffe)

MR 3358 I'm The Ukulele Man (MacDougal)*

On The Beat (MacDougal)*

*From the film *Spare A Copper*.

MR 3394 Bless 'Em All (The Service Song) (Hughes-Lake-Godfrey) Version One

Letting The New Year In (Formby-Gifford-Cliffe)

MR 3411 Guarding The Home Of The Home Guards (Formby-Latta)

I Wish I Was Back On The Farm (MacDougal)*

*From the film *Spare A Copper*.

Matrix TT-2623 *George Formby Entertains The Troops*: Dick Whittington Sketch (with Beryl Formby); With My Little Stick Of Blackpool Rock; Imagine Me In The Maginot Line; When I'm Cleaning Windows; Chinese Laundry Blues. Acetate, recorded live in France 23-3-40. UNRELEASED.

I'm shy (Formby-Gifford-Cliffe)*

*From the film *Spare A Copper*. Not recorded.

1941 (REGAL ZONOPHONE)

MR 3441 Bless 'Em All (The Services Song) Version Two.

Thanks Mr Roosevelt (Connor)

MR 3463 I Did What I Could With My Gas Mask (Lesley-Isaacs)

You'll Be Far Better Off In A Home (Box-Cox-Osborn)*

*Based on the march *El Abanico*, by Javaloyes.

MR 3472 Delivering The Morning Milk (Formby-Gifford-Cliffe)

It Might Have Been A Great Deal Worse (Formby-Gifford-Cliffe)

MR 3482 *Formby Favourites For The Forces*: Our Sergeant Major; The Lancashire Toreador; It's A Grand And Healthy Life; With My Little Stick of Blackpool Rock; I'm The Husband Of The Wife Of Mr Wu; When I'm Cleaning Windows.

MR 3512 You're Everything To Me (MacDougal)*

The Emperor Of Lancashire (MacDougal) With Beryl Formby & John Firman.

*From the film *Turned Out Nice Again*.

MR 3520 Auntie Maggie's Remedy (Formby-Latta) Version One. *

You Can't Go Wrong In These (MacDougal) With Beryl Formby*

*From the film *Turned Out Nice Again*.

MR 3521 The Left-Hand Side of Egypt (Gay-Bennett)

Who Are You A-Shoving Of? (Gay-Raymond) A Lupino Lane creation.

MR 3550 *George Formby Crazy Record*: Alexander's Ragtime Band; La Donna E Mobile; She'll Be Coming Round The Mountain; The Old (New) Sow. With Beryl Formby and John Firman.

MR 3553 Swing Mama (MacDougal)*

I Played On My Spanish Guitar (Lyons)*

*From the film *South American George*.

MR 3567 I'd Do It With A Smile (MacDougal)*

The Barmaid At The Rose And Crown (Formby-Arthurs)*
*From the film *South American George*.
La Donna E Mobile (from Verdi's *Rigoletto*).
Included in the above film, but not recorded.

1942 (REGAL ZONOPHONE)

MR 3599 *Formby Film Favourites*: When We Feather Our Nest; Our Sergeant Major; The Isle Of Man; Hitting The High Spots Now. Comprises badly-edited extracts of previously issued recordings.

MR 3619 Katy Did, Katy Didn't (Loesser-Carmichael)
Frank On His Tank (Formby-Gifford-Cliffe)

MR 3624 Smile All The Time (Formby-Coady)
Out In The Middle East (Godfrey)

MR 3640 Mr Wu Is Now An Air-Raid Warden (Latta)
Got to Get Your Photo To The Press (Latta)*
*From the film *He Snoops To Conquer*.

MR 3645 Talking To The Moon About You (Day)*
Delivering The Morning Milk (reissue)
*From the film *Much Too Shy*.

MR 3648 Andy The Handy Man (Latta)
They Laughed When I Started To Play (Formby-Cliffe)*
*From the film *Much Too Shy*.

MR 3654 Thirty Thirsty Sailors (Box-Cox)
Hold Your Hats On (Miller-Addinsell)*
*Sung by soldiers in the film *Troopship*.

MR 3663 Cookhouse Serenade (Twomey-Goodhart)
You Can't Love Two Girls At The Same Time (Formby-Godfrey)

Matrix CAR 6348-1 Sally The Salvage Queen (Formby-Gifford-Cliffe) UNRELEASED.

1943 (REGAL ZONOPHONE)
MR 3672 The Baby Show (Wise-Malcolm-Sanford)
When The Waterworks Caught Fire (Formby-Cliffe)
MR 3682 Spotting On The Top Of Blackpool Tower (Formby-Latta)*
Sentimental Lou (Formby-Gifford-Cliffe)
*Copyrighted as 'Sitting On The Top Of Blackpool Tower', the title used when Formby performed the song in the 1955 Royal Variety Show. 'Spotting' alludes to wartime 'fire-spotting' [BRC].
MR 3689 Get Cracking (Formby-Latta)*
Home Guard Blues (Formby-Gifford-Cliffe)
*From the film *Get Cracking.*
MR 3694 Under The Blasted Oak (Formby-Cliffe) **
Oh You Have No Idea (Godfrey)
*From the film, *Get Cracking.*
**'Mixed' from two recording sessions (11-10-42/8-7-43).
MR 3705 *American Medley*: My Old Kentucky Home; Camptown Races; She'll Be Coming Round The Mountain; Old Folks At Home; Oh Susannah; Over There; Anchors Aweigh: *British Medley*: Hearts Of Oak; Men Of Harlech; John Peel; On Ilkley Moor; Loch Lomond; Come Landlord Fill The Flowing Bowl; Auld Lang Syne.
MR 3710 Bunty's Such A Big Girl Now (Formby-Cliffe)
On The HMS Cowheel (Formby-Cliffe)
1944 (REGAL ZONOPHONE)
MR 3720 Bell-Bottom George (Parke-Parr-Davies)*
If I Had A Girl Like You (Parke-Parr-Davies)*
*From the film *Bell-Bottom George.*
MR 3733 Swim Little Fish (Parke-Parr-Davies)*
It Serves You Right (Box-Cox)*
*From the film *Bell-Bottom George*

MR 3736 The V-Sign Song (Sievier)
        The Old Cane-Bottom Chair (Formby-Cliffe)

1945 (REGAL ZONOPHONE)

MR 3475 Our Fanny's Gone All Yankee (Van Dusen)
        Unconditional Surrender (Cunningham-Towers)*
        *From the film *He Snoops To Conquer*.

MR 3750 Mr Wu In The Air-Force (Formby Latta)
        Blackpool Prom (Sievier)

MR 3760 The Daring Young Man (Formby-Cliffe)*
        I'd Like A Dream Like That (Formby-Cliffe)*
        *From the film *I Didn't Do It*.

MR 3761 She's Got Two Of Everything (Cunningham-
        Towers)*
        Up In The Air And Down In The Dumps
        (Cunningham)*
        *From the film *I Didn't Do It*.

1946 (COLUMBIA)

FB 3251 You Don't Need A Licence For That (Formby-Cliffe)*
        The Mad March Hare (Formby-Cliffe)*
        *From the film *George In Civvy Street*.

FB 3262 We've Been A Long Time Gone (Formby-Cliffe)*
        It Could Be (Cunningham-Towers)*
        *From the film *George In Civvy Street*.

Matrix CAX 9466-2 Get Cracking [Excerpt, live, 16-4-46,
        recorded at the Leicester Square Theatre,
        London, as part of the British Film
        Festival.] Orchestra: Sidney Torch.
        Released on Columbia DOX 823 [BRC].

1950 (DECCA)

F 9356 Come Hither With Your Zither (Miller-Noel-
        Donnelly)
        Aunty Maggie's Remedy (Version Two)*

*Minus two verses contained in Version One.
F 9444 Leaning On A Lamp Post (Version Two)
        When I'm Cleaning Windows (Version Two)
        All 1950 recordings, orchestra Harry Bidgood.

1951 (HIS MASTER'S VOICE)
B-10179 I'm Saving Up For Sally (Posford-Maschwitz)*
        The Pleasure Cruise (Version Two)
B-10180 Ordinary People (Posford-Maschwitz)
        Zip Goes A Million (Posford-Maschwitz) Finale
        All 1951 recordings from the stage-musical *Zip
        Goes A Million*. Orchestra: Debroy Somers.

1960 (PYE)
7N-15269 Happy-Go-Lucky Me (Evans-Byron)
         Banjo Boy (Niessen-Kay)

MISCELLANEOUS 1953–60
Between these dates George Formby sang the following songs,
not previously recorded or in the stated versions, on radio (R)
or television (T):

Sweet Georgia Brown (R): *In Town Tonight*, 5-10-53, BBC.
Leaning On A Lamp Post (T) with Terry-Thomas: *Top Of
    The Town*, 9-1-55, BBC.
Sara Maraise (Afrikaans song) (R): *In Town Tonight*, 16-4-55,
    BBC.
Ordinary People (T) with Petula Clark: *The George Formby
    Show*, 15-5-57, BBC.
MEDLEY: Some Of These Days; Dinah; Sweet Georgia
    Brown (T) with the Deep River Boys: *Formby Favourites*, 6-
    9-58, BBC.
Hello Canada (T): *Atlantic Showboat*, 13-12-58, BBC.
'Tain't No Sin To Take Off Your Skin and Piccolo Pete (T):
    Stepping Out With Formby, 25-4-59, BBC.

MEDLEY: Living Doll; 'Scotland The Brave'; Ma, He's Making Eyes At Me (T) with Morton Fraser & The Harmonica Rascals: *Showtime*, 29-11-59, BBC.

THE 'MISSING' SONGS

Around 100 George Formby songs were recorded on acetate between November 1935 and June 1945, few of which have been commercially released. Most are by the regular teams of Gifford and Cliffe, Eddie Latta and Formby himself, and Jack Cottrell. Some are in the EMI archives, but others may now be lost. In alphabetical order they are as follows:

All The Girls Serving On The Jury
Another Lucky Day
Antonio My Romeo
At Dusk
Because Of You
The Bell Tolled Out
The Bomb-Proof Shelter In The Garden
Bottle-Nosed Bertha From Bow
The Butcher's Meet
Bye And Bye
The Canal Boat Queen
Casey's Charabanc
A Couple O' Pounds Of Tripe
The Colonials Are Calling Me
The Coronation March
Cucumber Time At Kew
Down On Our Little Farm
Draw My Cigar
Drinkin'
Every Bit Of Help
Every Little Corner Of My Irish Home
George's Christmas Box
Give Me A Cosy Parlour

The Green Grass Grew All Around
Hello Canada!
He Said He Would Remember
He's Only A Learner
Hey, It's A Wonderful Day!
How I Play The Ukulele
Hurrah For The Rolling Sea!
I Ate One Too
I Could Do With A Day In Bed
I Couldn't Let The Boy Scouts Down
I Couldn't Miss A Chance Like That
I'm A G-Man
I'm A Sailor
I'm Daft When I'm In Love
I'm Going To Take Up Flying
I'm Leaving The Women Alone
I'm Leslie The Wrecker Of Women
I May Not Be Your First Love
I Must Have A Change With My Meals
In 1944
In My Little Store Of Melody
I Remember
I Said 'Ee, You're Welcome!'
It's All Through Mr Wu
It's No Laughing Matter
It's Only A Question Of Time
I Was Waggling My Magic Wand
I Was Touching My Lucky Charm
I Was Touching My Wishbone
Jolly-Polly Oliver
The Lancashire Scotch Brigade
Let George Do It
Let's All Go To A Holiday Camp
The Liverpool Song
Living On Our Avenue

Love On Wheels
Make A Start
Making The Most Of My Time
The Meditating Hindoo Man (Hindoo Man Version 2)
Murphy's Museum
My Little Boomerang
My Oasis Of Love
My Little Boomerang
My Perso-nality
My Ukulele Sweetheart
No One Understands
Now-Now, Come-Come!
Only Half A Day-Trip
O Pola-Nicola
The Piecan Eleven
The Plumber's Song
The Private, The Corp And The Sarge
Robbing Hood
Rollin' Into France
Shake Yourself A Sunshine Cocktail
Seringapatam
Seven O'Clock
The Sheik Of Araby
Shout At Auntie Lily
Sixpence Ha'penny
Somebody's Son
There'll Be No Performance Tonight
Thirty-Bob A Week
Those Were The Days
The Triumph Of Alceste
The Wart On Grandad's Nose
We Can't Make William Tell
When It's Cucumber Time
Who Told You That
The Wigan Butcher

The World Would Be Mine Once Again
You Never Can Tell With Me
You're A Great Big Beautiful Boy
You've Got To Make A Start Some Time

VINYL RE-ISSUES OF 78RPM RECORDINGS

Part One: Recordings issued during Formby's lifetime.

a) *45rpm Extended-Play* (All 1959)

George Formby And His Ukulele Vol 1 Decca EP-DFE 6144
Sitting On The Ice In The Ice Rink; Levi's Monkey Mike;
Chinese Laundry Blues; Do De O Do.

George Formby And His Ukulele Vol 2 Decca EP-DFE 6328
Leaning On A Lamp Post; When I'm Cleaning Windows;
Auntie Maggie's Remedy; Come Hither With Your Zither.

George Formby And His Ukulele Vol 3 Decca EP-DFE 6355
She's Never Been Seen Since Then; Swimmin' With The
Wimmin; It's No Use Looking At Me: You Can't Keep A
Growing Lad Down.

The Ukulele Man Vol 1 Columbia EP-SEG 7550
Mr Wu's A Window Cleaner Now; Hi-Tiddley-Hi-Ti-
Island; When I'm Cleaning Windows; Leaning On A Lamp
Post.

The Ukulele Man Vol 2 Columbia EP-SEG 7661
I'm The Husband Of The Wife Of Mr Wu; Grandad's
Flannelette Nightshirt; Under The Blasted Oak; Oh, You
Have No Idea.

Stepping Out With George Columbia EP-SEG 7936
Our Sergeant Major; Frigid Air Fanny; With My Little
Stick Of Blackpool Rock; Oh, Dear Mother.

Stepping Out With George Again Columbia EP-SEG 7964
She's Got Two Of Everything; When The Waterworks
Caught Fire; The Blue-Eyed Blonde Next Door; Like The
Big Pots Do.

b) *33⅓ rpm Albums* (1961)

George Formby Souvenir Decca ACL 1062
 When I'm Cleaning Windows; Why Don't Women Like
 Me?; Fanlight Fanny; Auntie Maggie's Remedy; I Told My
 Baby With My Ukulele; Believe It Or Not; Chinese
 Laundry Blues; My Ukulele; There's Nothing Proud About
 Me; As The Hours Roll By; Madam Moscovitch; Leaning
 On A Lamp Post.

VINYL RE-ISSUES OF 78RPM RECORDINGS
Part Two: Recordings issued since Formby's death. All are
albums.
Turned Out Nice Again (1963) Decca ACL 1145
 Sitting On The Ice In The Ice Rink; I Do Do Things I Do;
 If You Don't Want The Goods Don't Maul 'Em; The Best
 Of Schemes; The Wedding Of Mr Wu; John Willie's Jazz
 Band; I Went All Hot And Cold; The Old Kitchen Kettle;
 Levi's Monkey Mike; Do De O Do; The Fiddler Kept On
 Fiddling; In A Little Wigan Garden; Sunbathing In The
 Park; You Can't Keep A Growing Lad Down.
The World of George Formby Vol 1 (1969) Decca SPA 50
 When I'm Cleaning Windows; Why Don't Women Like
 Me?; You Can't Keep A Growing Lad Down; Swimmin'
 With The Wimmin; The Old Kitchen Kettle; With My
 Little Ukulele In My Hand; Chinese Laundry Blues; Sitting
 On The Ice In The Ice Rink; Running Round The
 Fountains; It's No Use Looking At Me; Fanlight Fanny;
 Leaning On A Lamp Post.
The World Of George Formby Vol 2 (1975) Decca SPA-446
 Auntie Maggie's Remedy; Believe It Or Not; I Do Do
 Things I Do; Do De O Do; The Fiddler Kept On Fiddling;
 The Best Of Schemes; Madam Moscovitch; Share And
 Share Alike; I Went All Hot And Cold; I Told My Baby
 With My Ukulele; Come Hither With Your Zither; There's
 Nothing Proud About Me.
With My Ukulele (1981) Decca RFL-8

My Ukulele; Chinese Laundry Blues; I Told My Baby With
My Ukulele; Baby; Sunbathing In The Park; Leaning On A
Lamp Post; She's Never Been Seen Since Then; When I'm
Cleaning Windows; The Wedding Of Mr Wu; Do De O
Do; If You Don't Want The Goods Don't Maul 'Em; The
Fiddler Kept On Fiddling; There's Nothing Proud About
Me; Believe It Or Not; I Went All Hot And Cold; I Do Do
Things I Do; In A Little Wigan Garden; As The Hours Roll
By.

A Chip Off The Old Block (1981) Living Era AJA-5003
George Formby Sr Sings: Twice Nightly; We All Went
Marching In; Looking For Mugs In The Strand; All Of A
Sudden It Struck Me; Did You See The Crowd In
Piccadilly?; I Had My Hand In My Pocket; The Bells Were
Ringing; Standing At The Corner Of The Street.
George Formby Jr Sings: All Going Back; John Willie's
Jazz-Band; Always A Willing Young Lad; I Parted My Hair
In The Middle; The Man Was A Stranger To Me; John
Willie Come On; Rolling Around Piccadilly; In The Congo.

I'm The Ukulele Man EMI Music For Pleasure MFP 1182
Leaning On A Lamp Post; Mother What'll I Do Now?;
Aunt Maggie's Remedy; Grandad's Flannelette Nightshirt;
In My Little Snapshot Album; With My Little Stick Of
Blackpool Rock; When I'm Cleaning Windows; The
Window Cleaner No 2; Mr Wu's A Window Cleaner Now;
Our Sergeant Major; The Lancashire Toreador; I'm The
Ukulele Man.

Turned Out Nice Again EMI Music For Pleasure MFP 1378
It's Cold In The Air; Oh, Don't The Wind Blow Cold?' On
The HMS Cowheel; They Can't Fool Me; Sitting On The
Sands All Night; Andy The Handy Man; Riding In The TT
Races; Oh, Dear Mother; Bell-Bottom George; Count Your
Blessings And Smile; Frigid Air Fanny; You'd Be Far Better
Off In A Home.

The Man With The Ukulele World Record Club WRC SH-126

The Wash House At The Back; Keep Your Seats Please;
Hindoo Man; When We Feather Our Nest; She Can't Say
No; I Blew A Little Blast On My Whistle; I Wonder Who's
Under Her Balcony Now?; My Little Wooden Tool Shed In
The Garden; It's Turned Out Nice Again; I'm The
Husband Of The Wife Of Mr Wu; Down The Old Coal
Hole; Bless 'Em All; I Played On My Spanish Guitar;
Delivering The Morning Milk; She's Got Two Of
Everything; Under The Blasted Oak.

George Formby And His Ukulele World Record Club WRC
SH-151
The Isle of Man; Hi-Tiddley-Hi-Ti Island; The Blue-Eyed
Blonde Next Door; Lancashire Hot Pot Swingers; The Left-
Hand Side of Egypt; Oh, Don't The Wind Blow Cold?;
Bless 'Em All; I'd Do It With A Smile; The Barmaid At
The Rose And Crown; Ordinary People; I'm Saving Up For
Sally; The Pleasure Cruise; On The Beat; Hitting The High
Spots Now; I Always Get To Bed Before Half-Past Nine;
On The Wigan Boat Express.

The Best of George Formby EMI OU-2072
When I'm Cleaning Windows; Grandad's Flannelette
Nightshirt; Riding In The TT Races; In My Little Snapshot
Album; I'm The Ukulele Man; It's In The Air; Count Your
Blessings and Smile; Mother What'll I Do Now?; Leaning
On A Lamp Post; Auntie Maggie's Remedy; With My
Little Stick Of Blackpool Rock; Mr Wu's A Window
Cleaner Now; Frigid Air Fanny; They Can't Fool Me; The
Lancashire Toreador; Our Sergeant Major.

COLLECTIONS
Leaning On A Lamp Post (1983) EMI Music For Pleasure
MFP-1032
1) Leaning On A Lamp Post; Mother What'll I Do Now?;
Auntie Maggie's Remedy; Grandad's Flannelette
Nightshirt; In My Little Snapshot Album; With My Little

Stick Of Blackpool Rock; When I'm Cleaning Windows;
The Window Cleaner No 2; Mr Wu's A Window Cleaner
Now; Our Sergeant Major; The Lancashire Toreador; I'm
The Ukulele Man.
2) Riding In The TT Races; Oh, Dear Mother; Bell-Bottom
George; Count Your Blessings And Smile; Frigid Air Fanny;
You'll Be Far Better Off In A Home; It's Turned Out Nice
Again; It's In The Air; They Can't Fool Me; The Wash
House At The Back; I Blew A Little Blast On My Whistle;
Hindoo Man.

The Man With The Ukulele World Record Club SM 351/352/
353/354
1) When I'm Cleaning Windows; Bunkum's Travelling
Show; Dare Devil Dick; Riding In The TT Races; Oh, Dear
Mother; The Window Cleaner No 2; You Can't Stop Me
From Dreaming; I Blew A Little Blast On My Whistle; She
Can't Say No; The Joo-Jah Tree; In My Little Snapshot
Album; Hitting The High Spots Now; It's A Grand And
Healthy Life; Dan The Dairy Man; Bell-Bottom George;
Formby Medley Parts 1 & 2.
2) Leaning On A Lamp Post; Hi-Tiddley-Hi-Ti Island;
Keep Your Seats Please; Mother What'll I Do Now?; Our
Sergeant Major; They Can't Fool Me; It's In The Air; I
Wonder Who's Under Her Balcony Now?; Rhythm In The
Alphabet; Frigid Air Fanny; It's Turned Out Nice Again;
Springtime's Here Again; You Can't Go Wrong In These;
Grandad's Flannelette Nightshirt; Mr Wu's A Window
Cleaner Now; Oh, Don't The Wind Blow Cold?
3) With My Little Stick Of Blackpool Rock; Lancashire
Hot Pot Swingers; A Lad From Lancashire; A Lancashire
Romeo; On The Wigan Boat Express; The Lancashire
Toreador; The Emperor Of Lancashire; Blackpool Prom;
You've Got Something There; Auntie Maggie's Remedy; I
Played On My Spanish Guitar; Under The Blasted Oak; On
The HMS Cowheel; Buntie's Such A Big Girl Now;

Sentimental Lou, On The Beat.

4) I'm The Ukulele Man; Have You Ever Heard This One?; Wunga Bunga Boo; I Can Tell It By My Horoscope; Letting The New Year In; I Wish I Was Back On The Farm; They Laughed When I Started To Play; Andy The Handy Man; Thirty Thirsty Sailors; Swim Little Fish; Keep Fit; She's Got Two Of Everything; The Mad March Hare; You Don't Need A Licence For That; Formby Crazy Record Parts 1 & 2.

Leaning On A Lamp Post (1986) Decca RECDL-4 (Double album)

When I'm Cleaning Windows; Fanlight Fanny; Chinese Laundry Blues; My Ukulele; Baby; I Do Do Things I Do; Sunbathing In The Park; I Went All Hot And Cold; The Fiddler Kept On Fiddling; Let's All Go To Reno; Leaning On A Lamp Post; Auntie Maggie's Remedy; I Told My Baby With My Ukulele; Believe It Or Not; In A Little Wigan Garden; Levi's Monkey Mike; She's Never Been Seen Since Then; The Wedding Of Mr Wu; If You Don't Want The Goods Don't Maul 'Em; There's Nothing Proud About Me; Madam Moscovitch; As The Hours And The Days . . .; Why Don't Women Like Me?; Running Round The Fountains; Sitting On The Ice In The Ice Rink; I Could Make A Living At That; John Willie At The Licence Office Parts 1 & 2; Come Hither With Your Zither; Do De O Do; John Willie's Jazz Band; Swimmin' With The Wimmin; You Can't Keep A Growing Lad Down; The Old Kettle; The Best Of Schemes; John Willie Goes Carolling Parts 1 & 2.

MUSIC CASSETTES AND COMPACT DISCS

These are too numerous to list in any detail and are largely compilations of the more popular Formby songs. There are, however, several notable exceptions which contain rare items:

Music cassettes:

The George Formby Library (1993) Mastersound MSR 141-50
10 volumes.
1) Chinese Laundry Blues; I Went All Hot And Cold; Since
I Parted My Hair In The Middle; Auntie Maggie's Remedy;
In A Little Wigan Garden; I Wish I Was Back On The
Farm; You Can't Keep A Growing Lad Down; I Played On
My Spanish Guitar; She's Got Two Of Everything; Our
Sergeant Major; Rolling Around Piccadilly; You Don't
Need A Licence For That; Swimmin' With The Wimmin;
I'm Making Headway Now (film s/track); If You Don't
Want The Goods Don't Maul 'Em; Home Guard Blues;
She's Never Been Since Then; We've Been A Long Time
Gone; Sally The Salvage Queen.
2) When I'm Cleaning Windows; Grandad's Flannelette
Nightshirt; Easy Going Chap; The Left-Hand Side Of Egypt;
I Could Make A Good Living At That; Banjo Boy; The Baby
Show; On The Wigan Boat Express; Katy Did, Katy Didn't;
My Plus Fours; Blackpool Prom; Down The Old Coal Hole;
I Promised To Be Home By Nine O'Clock (film s/track);
The Daring Young Man; Count Your Blessings And Smile;
Got To Get Your Photo Under The Press; Under The
Blasted Oak; I'm Saving Up For Sally; I'd Like A Dream
Like That (film s/track); Happy Go Lucky Me.
3) Leaning On A Lamp Post; On The Beat; I'm Going To
Stick To My Mother (film s/track); You Can't Love Two
Girls; When The Boys Of The Village Get Cracking (film
s/track); Up In The Air And Down In The Dumps; I Do
Do Things I Do; You'll Be Far Better Off In A Home;
Frigid Air Fanny; The Man Was A Stranger To Me; With
My Little Ukulele In My Hand; Hindoo Man; Keep Fit;
Madam Moscovitch; Swing Mama (film s/track); Bless 'Em
All No 2; Spotting On The Top Of Blackpool Tower; Tan-
Tan-Tivvy-Tally-Ho; Bunkum's Travelling Show;
Delivering The Morning Milk.

4) Riding In The TT Races; Mr Wu's A Window Cleaner
Now; I'd Do It With A Smile; I Was Always A Willing
Young Lad; Mr Wu's An Air Raid Warden Now; The Mad
March Hare; Said The Little Brown Hen; Talking To The
Moon About You; Thanks Mr Roosevelt; Let's All Go To
Reno; It's Turned Out Nice Again; Gallant Dick Turpin
(edited); Share And Share Alike; The Old Kitchen Kettle;
I'm The Husband Of The Wife Of Mr Wu; She Can't Say
No; Keep Your Seats Please; In The Congo; Springtime's
Here Again; On The Other Side Of The World (radio perf).
5) With My Little Stick Of Blackpool Rock; Smile All The
Time; A Farmer's Boy; Guarding The Home Of The Home
Guard (live); Hill Billy Willie; Goodnight Little Fellow
Goodnight (from 1960 farewell TV perf); Hitting The
High Spots now; I Blew A Little Blast On My Whistle; I
Did What I Could With My Gas Mask; Imagine Me In The
Maginot Line (live); Sitting On The Ice In The Ice Rink;
Sentimental Lou; Running Round The Fountains;
Somebody's Wedding Day; Swim Little fish; Swinging
Along Singing A Song; American Medley; Oh Dear
Mother; My Little Wooden Toolshed In The Garden; You
Can't Go Wrong In These (film s/track).
6) Out In The Middle East (live); Fanlight Fanny; The
Emperor Of Lancashire; Does Your Dreamboat Tell You
That; The Ghost; Five-And-Twenty Years; Mr Wu In The
Air Force; Bless 'Em All (live); Bunty's Such A Big Girl
Now; The Blue-Eyed Blonde Next Door; The Barmaid At
The Rose And Crown; Bell-Bottom George; Noughts And
Crosses; Quickfire Medley; Trailing Around In A Trailer;
The V-Sign Song; Cookhouse Serenade; The Window
Cleaner No 2; Why Don't Women Like Me?; The Pleasure
Cruise.
7) It's In The Air; It Might Have Been A Great Deal
Worse; It Serves You Right; It's A Grand And Healthy
Life; The Fiddler Kept On Fiddling; I'm The Ukulele Man;

I Told My Baby With My Ukulele; Pardon Me (film s/track); On The HMS Cowheel; They Can't Fool Me; The Isle Of Man; The Lancashire Toreador; Levi's Monkey Mike; Mother What'll I Do Now; They Laughed When I Started To Play; The Wash House At The Back; Biceps, Muscle And Brawn (film s/track); Letting The New Year In; Radio Bungalow Town; Thirty Thirsty Sailors.
8) When We Feather Our Nest; Frank On His Tank; You Can't Stop Me From Dreaming; If I Had A Girl Like You (film s/track); Sitting Pretty With My Fingers Crossed; You're Everything To Me; Come Hither With Your Zither; Have You Ever Heard This One?; You're A Li-a-ty; Who Are You A-Shoving Of?; Zip Goes A Million; Low Down Lazy Turk; Hi-Tiddley-Hi-Ti Island; Sunbathing In The Park; Hold Your Hats On; The Lancashire Hot-Pot Swingers; Kiss Your Mansy-Pansy; A Lancashire Romeo; I Always Get To Bed By Half-Past Nine; John Willie, Come On.
9) Swing It George Parts 1 & 2; Like The Big Pots Do; The Joo Jah Tree; Ordinary People; The Old Cane-Bottom Chair; The Wedding Of Mr Wu; Unconditional Surrender; Sitting On The Sands All Night; There's Nothing Proud About Me; Do De O Do; A Lad From Lancashire; I'm A Froggie; Ring Your Little Bell; Dare Devil Dick; The Best Of Schemes; Oh Don't The Wind Blow Cold?; Wunga Bunga Boo; When The Waterworks Caught Fire; You've Got Something There; Delivering The Morning Milk; Dan The Dairy Man.
10) Andy The Handy Man; Believe It Or Not; In My Little Snapshot Album; I Can Tell It By My Horoscope; My Little Goat And Me; John Willie's Jazz Band; I Don't Like; British Isles Medley; All Going Back; I Wonder Who's Under Her Balcony Now?; Rhythm In The Alphabet; It Could Be; Oh You Have No Idea; I Couldn't Let The Stable Down; Our Fanny's Gone All Yankee; It's No Use Looking At Me; As The Hours And The Days; Formby

Favourites For The Forces Part 1.

Compact discs:
Formby At War (1989) Grosvenor CDGRS-1224 Live
    recordings.
    Aunty Maggie's Remedy; Frank On His Tank; Guarding
    The Home Of The Home Guard; Chinese Laundry Blues;
    When I'm Cleaning Windows; With My Little Stick Of
    Blackpool Rock; Imagine Me In The Maginot Line; When
    The Lads Of The Village Get Cracking; Thirty Thirsty
    Sailors; Out In The Middle East; Mr Wu's An Air Raid
    Warden Now; It's In The Air; With My Little Ukulele In
    My Hand; Down The Old Coal Hole; Bless 'Em All.
George Formby: The Ultimate Collection (1997) Pulse PDS CD
    547
    1) Leaning On A Lamp Post; Hi-Tiddley-Hi-Ti Island;
    Happy Go Lucky Me; Banjo Boy; It's No Use Looking At
    Me; With My Little Stick Of Blackpool Rock; Our Fanny's
    Gone All Yankee; Bell-Bottom George; On The Beat; I
    Wish I Was Back On The Farm; I Blew A Little Blast On
    My Whistle; Andy The Handy Man; The Ghost; The
    Lancashire Toreador; Oh Dear Mother; Mr Wu's A
    Window Cleaner Now; Delivering The Morning Milk; Oh
    Don't The Wind Blow Cold; The Left-Hand Side Of
    Egypt; Chinese Laundry Blues.
    2) When I'm Cleaning Windows; The Pleasure Cruise;
    Levi's Monkey Mike; You're Everything To Me; Isle Of
    Man; Riding In The TT Traces; I'm Making Headway Now;
    I Couldn't Let The Stable Down; I Wonder Who's Under
    Her Balcony Now?; Fanlight Fanny; Hindoo Man;
    Springtime's Here Again; Sitting On The Ice In The Ice
    Rink; Grand And Healthy Life; Noughts And Crosses;
    Share And Share Alike; Grandad's Flannelette Nightshirt;
    Baby; We've Been A Long Time Gone; It's Turned Out
    Nice Again.

GEORGE FORMBY: FILMOGRAPHY

The following represents George Formby's complete output on celluloid, as far as is known. Shorts, clips and feature films were all shot in black and white. Some prints are of varying length, but the times stated are of those prints most commonly seen on cinema and television screens.

NO FOOL LIKE AN OLD FOOL [1915] BARKER FILMS
5 reels. No other details.

BY THE SHORTEST OF HEADS [1915] BARKER FILMS
Director: Bert Haldane, Script: Percy Manton/Jack Hulcup.
With Sidney Blackmer, Valerie Hobson, Moore Marriot, Jack Hulcup, Jack Tessier, Percy Manton, George Formby Jnr. 5 reels.

BOOTS! BOOTS! [1934] BLAKELEY PRODUCTIONS
Director: Bert Tracey, Script: Jack Cottrill [sic], George Formby.
Photography: Roy Fogwell. Music: Harry Hudson. Boots: George Formby, Snooky: Beryl Formby, Chambermaid: Tonie Ford, Manager: Arthur King. With Lillian Keyes, Donald Reid, Constance Fletcher, Myfanwy Southern, Wallace Roscoe. A scene featuring Betty Driver was cut from the finished print. 50 mins.
Songs: Baby; Why Don't Women Like Me?; Sitting On The Ice In The Ice Rink; I Could Make A Good Living At That;

Chinese Laundry Blues (music only).

OFF THE DOLE [1935] BLAKELEY PRODUCTIONS
Director: Arthur Mertz. Script: Arthur Mertz/ John Blakeley.
Photography: Sydney Leach. John Willie: George Formby.
With Dan Young, Beryl Formby, Clifford McLaglen, Wally
Patch, Tully Comber, James Plant, Constance Shotter, Stan
Pell, Daisy Maynard, Stan Little, Lew Martin. 69 mins.
Songs: With My Little Ukulele In My Hand; If You Don't
Want The Goods Don't Maul 'Em; I Promised To Be
Home By Nine O'Clock; I'm Going To Stick To My
Mother; Isn't Love A Very Funny Thing?; Surely There's
No Harm In A Kiss?; The Nearer The Bone The Sweeter
The Meat (sung by Dan Young).

GEORGE FORMBY CAVALCADE [1935] BLAKELEY PRODUCTIONS
This features all the Formby songs performed in *Boots, Boots*
and *Off The Dole.* 26 mins.

NO LIMIT [1935] ATP/EALING
Director: Monty Banks. Script: Tom Geraghty/Fred
Thompson. Photography: Roy Fogwell. George
Shuttleworth: George Formby, Florence Dibney: Florence
Desmond, Grandpa: Edward Rigby, Bert Tyldesley: Jack
Hobbs. With Peter Gawthorne, Alf Goddard, Florence
Gregson, Beatrix Fielden Kaye, Howard Douglas, Evelyn
Roberts. 77 mins.
Songs: Riding In The TT Races; Riding Around On A
Rainbow; In A Little Wigan Garden; Your Way Is My Way.

KEEP YOUR SEATS PLEASE [1936] ATP/EALING
Director: Monty Banks, Script: Tom Geraghty/Ian
Hay/Anthony Kimmins. Based on the play, *Twelve Chairs,*
by Eugene Petrov and Elie Ilf. George: George Formby,

Flo: Florence Desmond, Drayton: Alastair Sim, Max: Gus McNaughton. With Harry Tate, Fiona Stuart, Hal Gordon, Mike Johnson, Enid Stamp-Taylor, Tom Payne, Feldon Kaye, Clifford Heatherley. 82 mins.

Songs: Keep Your Seats Please; When I'm Cleaning Windows.

FEATHER YOUR NEST [1937] ATP/EALING

Director: William Beaudine. Script: Austin Melford/Val Valentine. Photography: Ronald Neame. Original titles: *Never Touched Me!*, *Marriage By Instalments*. Willie: George Formby, Mary: Polly Ward. With Enid Stamp-Taylor, Val Rossing, Davy Burnaby, Jimmy Godden, Ethel Coleridge, Jack Barty, Frederick Burtwell, Tom Payne. 88 mins.

Songs: When We Feather Our Nest; I'm As Happy As A Sandboy; Leaning On A Lamp Post.

KEEP FIT [1937] ATP/EALING

Director: Anthony Kimmins. Script: Anthony Kimmins/ Austin Melford.

Photography: Ronald Neame. George Green: George Formby, Joan Allen: Kay Walsh, Hector Kent: Guy Middleton, Ernie: George Benson. With Gus McNaughton, Evelyn Roberts, Edmund Breon, C Denier Warren, Hal Gordon, Leo Franklyn, Hal Walters, Aubrey Mallalieu. 82 mins.

Songs: Keep Fit; I Don't Like; Biceps, Muscle And Brawn.

CHRISTMAS GREETINGS OF 1937 [1937] ATP/EALING

Formby one of numerous participants in this trailer. 8 mins.

I SEE ICE [1938] ATP/EALING

Trailer with music/song extracts. 4 mins.

I SEE ICE ATP/EALING

Director: Anthony Kimmins. Script: Anthony Kimmins.
George Bright: George Formby, Judy Gaye: Kay Walsh,
    Martine: Cyril Ritchard, Galloway: Garry Marsh, Mrs
    Hunter: Betty Stockfield, Crooner: Gavin Gordon. With
    Ernest Sefton, Frederick Burtwell, Archibald Batty, Frank
    Leighton. 82 mins.
Songs: Mother What'll I Do Now?; In My Little Snapshot
    Album; Noughts And Crosses.

CHRISTMAS GREETINGS OF 1938 [1938] ATP/EALING

Formby one of numerous participants in this trailer. 10 mins.

IT'S IN THE AIR [1938] ATP/EALING

Director: Anthony Kimmins. Script: Anthony Kimmins.
    Photography: Ronald Neame. George Brown: George
    Formby, Peggy: Polly Ward, CO: Garry Marsh, Sergeant
    Major: Julien Mitchell, Craig: Jack Hobbs. With C Denier
    Warren, Esme Cannon, Hal Gordon, Jack Melford, Michael
    Shepley, Frank Leighton, OB Clarence, Scruffy. 84 mins.
Songs: It's In The Air; Our Sergeant Major; They Can't Fool
    Me.

TROUBLE BREWING [1939] ATP/EALING

Trailer with music/song extracts, 4 mins.

TROUBLE BREWING [1939]

Director: Anthony Kimmins. Script: Anthony Kimmins/
    Michael Hogan/Angus McPhail. Photography: Ronald
    Neame. Based on the novel by Joan Butler. George Gullip:
    George Formby, Mary: Googie Withers, Bill: Gus
    McNaughton, Madame Berdi: Martita Hunt, Brady: Garry
    Marsh. With Joss Ambler, Ronald Shiner, C Denier
    Warren, Beatrix Felden-Kaye, Basil Radford, Esme Cannon.
    85 mins.

Songs: I Can Tell It By My Horoscope; Hitting the High Spots Now; Fanlight Fanny.

COME ON GEORGE! [1939] ATP/EALING
Trailer with music/song extracts. 3 mins.

COME ON GEORGE! [1939] ATP/EALING
Director: Anthony Kimmins. Script: Anthony Kimmins/Val Valentine/Leslie Arliss. Photography: Ronald Neame. Music: Ernest Irving. George: George Formby, Ann Johnson: Pat[ricia] Kirkwood, Monica Bailey: Meriel Forbes, Squib: Ronald Stagg, Sergeant Johnson: George Carney. With Ronald Shiner, Cyril Raymond, George Hayes, Gibb McLaughlin, Hal Gordon, C Denier Warren, David Burnaby, James Hayter. 86 mins.
Songs: I Couldn't Let The Stable Down; I'm Making Headway Now; Pardon Me; Goodnight, Little Fellow, Goodnight.

LET GEORGE DO IT [1940] ATP/EALING
Trailer with music/song extracts. 3 mins.

LET GEORGE DO IT [1940] ATP/EALING
Director: Marcel Varnel. Script: John Dighton/Austin Melford/Angus McPhail/Basil Dearden. Photography: Ronald Neame. Music: Ernest Irving/Harry Bidgood. George Hepplewhite: George Formby, Mark Mendez: Garry Marsh, Mary: Phyllis Calvert, Iris: Coral Browne. With Romney Brent, Diana Beaumont, Torin Thatcher, Hal Gordon, Donald Calthrop, Bernard Lee, Helena Pickard, Percy Walsh, Johnny Schofield, Ronald Shiner, Gavin Gordon. 78 mins.
Songs: Grandad's Flannelette Nightshirt; Count Your Blessings And Smile; Mr Wu's A Window Cleaner Now; Oh, Don't The Wind Blow Cold.

SPARE A COPPER [1940] ATP/EALING

Director: John Paddy Carstairs. Script: Roger MacDougal/
Austin Melford/Basil Dearden. George Carter: George
Formby, Jane Gray: Dorothy Hyson. With Bernard Lee,
George Merritt, Beryl Reid, John Warwick, Elliot
Makeham, John Turnbull, Ellen Pollock, Warburton
Gamble, Edward Lexy. 77 mins.

Songs: I'm The Ukulele Man; On The Beat; I Wish I Was
Back On The Farm; I'm Shy.

TURNED OUT NICE AGAIN [1941] ATP/EALING

Director: Marcel Varnel. Script: Austin Melford/Basil
Dearden/John Dighton. Based on the play *As You Are* by
Hugh Mills and Wells Root. George Pearson: George
Formby, Lydia: Peggy Bryan, Mrs Pearson: Elliot Mason,
Uncle Arnold: Edward Chapman. With Mackenzie Ward,
O B Clarence, Wilfred Hyde White, Michael Rennie, John
Salew, Hay Petrie, Ronald Ward. 77 mins.

Songs: Auntie Maggie's Remedy; You Can't Go Wrong In
These; The Emperor Of Lancashire; You're Everything To
Me.

SOUTH AMERICAN GEORGE [1941] COLUMBIA

Director: Marcel Varnel. Script: Leslie Arliss/Norman Lee/
Austin Melford. Photography: Arthur Crabtree. Music:
Harry Bidgood. Tenor voices: Giovanni Martinelli [*La
Traviata*], Webster Booth [*Lucia di Lammermoor*]. George
Butters/Gilli Vanetti: George Formby, Carol Dean: Linden
Travers, Ricardo: Jacques Brown, Swifty: Ronald Shiner.
With Enid Stamp-Taylor, Felix Aylmer, Beatrice Varley,
Alf Goddard, Herbert Lomas, Gus McNaughton, Marie
Villiers, Muriel George, Eric Clavering, Norman Pierce,
Cameron Hall, Charles Paton, Rita Grant. 88 mins.

Songs: The Barmaid At The Rose And Crown; Swing Mama;

I Played On My Spanish Guitar; La Donna E Mobile; I'd Do It With A Smile.

MUCH TOO SHY [1942] COLUMBIA
Director: Marcel Varnel. Script: Ronald Frankau.
  Photography: Arthur Crabtree. Music: Harry Bidgood.
  George Andy: George Formby, Jimmy: Jimmy Clitheroe,
  Jackie Somers: Eileen Bennett, Miss Peabody: Kathleen
  Harrison, Lady Driscol: Hilda Bayley. With Joss Ambler,
  Brefni O'Rourke, Peter Gawthorne, Charles Hawtrey,
  Frederick Burtwell, Gus McNaughton, Eric Clavering,
  Gibb McLaughlin, D J Williams, Percy Walsh, Valentine
  Dyall, Clifford Buckton, Noel Dainton, May Norton, Wally
  Patch, Jack Vyvvyan, André Sacré, Marjorie Pointer,
  Eleanor William, Judith Helmes, Eve Chipman, Eleanor
  Hallam, Alf Goddard, Frank Atkinson, James Knight, Dave
  O'Toole, George Bishop, Ben Williams. 88 mins.
Songs: Andy The Handy Man; They Laughed When I Started
  To Play; Talking To The Moon About You; Delivering The
  Morning Milk.

GET CRACKING [1943] COLUMBIA
Director: Marcel Varnel. Script: L Du Garde Peach/Edward
  Dryhurst/Michael Vaughan/John L Arthur. Photography:
  Stephen Dale. Special effects: Fred Ford. George Singleton:
  George Formby, Mary: Dinah Sheridan, Everett Manley:
  Ronald Shiner. With Edward Rigby, Frank Pettingell, Mike
  Johnson, Wally Patch, Irene Handl, Vera Frances. 92 mins.
Songs: Under The Blasted Oak; Home Guard Blues; When
  The Lads Of The Village Get Cracking.

BELL-BOTTOM GEORGE [1943/4] COLUMBIA
Director: Marcel Varnel. Script: Peter Fraser/Edward
  Dryhurst/Peter Cresswell/Richard Fisher/John L Arthur.
  Photography: Roy Fogwell. George Blake: George Formby,

Pat: Anne Firth, Jim Bennett: Charles Farrell, Henry
Shapley: Peter Murray Hill, Birdie Edwards: Reginald
Purdell. With Elliot Makeham, Manning Whiley, Jane
Welsh, Denis Wyndham, Hugh Dempster, Charles
Hawtrey, Peter Gawthorne, 94 mins.
Songs: Swim Little Fish; It Serves You Right; If I Had A Girl
Like You; Bell-Bottom George.

HE SNOOPS TO CONQUER [1945] COLUMBIA
Director: Marcel Varnel. Script: Howard Irving-Young/
Norman Lee/Stephen Black/Langford Reed/Michael
Vaughan. Photography: Roy Fogwell. George Gribble:
George Formby, Sir Timothy Strawbridge: Robertson Hare,
Jane: Elizabeth Allen, Oxbold: Claude Bailey. With James
Harcourt, Gordon McLeod, Vincent Holman, Aubrey
Mallalieu, William Rodwell. 97 mins.
Songs: Hill Billy Willie; Got To Get Your Photo In The Press;
Unconditional Surrender.

I DIDN'T DO IT! [1945] COLUMBIA
Director: Marcel Varnel. Script: Howard Irving-Young/
Norman Lee/Stephen Black/Peter Fraser/Michael Vaughan.
Photography: Roy Fogwell. Music: Harry Bidgood. George
Trotter: George Formby, Vance: Carl Jaffé, Tiger Tubbs:
Billy Caryl, O'Rourke: Jack Daly, Betty Dixon: Marjorie
Brown. With Hilda Mundy, Gaston Palmer, Wally Patch,
Ian Fleming, The Boswell Twins, Vincent Holman,
Georgina Cookson, Dennis Wyndham, Gordon McLeod,
Merle Tottenham, Jack Raine. Claude Bailey, William
Rodwell. 93 mins.
Songs: She's Got Two Of Everything; I'd Like A Dream Like
That; The Daring Young Man.

GEORGE IN CIVVY STREET [1946] COLUMBIA
Director: Marcel Varnel. Script: Peter Fraser/Ted Kavanaugh/

Max Kester/Gale Pedrick. Photography: Philip Grindrod. Music: Johnny Claes and His Band. George Harper: George Formby, Mary Colton: Rosalyn Boulter, Fingers: Ronald Shiner, Shadrack: Ian Fleming, Jed Brindle: Frank Drew, Lavender: Philippa Hiatt. With Wally Patch, Mike Johnson, Enid Cruickshank, Robert Ginns, Moore Raymond, John E Coyle, Roddy Hughes, Lynn Evans, Daphne Elphinstone. 76 mins.

Songs: The Mad March Hare; We've Been A Long Time Gone; You Don't Need A Licence For That; It Could Be; I Was Christened With A Horse-Shoe; You Don't Need Them (sung by Daphne Elphinstone).

FAREWELL PERFORMANCE [1960, RESTORED 1994] MASTERSOUND

Formby's legendary *Friday Show*, brilliantly restored and serving as his epitaph. The opening caption reads:

In December 1960, one of the world's greatest stars said his farewell in a musical concert which revealed many surprising details of his life. The business deals, the first films, his poor education, the famous father, the regrets of his private life, and those exciting wartime years. Supported by a full orchestra and ten hit songs, this is a recording to enjoy and treasure. Ten weeks later, the cheerful Emperor of Lancashire lost his long battle against ill-health.

Songs: With My Little Stick Of Blackpool Rock; It Serves You Right; George Was A Miner (Down The Old Coal Hole); Swim Little Fish; Guarding The Home Of The Home Guard; Goodnight Little Fellow Goodnight; Sitting On The Ice In The Ice Rink; When I'm Cleaning Windows; Chinese Laundry Blues; Leaning On A Lamp Post. 36 mins.

There have been many documentaries, videos and inclusions in film soundtracks. The best are:

The Singing Cinema (1964); *Looking Back At George Formby* (1967); *The Ukulele Man* (1971 & 1973); *To See Such Fun* (1977); *40 Minutes, The George Formby Story* (1982); *The South Bank Show* (1992); *Heroes Of Comedy* (1992); *The Songs That Won The War* (1994).

GEORGE FORMBY: STAGE PLAYS

ZIP GOES A MILLION! 20-10-1951 PALACE THEATRE, LONDON

An Emile Littler Concept/Presentation. Libretto: Eric Maschwitz. Music: George Posford. Producer: Charles Hickman. Musical Direction: Debroy Somers. Based on *Brewster's Millions* by George Barr-McCutcheon and Winchell Smith. Previewed Coventry/Manchester in September 1951. Formby left the production in April 1952. Cast: George Formby, Ward Donovan, Barbara Perry, Wallace Eaton, Sarah Gregory, Ian Stuart, Wilfred Kirkness, John Marquand.

Songs: Zip Goes A Million; Riding Into Town; Raratonga; I'm Saving Up For Sally; The Story Of Chiquita; The Thing About You; It Takes No Time To Fall In Love; Nothing Breaks But The Heart; Thou Art For Me; I Owe You; Big Business; Ordinary People; Running Away To Land; Garter Girl; The Pleasures Of A Pleasure Cruise.

TOO YOUNG TO MARRY 1954–56 TOURING

An Emile Littler Concept/Presentation. Libretto: Martin Flavin, revamped by Emile Littler. Director: Maxwell Wray.

Cast: George Formby, Arthur Hoskins, Eric Yorke, Shaun O'Riordan, Sydney Arnold. Song: If You Don't Want The Goods Don't Maul 'Em.

BESIDE THE SEASIDE: A HOLIDAY ROMP! MARCH–MAY 1958

Script: Leslie Sands. Presented by Derek Salberg. Director: Maxwell Wray. Cast: George Formby, Barbara Mitchell, Nancy Roberts, Doreen Andrew, Michael Lomax, Rosemary Towler, Anne Jameson, Susan Neil, Denis Spenser. Songs: Leaning On A Lamp Post; Swimmin' With The Wimmin.

GEORGE FORMBY: IMMEDIATE FAMILY

Eliza Ann Hoy (1879–1981) m George Formby Sr (1875–1921)

Children:
1 Louisa (1900)
2 Beatrice (1901–2)
3 Edith Lillian (1903)
4 George Hoy (1904–61)
5 Unknown (c. 1905)
6 Louisa (1906–)
7 Unknown (c 1907)
8 Frances (1908–9)
9 Ella (1910–98)
10 Mary (1912–87)
11 Frank Allen (1913–83)
12 Ethel (1915–98)
13 Edward (1918–)

THE GEORGE FORMBY SOCIETY

by Dennis Taylor, President

The George Formby Society was formed in 1961 for the purpose of perpetuating the ukulele style of music and memory of George Formby, renowned ukulele entertainer, song writer, actor and comedian. After almost 38 years, it has grown into a thriving organisation of almost 1,000 'happy go lucky' members and their families from all over the world, ranging in age from four years old to a few elder statesmen in their late seventies.

The Winter Gardens complex in the holiday resort of Blackpool is where this dedicated group of avid George Formby fans meet four times a year. In March, June, September and November, 250 to 300 Formby fans meet in one of the large halls within the Winter Gardens for the weekend to share in ukulele fun, George Formby style of course, with concerts by members, young and old, who wish to perform, plus films of George Formby himself for viewing. These lively gatherings generally attract media coverage of some kind, resulting in information about the George Formby Society being spread not only nationally but also internationally.

Members communicate through a quarterly magazine called the *Vellum*. Lots of letters are received by the Editor, not only from the UK, but also from our members all over the world, for publication. Also included are articles and information on

George Formby and his wife, Beryl, his family and the songs and, of course, tips on how to play the ukulele.

And finally . . .

Did George Formby play the ukulele or a banjo?

George did indeed play a ukulele. In fact, it's all he plays in his first two films. In his first film for ATP, made at the Ealing Studios entitled *No Limit*, which is about the TT races, in one scene on a train he sings 'Riding In The TT Races' again to the accompaniment of the little wooden ukulele. He again plays one in his next film, *Keep Your Seats Please* when he sings the 'Window Cleaner' for the first time.

A ukulele is a small wooden guitar-shaped instrument. Invented in Hawaii at the end of the nineteenth century, being a modified instrument similar to the ones brought in by the sugar cane cutters from Madeira, it was named by the Hawaiians who thought that the action of the players' fingers in strumming the instrument resembled dancing insects – the word 'uku' meaning flea and 'lele' meaning dancing – hence 'ukulele', the 'dancing flea'.

Although the instrument became very popular in America from about 1910 onwards it had one major drawback. It wasn't very loud and as variety artists were using it in their acts it was a problem in a large hall to hear it. Alvin D Keech and his brother went over to the West Coast to teach the up-and-coming stars of the day how to play the ukulele. They soon realised its drawbacks and decided to improve the sound by inventing a new instrument. By combining the ukulele and the big American banjo, Alvin Keech produced a new instrument which he called a banjulele. He patented that name. The main difference was the fitting of a drum with a tight calfskin vellum and a resonator to amplify and project the sound forward – the sound being transmitted from the strings via a bridge seated on the vellum.

Other manufacturers began to produce these instruments such as Gibson and Ludwig, but had to call them banjo-ukuleles or ukulele-banjos.

This was the type of instrument which George reputedly purchased for fifty shillings from another entertainer with whom he shared a dressing room at the Alhambra, Barnsley. There *are* photographs of George holding a Keech banjulele but, in fact, instruments made by other manufacturers were far superior in quality and sound.

George's main instruments were made by Ludwig and Gibson which were American companies. The Abbott Monarch Banjo Ukulele was made by Jack Abbott, a London instrument maker, especially for him in the late 30s. George sponsored a range of banjo ukuleles made by John E Dallas and Sons Ltd., London, which probably sold thousands into the home market. Each had his autograph stamped on the vellum, and had either a metal plate on the peghead with a picture of George or, on the better ukes, an inlaid piece of mother of pearl with George's signature. George can be seen playing all of these instruments in his various films. He perfected a style of his own which is very difficult to replicate – although many still try.

BIBLIOGRAPHY:

PRIMARY & SECONDARY SOURCES

BOOTH, Eliza: *Interviews with David Sharpe*, 1974.

BRET, David: *Gracie Fields: The Authorised Biography* (Robson, 1995).

DANCE MUSIC POLICY COMMITTEE: Minutes (unpublished, 1944).

DUNN, J H: *Letters from Palestine* (unpublished, 1943).

ELLIS, Sqd-Leader Frank: *Letters from North Africa* (unpublished, 1943).

FORMBY, Beryl: *War Diary* (unpublished, 1940).

FORMBY, George: *In The Days Of My Youth* (unpublished, 1936).

FORMBY, George: '£84,000 A Year' (Interview, *Sunday People*, 1952).

FORMBY, George: *Interviews with Brian Hargreaves* (unpublished 1956–61).

FISHER, John: *George Formby* (Woburn-Futura, 1975).

HIGH COURT OF JUSTICE: Probate, Divorce & Admiralty (Papers 1961–6).

HOWSON, Fred: 'Interview' (*Sunday Express*: 1971).

HOWSON, Patricia: Interviews (published/unpublished, 1961–6).

RANDALL, Alan & SEATON, Ray: *George Formby* (W H Allen, 1974).

SMITH, Phyllis ('Sylvia'): *Journals* (unpublished, 1936–44).

SMITH, Phyllis ('Sylvia'): *Interviews with Beryl Formby* (unpublished, 1956–60).
TAYLOR, Jack: Letters (unpublished, 1943).

PUBLICATIONS

GREAT BRITAIN: *Daily Telegraph*; The *Stage*; The *Independent*; *Blackpool Evening Gazette*; *Tatler*; *The Times*; The *Daily Mail*; *Sunday Express*; *Daily Herald*; *Daily Express*; *Daily Mirror*; *Variety*; *Sunday Mirror*; *People*; *Pictorial*; *Daily Film Renter*; The *Guardian*; *Sunday Times*; The *Daily Worker*; *Today's Cinema*; The *Vellum*; *Picturegoer*; *Film Weekly*; *Kinematograph Weekly*.

AUSTRALIA: *Adelaide Advertiser*; *Sydney Current Affairs Bulletin*; *Sydney Morning Herald*.

CANADA: The *Hamilton Spectator*; *Toronto Globe & Mail*; *Toronto Star*; *Vancouver Sun*.

SOUTH AFRICA: *Cape Times*; *Johannesburg Sunday Times*; *Durban & Natal Mercury*; *Pretoria News*.

ZIMBABWE: *Bulawayo Chronicle*; *Bulawayo Sunday News*.

JOURNALISTS/CONTRIBUTORS (living and deceased): Chris Arnot; Michael Berry; Sydney Brennan; Arthur Brooks; Peter Clayton; Hubert Cole; Kevin Daly; Russell Davies; Jane Fickling; Clifford Greenwood; John Gale; Brian Hargreaves; Ed Hocura; Fred Bruce Lockhart; Kerstin McClure; Morrissey; David Nathan; Harry Scott; David Sharpe; Hannen Swaffer; Leonard Wallace; Michael Walsh; Cecil Wilson.

INDEX